Conquer the Clutter

Elaine Birchall &
Suzanne Cronkwright

Conquer the Clutter

Strategies to Identify, Manage,
and Overcome Hoarding

JOHNS HOPKINS UNIVERSITY PRESS
BALTIMORE

Johns Hopkins University Press
2715 North Charles Street
Baltimore, Maryland 21218-4363
www.press.jhu.edu

Library of Congress Cataloging-in-Publication Data

Names: Birchall, Elaine, author. | Cronkwright, Suzanne, author.
Title: Conquer the clutter : strategies to identify, manage, and overcome
    hoarding / Elaine Birchall and Suzanne Cronkwright.
Description: Baltimore : Johns Hopkins University Press, 2019. | Includes
    bibliographical references and index.
Identifiers: LCCN 2018054665 | ISBN 9781421431505 (hardcover : alk. paper) |
    ISBN 1421431505 (hardcover : alk. paper) | ISBN 9781421431512 (pbk. : alk.
    paper) | ISBN 1421431513 (pbk. : alk. paper) | ISBN 9781421431529
    (electronic) | ISBN 1421431521 (electronic)
Subjects: LCSH: Compulsive hoarding—Treatment. | Obsessive-compulsive
    disorder—Treatment.
Classification: LCC RC569.5.H63 B57 2019 | DDC 616.85/227—dc23
LC record available at https://lccn.loc.gov/2018054665

A catalog record for this book is available from the British Library.

Special discounts are available for bulk purchases of this book.
For more information, please contact Special Sales at 410-516-6936 or
specialsales@press.jhu.edu.

Johns Hopkins University Press uses environmentally friendly book materials,
including recycled text paper that is composed of at least 30 percent post-
consumer waste, whenever possible.

We would like to dedicate this book to
those struggling with hoarding disorder and
those who care about them.

Many people must deal with life circumstances that make progress an
uphill struggle. The courage of those who hoard and that of their families
demonstrates that being willing to open old wounds, challenge limiting beliefs,
and step forward into unfamiliar and unknown territory mentally, physically, and
spiritually is genuinely humbling and inspiring to peers and professionals alike. To
face one's fear of judgment and continue to work toward success takes courage and
fortitude, especially in the face of harsh and unrealistic opinions about hoarding.
Continued hope and perseverance deserves acknowledgment and respect. Our society
needs to work toward redefining success in our spaces, from "picture perfect"
to safe and healthy, respecting the priorities of the people living there.

Contents

PART III

Getting There: Resources, Tips, and Tools

Acknowledgments

THIS BOOK HAS BEEN ACCOMPLISHED with a great deal of help and support from *many* people.

We would first like to thank our husbands, Ray and Mike, for continuous support, encouragement, and technical expertise.

We are grateful to Jane Burka, PhD, and Lenora Yuen, PhD, for their generous permission to include material from the discussion Elaine and Jane shared on Elaine's VoiceAmerica Variety Channel show *Take Back Your Life: When Your Things Are Taking Over.* They also permitted us to use their material to develop a procrastination worksheet, "Knowing Yourself" (see chapter 5), to help readers progress in combating their procrastination habit.

We thank Dr. Carole Menard-Buteau for helping ensure that we stayed true to our goal of remaining user friendly and relatable to those who hoard, those who care about them, and the professionals working with real people who are truly stuck.

"Lucy/Lucinda" has our gratitude for her story and contribution to chapter 15, "The Last Word," as well as her excellent suggestion that illustrating actual levels of risk would be invaluable to those who hoard.

We thank Howard Sonnenberg, our director of photography, who helped turn Lucy's vision into a reality.

We thank Katherine, Raedeen, Helen, Rachel, and Ruth for allowing us to include their stories and real-life pictures in the book.

Donna, Olivia, and Spring provided invaluable assistance with research, tabulation, and myriad other administrative tasks. Olivia also acted as our photographic production assistant and animal-hoarding contact person. Donna saved the day when she found the missing memory stick containing the manuscript. Thanks also to John for keeping Elaine fed and watered, as well as running a hundred other errands for this book.

We wish to thank the Hilton Mississauga/Meadowvale management and staff, who have cared for Elaine, and sometimes Sue, as family every week for the past six years: upgrading us, feeding us like "nonnas," laughing with us, and sharing their lives. Printers arrived miraculously, as did extras of necessities forgotten at home. There were hugs, encouragement, inquiries about how the book was proceeding, and offers to help. Their generosity was far above normal customer service standards, and we are enormously grateful.

Joe Rusko, the health and wellness editor at Johns Hopkins University Press, kept us on track through his enthusiastic coaching, which improved this book immensely.

We would like to thank our anonymous hoarding-informed expert reviewers, whose feedback helped us see the manuscript through the eyes of its diverse readership.

This book would not have happened without Jacqueline Wehmueller, former executive editor at Johns Hopkins University Press. She championed this book right from the beginning, and we are forever in her debt. She shared and nurtured our belief in a gentle, holistic approach to hoarding.

And last, but not least, thank you to all our friends, family, and colleagues who supported us along the way with their words of encouragement. You kept us energized during the past six years.

How to Navigate the Book

THIS IS A BOOK ABOUT HOPE AND PERSEVERANCE. I have divided it into three parts to illustrate and resolve three essential components for those living with hoarding disorder and those assisting them.* These components are *assessment*, *motivation*, and *tools and strategies*. This book assists individuals to reach and maintain necessary goals to take back their lives when their things are taking over.

I have deliberately designed this book as a companion to the more theoretical, formal books on hoarding based on cognitive behavioral theory, or CBT. I see no benefit to anyone in repeating what has already been done well by so many academic authors. CBT is a valuable treatment tool, but in my experience, some clients—even the highest-functioning individuals—are at times not able to engage with a CBT model because of various factors, including feeling overwhelmed (which is typical of hoarding situations). Although I do use CBT in my practice, I also use other models of intervention, whatever is appropriate to my client's needs at a given time (including harm reduction, solution-focused treatment, crisis counseling, Satir therapy, and psychodynamic strategies).

I see the people who come to me as whole individuals, and I firmly believe that I need to respect that wholeness. Therefore, I do not focus solely on the psychological aspect of hoarding, because hoarding never happens in isolation. It happens in the context of the whole person's life. I have seen no evidence in my practice that progress is sustainable with hoarding treatment that doesn't also address other life challenges. People come to me for help with their hoarding disorder, but the work I do weaves

---

* For simplicity, we use first-person (e.g., I, me, etc.) throughout to refer to Elaine alone and to Elaine and Sue collectively.

learning, skills, theory, and reclaiming self-respect into the fabric of each unique life. I have found that knowing the theory is important as a clinician, but I believe it is my responsibility to treat based on the needs of each individual. I have developed this approach over 17 years working with individuals "in the trenches"—the environments where the hoarding actually occurs, at all levels of severity.

Part I. Understanding Hoarding and What It Takes to Clear Your Path

The first part of the book introduces you to hoarding disorder and coaches you on how to carry out an accurate assessment of your particular clutter situation. Once you have assessed your environment, you'll learn how to set goals to move forward. You can then follow my decision-making process to do the work needed to clear your spaces. In part I, you'll find a clear, step-by-step process to help you actually make decluttering and other non-hoarding-related decisions happen and take back your life.

- **CHAPTER 1** provides an overview of hoarding disorder, including
    - *scope, prevalence, and diagnostic criteria according to the* Diagnostic and Statistical Manual of Mental Disorders, *5th Edition (DSM-5)*;
    - *a quick five-question quiz to identify five red flags that might mean you are hoarding;*
    - *a full quiz to identify where you are on the hoarding continuum, from "not at all" to "extreme";*
    - *a checklist to confirm that you either have a hoarding disorder or are somewhere on the path to hoarding;*
    - *the difference between hoarding and cluttering;*
    - *definitions of the five types of hoarding;*
    - *how hoarding affects others around you;*
    - *three paths to hoarding and how a person develops a hoarding disorder;*
    - *debunking of some common misconceptions about hoarding and about those who live with hoarding disorder.*

- **CHAPTER 2** offers tools for assessing your environment and yourself, including
    - *a checklist to identify the problem areas in your environment so that you can prioritize the areas to work on first;*
    - *a worksheet you can use to look realistically at how the clutter in your environment is affecting the way you live in your spaces, such as by making adaptations in order to function amid the clutter;*
    - *a photo collection illustrating what actual safety risk levels look like (not severity level by volume) to help you identify such risks in your environment;*

o *an assessment for determining the risk your spaces pose for yourself and anyone else living with you or nearby;*

o *an eight-step self-assessment to determine the level of depression, anxiety, and isolation you are living with as you move forward.*

- **CHAPTER 3** provides definitions of SMART goals and types of goals, including goal-setting instructions and a blank worksheet.

- **CHAPTER 4** outlines the decision-making method during onsite clutter coaching, including the *scaling process* to rank items in order of importance. This is a key chapter in the book to help you achieve success in taking back your life.

- **CHAPTER 5,** on procrastination, takes a slightly different format, including discussion from an informative interview of Jane Burka, one of America's leading experts on procrastination, on my weekly radio series in 2017. In preparation for this book, I surveyed my clients about whether they felt procrastination information was important to their recovery from hoarding disorder. Every single one of them said that procrastination was a problem in multiple areas of their lives, including in their hoarding disorder, and asked that I include this topic in the book.

Part II. Moving Forward: Inspiration from Those Who Have Gone before You

Part II will help you maintain your motivation when perseverance is necessary.

The real-life stories and those that are a montage of hundreds of other lives illustrate realistic choices others have made to reach their goals and maintain their progress in "clearing their paths." In chapters 6 to 15, these accounts illuminate people's history and struggles with hoarding, including what worked and what didn't, as they moved forward to reclaim their spaces and lives from excessive clutter.

The stories also demonstrate for those assisting you how to coach and support using gentle, holistic techniques that respect your priorities and your pace.

And if you live with any *comorbid factors*—coexisting conditions that complicate the lives of those who hoard and those who live with chronic disorganization and the resulting excessive clutter—the stories offer hope.

- **CHAPTER 6** introduces the family of Joan and Paul, who both suffer from myriad disorders, and describes how this situation affects their children.

- **CHAPTER 7** discusses the role of grief and loss in hoarding disorder.

- **CHAPTER 8** is a montage of many people who look to shopping to restabilize their mood and who deal with compulsions and rituals to self-soothe. It offers tools and strategies for making conscious choices to take back your life from the need to buy impulsively or compulsively.

- **CHAPTER 9** provides two of many possible examples of accumulation common to the sandwich generation: (1) a woman overwhelmed with bequeathed items, and (2) a family accumulating too many items from parents as well as from adult children in transition.

- In **CHAPTER 10,** two stories illustrate the effects of Diogenes syndrome, a condition involving neglect of self and surroundings, and the severe risks associated when hoarding disorder develops.

- **CHAPTER 11** focuses on an individual who has a successful professional practice but returns at the end of the day to chaos, piles, and pathways in her hoarded home.

- **CHAPTER 12** describes the additional burdens that a disabled person faces when suffering from hoarding disorder.

- **CHAPTER 13** discusses an individual whose hoarding disorder stems from unresolved attachment issues.

- **CHAPTER 14** offers the stories of others who are affected by hoarding: adult children of those with hoarding disorder, seniors living with others who hoard, and neighbors unaware of the risks they face from nearby hoarded environments.

- **CHAPTER 15** consists of real-life accounts from my clients, describing their hoarding experiences and which strategies did and did not work. It was important to them to speak to those picking up this book, who likely feel as overwhelmed as they did at the outset.

Part III. Getting There: Resources, Tips, and Tools

Part III provides a wealth of excellent and differing resources to assist you and those helping you (whether family, friends, or professionals) complete the work ahead and take back your life. I encourage you to reproduce the resources provided in chapter 16 and online (jhupbooks.press.jhu.edu/title/conquer-clutter) as tools for your progress, or to share with others you are concerned about or those who come to you as clients.

The appendix provides the results of informally reviewing a random sampling of my case files from a 10-year period to study the demographic data. During the summer of 2017, I collected data from 214 cases files for comparison to general hoarding research over the past 10 years and to drill down to a deeper understanding about the hoarding cases and their demographics.

Although all information in this book will likely be of interest to people who hoard, I use a key-shaped icon to highlight especially important concepts. A second icon draws attention to useful ideas for helpers (including family members and clutter coaches), and a third icon signals information particularly relevant to mental health professionals.

The information these last two icons highlight is also equally important to those who hoard.

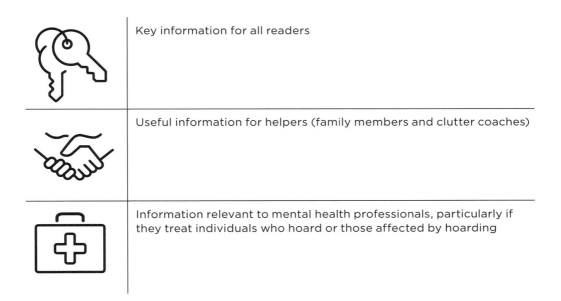

	Key information for all readers
	Useful information for helpers (family members and clutter coaches)
	Information relevant to mental health professionals, particularly if they treat individuals who hoard or those affected by hoarding

Conquer the Clutter

Prologue

AS A SOCIAL WORKER WITH 30 YEARS' EXPERIENCE and a specialist in hoarding for the past 17 years, I hear a single word on a daily basis: *overwhelmed*. That's because I specialize in working with those who hoard and those who care about them. Feeling overwhelmed continues to happen for good reasons. Professionals can also be overwhelmed when working with hoarders, so I train specialists across Canada and the United States. I also consult internationally on hoarding.

This book is meant for you:

- ✔ if you are overwhelmed and even fleetingly want "to take back your life when your things are taking over";
- ✔ if you care about someone who hoards;
- ✔ if you fear that things could, or are beginning to, get out of control; or
- ✔ if you are a professional working "in the trenches" with hoarders.

If you fall in the last category, the stories and holistic strategies included in each chapter will give you a fuller appreciation of the teamwork and "thinking outside the box" approach that is often necessary to provide the support needed for sustainable success.

I am committed to helping people get unstuck. Seeing insight dawn in someone's eyes and then seeing that person use that vision to make his or her life more meaningful is like no other feeling in the world.

There are three ways to motivate: (1) a carrot, (2) a stick, or (3) a change in our relationship to whatever is causing a problem. All three motivators work. The stick (fear, pain, shame) will get us started, but it will only keep us motivated until the actual or perceived threat of discomfort disappears. The carrot (pride, pleasure, security, safety) will keep us moving toward our goals and beyond, because pleasure and self-esteem will continue to create joy and meaning in our lives.

Changing our relationship to the things causing us problems trumps both carrot and stick. This approach alone will give us peace and stability, putting us in a secure position to make more conscious, sustainable choices we can live with. This strategy is powerful because choices made in this way truly reflect who we are today—moving forward toward our goals—not who we used to be or wish we could be.

I work from the belief that we get only one life (that we can be sure of), and it's a shame to waste it being stuck, missing all the good that could bring us joy and meaning. When we are stuck, we also miss the not-so-good moments. These moments often turn out to be life lessons that can give us the impetus to grow and make changes—if only to escape discomfort. When we persist during these times, we often experience moments of clarity, revealing a path through the obstacles of doubt ("I don't think I can do it") and shame ("I don't want anyone to discover how I live").

Sometimes events we believe are losses, failures, or mistakes turn out to be course corrections, leading to opportunities we never imagined. These moments will pass us by, however, if we don't make ourselves *aware* and *available* to take a step farther down that path.

You picked up this book in just such a moment of awareness.

Seize the moment now.

Invest in yourself enough to remain available to read and reflect on the information in this book. The wisdom and learning of others who have struggled as you are struggling can support you in *clearing your path.*

The purpose of this book is to offer you just such a moment—an opportunity to figure out who you are today, who you want to be moving forward, and what you really need and love. You will then be prepared for the next step: letting go of the things weighing you down in your life. Your things will *never* love you back, and they won't miss you when you're gone. These things will never give you the pride and meaning in your life that you deserve and were truly meant to have.

As you read and begin clearing your path, keep a few points in mind:

- Be gentle with yourself.
- You will never overcome anything difficult by looking down on yourself.
- We *all* make mistakes, whether or not we hoard, and we all go through periods when success eludes us.
- We are *all* flawed, imperfect human beings, just the way we are supposed to be.
- We are *all* more than the problems or limitations we have.

With the right support and perseverance, we can all do things we never dreamed possible, just like the people whose lives and struggles appear in the pages to follow.

You are not the first. You are not alone. They have cleared a path, and so can you.

Introduction

I COUNSEL PEOPLE WHO CREATE HOARDED ENVIRONMENTS and help them declutter their homes and lives. I also counsel their families, who try valiantly to offer support and help, which is often not well received. The accumulation that overwhelms people is made up of things, but what really overwhelms people are the hurts, setbacks, loss of self-respect, and fractured relationships that they carry around with them throughout their lives. Paths are blocked by tangible objects, but intangibles like feelings and beliefs also get in the way.

Successful outcomes are not achieved solely by cleaning up. Sometimes, sadly, the situation reaches a crisis level in terms of personal and public health and safety and must be dealt with quickly and intensively. I believe we always increase the damage to the person struggling with hoarding by intervening, even when we do so reluctantly, in this way. For this reason, quick, intensive intervention should be an absolute last resort. *Success is gained by helping people who hoard change their relationship with their things to achieve a healthier balance with things in their lives.* In helping people take their lives back when their things are taking over, I use a holistic approach because hoarding *never* happens in isolation. A cleaned-up house isn't going to stay that way for long if the person who hoards doesn't also get help with other destabilizing, non-hoarding-related practical issues.

I could start with a story about one of my amazingly brave, lovely, and yet distressed clients so that you could learn from their courage and perseverance, but I want you to know a little bit more about the coach and guide who is offering you hoarding and strategies that have helped and healed others.

I think it is only fair to share moments of "walking the talk" from my own life. Even though I am a social worker who counsels others, and I don't hoard, I have experienced the feelings and emotions you likely feel and have journeyed through them, sometimes with support, sometimes with "gifts" that at first seemed to only block my way.

Life sends us all pain and challenges that test us sorely and cause us to plumb our depths. Perhaps these difficult life events can also help us develop and strengthen parts of ourselves we never knew we had.

I believe each of us is sent at least one person, someone who gets us. When we see ourselves reflected in this person's eyes, we feel validated for our authentic worth. One of my "someones" was my father, who had just passed away.

I was running on empty—physically, emotionally, and spiritually. Being overwhelmed can leave you feeling hollow, immobilized, and disoriented, even if you are a social worker. I'd read all the books explaining "Life is what you make it," but I guess I just wasn't ready to understand the concept. Reading is very different from living. I can attest to that.

My days were miserable because of this aching loss.

Every day I got up, got ready for work, and, in the bathroom mirror, looked myself squarely in the eye and repeated, "You are Ken Birchall's daughter, and you can do this!" Slightly more reinforced, I would head off, gut clenched and shoulders hunched, to face what I believed would be another predictably miserable day.

At one particularly low point, on my long drive in to work, I said aloud, "Whoever up there is on my side"—someone always is, even though we often forget this— "please send me something, anything, to offset the dismal day ahead." Seconds after making this plea, I witnessed the most glorious sunrise I have ever seen. Although this small event occurs every single day, I had never left myself open to really noticing it before. The beautiful sunrise filled me with a hint of happiness and elation and released me from the stress that had been bearing down on me. True, those emotions lasted for only a short time that day, but my overall sense of loss and of being overwhelmed lessened just a little. Those few minutes of feeling buoyed up were a gift and gave me a bit of additional strength to deal with the day's challenges.

I had made that long drive every day for years and never noticed the sunrise. I hadn't needed it or made myself available to notice it. The change was in *me*, not what was available to help me.

The next morning, I got up, repeated, "You are Ken Birchall's daughter, and you can do this!" in the bathroom mirror, and headed out to work, wondering if the splendor of the previous day's sunrise had been just a one-off event. But there it was again, completely different but magnificent all the same. It was like having a private viewing of a work of art on display for only one day. Sunrise Day 2 was just as much a gift as Day 1. It buoyed me and left me with a little jolt of joy, something extra to fortify myself.

I promise I won't take you through every sunrise since then, but let me tell you about Day 3.

I woke up with the familiar gut-tightening dread of the "predictably miserable day" to come, but this time I noticed a little bubble of excitement with my second thought: *I wonder what the sky will be like today?* I found myself looking forward to something happy. By the time my feet touched the floor, the horrible gut-wrenching dread had been lessened a great deal by my hope and belief that despite what I couldn't change right away in my life, gifts would be available to me throughout the day if only I chose to notice the positives on my path—gifts for the taking. Without pretending everything was rosy, feeling better really was a matter of choosing what to focus on. Both the positives, the things that can sustain us, and the negatives, the things that weigh us down, are present at the same time. Will you choose healing and take back your life, or will you choose to continue feeling as overwhelmed as you likely feel right now?

My hope is that right now you choose to take back your spaces and your life for today and for all the tomorrows to come.

PART I

Understanding Hoarding and What It Takes to Clear Your Path

CHAPTER 1

Overview of Hoarding

DAVID, A WELL-RESPECTED, SUCCESSFUL LAWYER who regularly wins landmark cases, has to step up two feet over piles of mail and packaging as he tries to push open the front door to his home and wedge himself through it. Once inside, he faces pile after pile of items awaiting decisions about whether to keep them or let them go. At this point every day, he is suddenly hit with a tsunami of overwhelmed feelings, which leaves him feeling completely empty and reaching for his recliner for a few hours of reprieve immersed in his favorite video game *NieR: Automata*. Those few hours regularly turn into early mornings. But before escape becomes possible, as he waits for the game to load, David's clutter blindness slips, just for a second, allowing him to see that the front entry piles extend to every room in sight. This time reality sinks in. Why at the end of every workday is he suddenly so numb and overwhelmed? He pauses the game, reaches for his cell phone, and makes an appointment with his family doctor to find out whether there is something wrong with him.

———

JOAN AND PAUL LOOK AT EACH OTHER in a state of panic, helplessness, and ultimately defeat as they realize that the only choice they feel capable of acting on is to surrender their three boys to Child Protective Services (CPS) instead of dealing with the extreme clutter in their home to make it safe for all of them. How has it come to this? They had tried to think of every possible way to avoid today's decision and had come up empty. Their home is 70 percent filled, three-dimensionally. There is nowhere to sit, nowhere to eat as a family. They are always running to meet deadlines but never making them. There is no space in their home for their beloved children to have a safe and normal life. Heartbroken, Joan and Paul agree to relinquish their children to CPS, and their caseworker suggests a two-step plan. First, the children will go to foster care together; second, she will give Joan and Paul the name of someone who can help them address their hoarding situation.

———

MAUREEN HAS A SINKING SENSE OF DREAD as she begins to feel the rushing euphoria and racing mind that precede her daily buying episodes—which sometimes reach thousands of dollars. When she considers the state of her credit cards, the lump in her throat tightens, and sweat breaks out on her forehead and on the back of her neck. *There's always the home equity line of credit*, she thinks. But suddenly she can't get a breath, and her face is burning and tingling, as it dawns on her that she can't make the monthly payment on the line of credit in time, because she doesn't get paid before it comes due. There is no money left available to her, and the house is so full she can hardly move.

Panicked, she decides to return some recent purchases to cover the upcoming payment. Her stomach clenches at the thought of having to face the same sales staff who sold her the items just days ago. Feeling ashamed, cornered, and confused, Maureen promises herself over and over again, "This is the last time." Before she leaves, with bags filled and receipts in hand, she sits on the bottom step of her staircase with her head in her hands. After a while, she makes up her mind that when she returns, she will go online and find some help to ensure this really is the last time she has to shame herself to survive her shopping addiction.

———

TERRI FACES MIDDLE AGE FEELING A HEAVY LOAD OF RESPONSIBILITY for her ailing parents and their things. The plan is to move her parents to manageable, safe accommodations, but the question is, What will she do with their extra stuff? A deluge of overwhelmed feelings and obligation overtakes Terri when considering her parents' values and feelings about their things versus the reality of how much is needed and will fit in the new condo. Wanting to respect their values and feelings, Terri believes the solution is for other family members to make space in their lives for Mom and Dad's things, preserving family memories by valuing the legacy these possessions represent. A struggle arises when family members tell Terri that these objects do not represent who they are, or want to be, and they feel they don't have enough space to accept the offer. Not wanting to give up family memories associated with this collection of furniture, collectibles, and family records, Terri feels compelled to make space available in her already filled home.

Moving day arrives, and Terri brings home the leftover items that would not fit in the condo. Very quickly all free space disappears, and the only alternative is to put what's left in the basement. Terri feels reassured by doing the right thing in preserving family memories and history, as well as pride in meeting her obligation and in knowing that she's done her best for her parents and her other family members. Exhausted from the move, Terri retires for the night.

Morning brings excitement and pleasure in having valued possessions and history close by. As one day turns to another, however, feelings of pride, reassurance, and pleasure are gradually replaced by tightness in her chest, spasms in her gut, and an inability to take a full breath. Terri feels increasingly suffocated as she tries to live normally with so little free space. When these new symptoms persist weeks later, she realizes that making day-to-day decisions has become impossible. In an overwhelmed fog, Terri reaches out to a friend for support. When the friend hears that Terri has taken full responsibility for all the leftover things from the family home, he explains to Terri that if the current situation becomes her new normal, it will be hoarding, even though that was not Terri's intention. Together, they call for help to understand and deal with the underlying reasons this crisis has developed as well as support to decide how to deal with the items and Terri's vulnerability to keeping them.

––––––––––

AT THE END OF ANOTHER WORKDAY, NANCY leaves her medical practice with the now-familiar feeling of not quite being present. She aches to rest her mind and body but dreads her bedtime, knowing that she won't be able to make herself go to bed, even as exhausted as she is. She feels like she is drifting on autopilot.

As she approaches her front door, she feels a little thrill that quickly turns into a chilling anxiety. She has done it again. The evidence is hanging on her front door knob. Packages have arrived. Nancy breaks out in a cold sweat as she scours her memory of last night and the night before—actually, every night as far back as she can remember. What did she buy? Was it the jewelry from the advertising channel or the figurines from the online auction? A struggle of ambivalence takes over inside her. Bubbles of excitement crash against rising fear and dread that she will not be able to make her mortgage payment this month.

She reaches for the pickup notices dangling on the front door, opens the door, shuts her eyes, and takes a deep breath before facing the chaos in front of her. She tries to put her keys on the hall table, but they fall to the floor because the table (like every other flat surface in the house) is piled high. That familiar overwhelmed feeling wraps around her like a blanket. Nancy decides that a little distraction is what she needs—a little wine, some mindless TV—so she makes her way to the kitchen for a bottle of chardonnay, stepping over piles and navigating narrow pathways. She is momentarily aware of an internal conflict brewing between her need for rest and her need for escape. *If only I could go to bed on time and get the rest I need*, she thinks, but she picks up the TV remote instead and cruises for relaxing programming. *I won't watch advertising channels*, she promises herself, *and I won't get on my laptop to scan online auction sites*.

Despite her resolve, she ends up browsing art and other collectibles because this is the only activity that interests her. *But I won't buy*, she declares to herself, looking around at previous purchases already covering her walls. In fact, not only is every wall completely filled, but most floor spaces within her field of vision are strewn with unopened or partially opened delivery boxes. Her excitement and interest in any item she purchases seem to fade once she opens the package, at which point she drops the object where it lands and moves on to the next package. After she has opened and dropped in place five packages, she stops abruptly. *What am I doing?* she wonders. *Do I really just want to open packages for the rest of my life?*

Nancy mutes the TV, puts down the remote, and for the first time in years, she takes a long, hard look around her. *Dear Lord*, she thinks, *when did this happen? How am I ever going to get out from under?* She sits for a second, trying to quiet her mind, then opens her laptop, begins a search for help with clutter, and discovers the term *hoarding*.

What do all these people have in common? They are among the more than 21 million people (a conservative estimate[*]) who suffer from compulsive hoarding in North America today.

What Is Hoarding?

You have picked up this book because you are concerned that you might hoard. Or you are trying to help a loved one whom you suspect or know hoards. To get started, let's look quickly at a simple definition of hoarding. In chapter 16, I discuss the full clinical definition of hoarding according to the *Diagnostic and Statistical Manual of Mental Disorders*, 5th Edition (*DSM-5*) (APA 2013) and go into more detail about the types and impact of hoarding.

Hoarding is defined by all three of the following criteria, even to a minimal degree:

1 Excessive accumulation and failure to discard (proportionately) things, animals, or both, even when items appear to be of questionable value.

2 Impaired activities of daily living because spaces cannot be used for their intended purpose (for example, not being able to cook on the stove or eat at the table intended for meals).

3 Distress or difficulty functioning in the environment. Hoarding can also be a problem in other areas of your life (for example, office, car, computer hard drive, paper records, or even your purse), creating heightened anxiety that you carry with you everywhere, every day. This criterion includes "reasonable" distress that you might feel if the condition of your property puts you and others at risk, even if you are able to conceal the reality of your environment well enough that those who might have legitimate concerns aren't actively distressed.

---

* Based on the United Nations' current North American population estimates, 328,158,467 (United States) and 36,970,055 (Canada), as well as research showing that up to 6 percent of the population hoards (Timpano et al. 2011).

Note that individuals can exhibit behaviors associated with hoarding without meeting the *DSM-5* criteria for having hoarding disorder. *Adaptive hoarding*, for example, refers to behaviors like stockpiling for a purpose, without waste due to elapsed expiration dates. *Maladaptive hoarding* refers to accumulation that is out of control and causing problems for the people who hoard and those who share their environment. (See "Common Misconceptions about Hoarding" later in this chapter.)

Because maladaptive hoarding is widely acknowledged to be a compulsive behavior, it can create the following conditions as it progresses:

- Unhealthy living conditions due to deterioration, infestation, or contamination (for example, dangerous breathing conditions as a result of poor air quality, thick layers of dust, mouse scat, or mold)
- Unsafe living conditions due to fire, flood, tripping, or toppling risks, for example,
  o *rodents chewing on electrical cords, which could start a fire*
  o *an excessive accumulation of combustible items, providing fuel that could greatly intensify, prolong, and expand a fire*
  o *items getting wet, which can put a dangerous load on the structural integrity of the building*

Three additional facts about hoarding are important to understand:

1 Hoarding occurs in all cultures, at every income and education level, and for many different reasons.
2 Hoarding interventions can be costly and require time for the person to be ready to truly let go of their things, not just discard them. Extreme cleanups should be done as a last resort because they can be very destabilizing to the person hoarding.
3 Hoarding is a compulsive behavior. Without treatment, conditions will continue to deteriorate, often until the health and safety of the individual and community are put at risk.

Scientific literature, client experiences, as well as my professional clinical experience has taught me that the keys to successful outcomes are

- providing counseling, support, and coaching for the underlying reasons that people hoard; and
- decluttering their spaces, which are cluttered as a result of people not getting the help they need in time.

More than a Mental Health Issue

Hoarding was not considered a discrete disorder until the release of *DSM-5*, in May 2013. It is not, however, simply a mental health issue. Hoarding can also be a legal, personal, and public health and safety issue. Without identification and treatment, people living with hoarding disorder will likely continue to experience further deterioration in their mental health status as well as in their living conditions. Without hoarding-informed supportive interventions, people who hoard often put themselves and others at risk.

How Widespread Is Hoarding?

Research originally reported in 2003 by Gail Steketee and Randy Frost (2007) estimated that 1 to 2 percent of the general US population hoarded. The 2013 inclusion of hoarding disorder in the *DSM-5* has generated limited research on its prevalence rate. As the Shaw Mind Foundation (2016) notes in its report on hoarding, *Hoarding Disorder*, more research is needed to overcome the problem of data gathering from studies conducted before the new diagnosis classification, because that earlier research examined hoarding symptoms as part of other disorders. Under-reporting of incidence, severity, and self-identification were also noted in the report as common factors affecting accuracy. With these limitations in mind, we can still get an idea of how widespread hoarding disorder is:

- International studies found that the disorder affects between 2 and 6 percent of the population.
- UK-based studies suggested a prevalence of between 2 and 5 percent, indicating that the international estimate likely represents actual rates.
- German studies have put the rate of hoarding at approximately 5.8 percent.
- A Netherlands-based twin study estimated prevalence rates of 2 to 4 percent and found evidence that as people age, the prevalence among their age group increases, to 6 percent for those over 55 years old.
- Australian researchers estimated that hoarding occurred in 1 to 2 percent of the population, but critics of that research argued that the more accurate rate was in line with the international estimate, between 2 and 6 percent.
- In Japan, the study cited in the Shaw Mind Foundation report correlated obsessive-compulsive disorder, or OCD, with hoarding and found that more than one-third of participants with OCD also compulsively hoarded.
- In Canada, estimates suggested that between 3 and 6 percent of the population hoard.
- US estimates of the number of people who hoard ranged between 5 million and 14 million Americans. Given that the US general population was listed at 323.1 million in 2016, the range translates to between 1.5 and 4 percent who hoard.

In 2003, the rate cited by Steketee and Frost (2007) was 1 to 2 percent. Eight years later, in 2011, prevalence rates were revised to between 5 and 6 percent. I don't believe that the prevalence rates have increased. We may simply be better able to recognize a wider range of symptoms, giving us a more accurate picture of how prevalent this disorder actually is.

Clearly more research is needed internationally to determine with greater certainty what the actual hoarding prevalence rate is in the general population. Unfortunately, the lack of research funding limits our ability to determine actual prevalence rates. As further research with larger samples becomes available and can be replicated, I would not be surprised to find that the full continuum of hoarding occurs at a much higher rate than we can now substantiate. By *full continuum*, I mean the range of hoarding behavior that is sufficient to disrupt lives, rather than the smaller group of more severe symptoms used to determine hoarding prevalence in the research to date.

I can verify that hoarding is a concern throughout the world. My website, Birchall Consulting (www.hoarding.ca), regularly has visits from Norway, Denmark, Finland, Vietnam, Russia, Sri Lanka, Australia, South America, the United Kingdom, Canada, the United States, Central America, Malaysia, Indonesia, and Japan. I also receive daily phone calls, emails, and online requests from those who hoard, other professionals, and concerned family members worldwide, looking for advice on how to help themselves or the individuals they are concerned about. For advice on how you can help, see the video "Are You Worried about Someone's Collecting or Hoarding Behavior?" in the "Resources" section of my website. Other videos are being developed to provide support for those who hoard and for the professionals trying to respond effectively. You may also find these websites helpful:

International OCD Foundation, www.hoarding.IOCDF.org (US)
Children of Hoarders, www.childrenofhoarders.com (US)
Compulsive Hoarding, www.compulsive-hoarding.org (UK)
Australian Ageing Agenda, www.australianageingagenda.com.au (AU)

In the past, hoarding was thought to be an infrequent occurrence (affecting only 1 to 2 percent of the general population), yet everyone seemed to know someone who hoarded, and many had family members facing this challenge. In my experience as a trainer, therapist, and community developer, I can't mention hoarding anywhere without individuals taking me aside to tell me about their hoarding problem, discuss the hoarding of a loved one, or tell me a story about someone they know who hoards.

Although my practice is fee-for-service, I also do pro bono work and provide a manageable process for accessing services. I coach family members to help their loved ones, and I provide unlimited cost-free peer consultations to increase the options available for people to get the help they need when they need it, not just when they can afford it. For this reason, my practice is very diverse. This diversity widens my understanding every day of the many different people struggling with hoarding, the complex dimensions of their lives as a whole, and how this complexity can inspire adaptations and alternative strategies for changing their relationships with their things. In turn, what I learn from each person who comes to me for help becomes part of an ever-expanding toolbox for helping others.

Five Red Flags of Possible Hoarding

If you are unsure whether hoarding is becoming a problem for you or a loved one, ask yourself the following questions:

- ☐ Are there areas of your home that can't be used for their intended purpose, without shifting things around?
- ☐ How easy is it for you to find things when you want them?
- ☐ Does clutter make it difficult to walk through any of the rooms in your home?

TABLE 1.1

Are You a Hoarder in the Making?

RATING SCALE 0 = not at all; 2 = mildly; 4 = moderately; 6 = severely; 8 = extremely	YOUR RATING (0–8)
1 Considering the number of possessions you have, how difficult is it to use the rooms in your home?	
2 How much does your home's current condition upset you?	
3 How upset or concerned are others about your home's current condition?	
4 How concerned are other people or agencies with your clutter, to the point of trying to intervene (e.g., offering to help you tidy up)?	
5 How difficult or distressing is it for you to get rid of things?	
6 How difficult is it to resist buying something when you don't have the money to spend?	
Add up your ratings for questions 1–6 to get your total:	

☐ To what extent are flat surfaces cluttered?

☐ When you see things you want, do you feel compelled to have them?

If any of these areas are a problem for you, you can gain more understanding by taking the full quiz in table 1.1.

10 Most Common Things Hoarded

Now, armed with the information you have gathered, you are closer to a better assessment of your acquiring behaviors. Check the list in the box on page 18 to see how many of these items are accumulating in your home.

If you want to support someone who hoards, be sure to review Resource 16.6, "Dos and Don'ts for Coaches in Hoarding Situations," *before* you start the process. This information will help you avoid starting out on the wrong foot when trying to help someone who hoards.

RESULTS

0–10 = You probably have a mild clutter situation in your home. Welcome to the real world.

11–20 = The clutter in your home is at a moderate level. It's time to have a closer look at why it keeps happening. An ounce of prevention is worth a pound of cure.

21–36 = The accumulation in your home is at, or approaching, a severe level. This is about more than being "messy" or "too busy." Would you agree that you are overwhelmed? Do you repeatedly start but get nowhere? It's time to get the help you need.

37–48 = The accumulation in your home is extreme. The people (and animals) in the house may be in danger. If you live in attached housing, your neighbors share your risk. Without a doubt, it is time to get help. Please make the call now.

QUESTION SPECIFIC RESULTS

✔ **If you rated questions 1, 4, or 5 above a 2,** assess your situation and ask for feedback from someone you trust who knows you, then ask for help if needed.

✔ **If you answered 2 to most questions,** keep an eye on your situation. These questions are red flags. Many people who hoard "wake up" one day and ask, "When did this happen?"

✔ **If you answered 4 or higher to questions 2, 3, or 6**, ask for feedback from a trusted friend who knows you. Search yourself for the reasons for your ratings and assess your ability to tackle the problems on your own. If you need to try to do it yourself but are not making progress in a month, call for help. A month easily becomes a year.

✔ **If you have tried to declutter numerous times without success,** seek help to manage what may develop (or has already developed) into a more serious problem.

---

10 Most Common Things Hoarded

1 Paper, especially newspapers, magazines, and flyers—or electronic data

2 Things used in everyday life that don't get put away: food containers, clothing, laundry, shopping and grocery bags, mail

3 Excessive recycling materials that don't get recycled, such as flyers, newspapers, biodegradables

4 Clothing

5 Plastic bags

6 Sentimental things that tell a story of significant life events or happier times

7 Mechanical objects, car parts, electronic equipment and components, tools, nuts, bolts, screws, building materials, leftover pieces of partially used materials that are kept "just in case"

8 Wool, fabric, craft supplies for use in the near future, or for use in potential projects far into the future while current project remains unfinished

9 Furniture and household or work-related items thought to be too good to get rid of, despite no foreseeable need for them, or items discovered by the side of the street believed to be too good to miss

10 Animals

Diagnostic Criteria from the *DSM-5*

The *Diagnostic and Statistical Manual of Mental Disorders*, 5th Edition (*DSM-5*), is the official source for the clinical definition of hoarding disorder. The *DSM-5* is widely used as the standard for diagnosing mental disorders, using comprehensive lists of criteria, in people experiencing compromised mental health and wellness.

 Refer to chapter 16, "Resources," for a full description of hoarding disorder according to the *DSM-5*.

Hoarding's inclusion in the *DSM-5* confirms it as a separate disorder in its own right. In the past, many thought of it as a syndrome of OCD (obsessive-compulsive disorder). We now accept that hoarding is different. The disorder now has its own diagnostic criteria and treatment requirements.

How many people who hoard have OCD? Research results vary within a range of 15 to 33 percent. The average in my practice is 19 percent (see appendix). These people are living with OCD symptoms and behaviors that interfere with achieving important life goals. Many went unidentified and untreated until they called me for help.

On the Path to Hoarding?

Table 1.2 provides the working definition of hoarding that I offer my clients to determine where they are on the path to hoarding. If you check *any* of the boxes in the table, you are either living with hoarding or somewhere on the path to hoarding.

TABLE 1.2

Where Are You on the Path to Hoarding?

☐ The accumulation (no matter what the items are or what the price tag says) is what most people would describe as excessive.

☐ You are unable to manage the items so that each has a permanent place and does not require you to adapt your life to access it.

Some or all areas in the environment can't be used for their intended purpose. People have to regularly take *adaptive* action to access or use the space in the home. Adaptations include:

☐ *walking on objects*

☐ *stepping or climbing over things, such as climbing over a gate to go up and down stairs because so many animals are in the house, meaning the gates need to remain in place night and day*

☐ *moving items to be able to use the space*

One or more people are *or* have become concerned about the condition of your environment, *or* they would be concerned if they knew the truth about the situation. They might be any of the following:

☐ *Family members*   ☐ *Local bylaw officials*

☐ *Friends*   ☐ *Child protection officials*

☐ *Neighbors*   ☐ *Animal protection officials*

☐ *Landlords*   ☐ *Home insurance providers*

☐ *Local fire department officials*   ☐ *Mortgage company*

What Is the Difference between Hoarding and Cluttering?

You may hear the terms *hoarding* and *cluttering* used interchangeably. There is a difference. The distinction is that generally people who clutter, although they may keep excessive quantities of things, don't hold on to as many things as people who hoard. The other difference is that people who clutter usually do not have the same difficulty making decisions about how to dispose of enough items to maintain healthy and safe environments. Only in retrospect can you say with certainty whether your behavior was clutter or early onset hoarding, and ultimately you need to be guided by the fire regulations as they relate to Risk Levels 0–5 (see "What Is Your Level of Risk?" in chapter 2).

Here is what we *don't* know: whether cluttering is really a stage in the life cycle of hoarding.

Every person who has clutter does not necessarily go on to hoard. But conversely, in the 17 years I have worked with those who hoard, every single person has told me that creating clutter was the starting point.

You decide. Is your clutter manageable?

Five Types of Hoarding

I divide hoarding into five distinct types.

1 *Indiscriminate hoarding:* when people who hoard gather and acquire indiscriminately.

If you hoard indiscriminately, you are likely tempted to keep everything that comes into your area of control. You generally acquire and hold on to things, with few limits, until you are discovered and persuaded to reduce your collection. Many of the people described in chapter 6, "The Impact of Hoarding on the Family," hoard indiscriminately, acquiring and holding on to many of the top 10 hoarded items listed earlier in this chapter. Those who continue to hoard rarely wake up one day and say, "Gee, I think I have enough." There is always the next deal, the next find, the next one-of-a-kind or "just in case" acquisition. Given enough time, if those who hoard indiscriminately are unidentified and untreated, they will go on to create personal and public health and safety hazards. Hoarding is a compulsive behavior, and therefore if nothing changes, indiscriminate hoarding will continue compulsively.

An example of *indiscriminate hoarding:* a cluttered garage in which the floor has been completely covered with all types of items

2 *Discriminate hoarding:* when people who hoard discriminate between items they see as extremely desirable and those they do not, acquiring a specific type or group of items excessively.

Another way to hoard is to respond intensively to items with particular characteristics. These types of items have high attraction and reward value to the person hoarding them, who places few, if any, limits on the importance of acquiring these items. For example, in the chapter 6 case study, Paul has a massive music collection of both vinyl records and CDs. He also has bookcase after bookcase, throughout many rooms, filled with books and magazines on specific topics.

3 *Combination hoarding:* both a type and a stage of hoarding, when the excessive accumulation reaches a point where the valued items are mixed up in piles with large numbers of unimportant things.

An example of *discriminate hoarding*: an accumulation of clothes piled on top of a living room chair

FACING PAGE:
An example of *combination hoarding*: a craft/playroom with a combination of items appropriate for the space and unrelated objects piling up on containers

This third way to hoard combines both discriminate and indiscriminate hoarding, resulting from not processing everyday items, such as dishes, empty food containers, garbage, food scraps, newspapers, magazines, flyers, and furniture. Among the developing piles of everyday things are highly valued items. These piles are often chaotic and present a problem for safe mobility throughout the environment, the pathways ending up surrounded by higher and higher piles.

4 *Hoarding in Diogenes syndrome:* when the hoarding is one of several signs that a person is suffering from Diogenes syndrome, sometimes referred to as *senile squalor syndrome.*

Diogenes syndrome is characterized by extreme self-neglect; domestic squalor; social isolation; compulsive (combination) hoarding of everything, including garbage; and apathy about, among other things, the conditions the person has created. In extreme cases, individuals are so apathetic that they appear to be in a fog or stupor.

An example of *compulsive combination hoarding* related to *Diogenes syndrome:* a kitchen in which mixed accumulations of food, garbage, and kitchen supplies contribute to the squalor characteristic of the syndrome

FACING PAGE: An example of *animal hoarding*: a large number of dogs sharing a relatively small space

They are often suspicious and hold paranoid beliefs, especially concerning public officials and authority figures. In the chapter 10 case studies, Mario's hoarding is related to Diogenes syndrome.

5   *Animal hoarding:* when a person accumulates a sufficient number of animals to the point where human and animal health and safety are compromised. The definition of animal hoarding does not contain any actual number of animals.

Animal hoarding can be seen in some ways as a complex subset of discriminate hoarding. It is defined as an accumulation of animals to the extent that there is:

- failure to provide minimal nutrition, sanitation, and veterinary care;
- failure to act on the deteriorating condition of the animals or the environment; and
- failure to act on or recognize the negative effects of the deteriorating condition of the animals on the individual's own health and well-being.

For more information on animal hoarding, including how it is explained by five different psychiatric models, see "Animal Hoarding: Devotion or Disorder?" in this book's supplemental online resources (jhupbooks.press.jhu.edu/title/conquer-clutter).

What Hoarding Costs You

Hoarding can cost you so much of your life, as the first-person accounts in chapter 15 attest. It could cost you relationships that would have enriched your life and sustained you. By investing in your relationship with your possessions, you spend your time, focus, and emotional energy with objects, which can't love you back. They are just things, inanimate things. They have no value on their own except the cost of replacing them. *You* bestow importance to them beyond their dollar value.

Should anything ever happen to you, your things will never miss you. They can't empathize or respond when you are sad, lonely, or afraid. They don't care that you enjoy having them as part of your life, and you are not part of theirs. They don't have other loved ones who miss them, worry about them, or grieve the rupture that exists in what should be their closest relationships. Your things are not changed by missing the chance to build memories, laughter, and loyalty with others of their kind. Most people I work with, whether they hoard or love someone who does, tell me that hoarding has cost them many of these benefits of human connection.

Hoarding also deprives you of peace of mind. Many people who hoard go to great lengths to manage events in their lives to avoid discovery of their hoarding by family, friends, acquaintances, landlords, neighbors, the fire department, or local enforcement officials. Depending on where you live, enforcement officials might include bylaw officers, code enforcement officers, property standards officers or code compliance inspectors if you live in a multi-unit dwelling, child protection officials, and animal protection officials. Hoarded environments are also a concern to mortgage companies and home insurance companies.

At an absolute minimum, hoarding costs you a functional and comfortable space to live. The accumulation may also be costing you a safe and healthy environment.

Most of the people who come to me for help tell me that in their quiet moments, when they tell themselves the truth, they acknowledge that hoarding also, sadly, costs them their self-esteem and self-respect. Quite often they acknowledge it only to themselves. They don't want to live any longer in chaos and, for some, squalor. They dream of a different life and want to feel normal again; if only they could figure out how to undo the chaos they have created.

Let this book be a part of your process to reestablish your dreams and reach your goals. There is help available. This book is part of the collective of excellent sources that can assist you to find the help you need to take back your life when your things are taking over. See resource 16.4, "Hoarding Disorder and Associated Resources."

Three Paths to Hoarding

How does a person become someone who hoards? When I consider all the research and everything I've read on hoarding, along with my clinical experience and what other professionals and my clients have told me, three paths to hoarding emerge: genetics—inheriting the vulnerability to hoard as a result of genetics or environmental factors, for example, by mirroring beliefs and behaviors due to the genetics of your family of origin; having a high-risk comorbid factor; or being (even mildly) chronically disorganized and then becoming vulnerable.

1. Inheriting the vulnerability to hoard, genetically or environmentally. Research shows that 84 percent of people with OCD who hoard have a first-degree relative who also hoards, but only 37 percent reported a family history of OCD (Feusner and Saxena 2005; Winsberg et al. 1999). In other words, 84 percent of the study participants have a mother, father, sister, brother, or child who hoards.

Some genetic research points to four chromosomes (long strings of genes) with markers in common among some people who hoard. Three of the chromosomes identified in one study were 4, 5, and 17, indicating an *autosomal recessive inheritance pattern* (Zhang et al. 2002), meaning a person would have to inherit a trait or condition from both parents to actually have that trait or condition. To understand the significance of the chromosome numbers, you may recall that each cell in the body has 46 chromosomes arranged in 23 pairs: one pair of sex chromosomes and 22 pairs of *autosomal* chromosomes. One of each pair is inherited from the mother and the other from the father. The autosomal chromosome pairs are numbered, enabling researchers to identify specific chromosomes, such as those associated with hoarding in the studies above.

The OCD Collaborative Genetics Study, led by Johns Hopkins Medicine researchers, also linked compulsive hoarding to chromosome 14 (Samuels et al. 2007). This extensive study found that compulsive hoarding is a serious health problem for the sufferers, their families, and the community at large. It appears to be highly prevalent and to run in families, which could be the result of genetic inheritance, but not necessarily. Hoarding behaviors can be passed down from one generation to the next as a result of environmental factors, for example:

- growing up in a home where cluttering and hoarding beliefs and behaviors were modeled for impressionable children;
- being raised by a parent incapable of teaching boundaries and limits or leading by example; or
- having a parent who cannot teach effective life strategies to deal with loss, fear, and compulsions and who models substituting things for healthy processing of feelings

To review more of the research done on genetic links for hoarding, see this chapter's section of the references near the end of this book.

2. Having a high-risk comorbid factor. The term *comorbid factor* refers to another disorder coexisting with hoarding. Comorbid disorders or life situations don't *cause* hoarding, but they do make it more complicated to manage. The extra layer of need can interfere with progress and require additional treatment.

A *high-risk* comorbid factor means that the presence of a certain factor makes another specific factor more likely. People who have any of the disorders or other issues listed below are at a higher risk for developing hoarding disorder. Is it a certainty? No. But please take note of the excellent research cited for certain disorders to obtain more information about how they affect individuals who hoard. Also note that risk of hoarding disorder is not equal from one comorbid factor to the next. The prevalence rate of hoarding disorder co-occurring varies with each disorder listed.

- Anxiety disorders
- Eating disorders
- Addictions (drugs, alcohol, gambling)

- Tics, Tourette syndrome
- Autism
- Schizophrenia
- Dementia and Alzheimer's (Hwang et al. 1998)
- Attention deficit disorder, or ADD, attention deficit/hyperactivity disorder, or ADHD (Hartl et al. 2005)
- Social isolation
- Social phobia
- Depression
- Personality disorders such as obsessive-compulsive, avoidant, dependent, paranoid
- Aging with mobility issues
- Biological factors, such as differences in the brain (Emergence Health Network 2018)

See the appendix for a breakdown of the comorbid factors present in a random sample of my clients.

3. Being (even mildly) chronically disorganized and then becoming vulnerable.
Many people lead mildly disorganized lives, never quite getting on top of things, including their living and working spaces, finances, maintenance of healthy relationships, and physical, mental, and spiritual well-being. Some may be at additional risk of developing hoarding disorder when they become vulnerable because of a major negative event or a series of lesser events that occur in a compressed period and prevent them from restabilizing between setbacks. They do only what they have to do to keep things barely manageable. This means that they are consistently living on the verge of spinning out of control and becoming overwhelmed.

Then something challenging happens (as it does to all of us). If it isn't a major setback, they usually manage to get themselves back on track.

There is an expression that "bad things happen in threes." Whether or not this is true, many people have a tendency to believe it. Several challenging events happening in too compressed a period can make it very difficult for the person to recover and restabilize before the next setback happens. This onerous period in their life can leave them disoriented, destabilized, and overwhelmed. Remember, feeling overwhelmed is a dangerous state of mind to allow yourself to get mired in, and you should never allow yourself to get stuck or remain there. Feeling overwhelmed robs you of the very tools you need (ready access to your brain's executive functioning) and the capacity to figure things out, to regain your equilibrium and your life along with it.

When I am called in to help people who hoard and find themselves overwhelmed, I often find that they have made one of two choices to cope.

CHOICE 1: to acquire and save things to soothe themselves and fill the void.
The things have become their primary positive focus and a source of comfort, security, and stability. The things are their friends. The more things they have, and the closer they keep those things around them, the better they feel. At a minimum, relationships have started to become more distant. In most cases, by the time people who have made this choice realize how serious the situation has become (the call for help is usually prompted by an impending crisis), many of their relationships have become burned out or ruptured. Loved ones (even though they may still care and worry about the person) pull away and detach themselves to avoid being pulled into the vortex of chaos and crisis.

CHOICE 2: to stop processing the things of everyday life and shut down.
People who make this choice compartmentalize their lives in the extreme. They may still go out to work every day and act as if nothing is wrong. No one would guess their internal turmoil based on how well groomed, well presented, and capable they are by day. No one would guess that they return to severely hoarded living conditions each evening. Having more things does not in reality create a haven or cocoon, even though becoming immune to the growing clutter does protect people from having to come to terms with the state of their lives at that time. The clutter creates a place where, for example, a person may have only one available chair, one place to sit. No one is invited in. Elaborate ruses and explanations are used to keep others away, even to the extent of letting cherished loving relationships deteriorate, because the things (which are not their friend) have taken over, and the thought of reclaiming the environment feels insurmountable. They are in survival mode, often not even noticing the reality of what is developing around them.

For those reading this who have already arrived at either of these two points, know that with the right hoarding-informed help and support, living the life you really, really want is not out of your reach.

For those reading this who haven't gotten to the point of making these choices yet, or who don't believe they ever could, know that *no one ever set out to hoard*. Many felt just like you.

There are four questions to ask yourself:

1 How well am I taking care of my physical, mental, and spiritual health? (Belonging to a formalized religion is only one option for expressing and living the spiritual side of ourselves; there are other ways to honor your spirit.)
    Consider:

- *What is the meaning and purpose of my life?*
- *What do I stand for and believe in?*
- *What unique gifts and talents do I possess?*

- *Have I lost touch with what my gifts and talents are? (Like everyone else, you have them. Yes, you do.)*
- *Do my things represent who I am today, moving forward, or do my things represent me in the past and are no longer the me of today?*
- *Does the current accumulation block me from being who I am today, with a future, including a vision and goals?*

2 What would it take to overwhelm me? How close am I right now?

3 How would I react to becoming overwhelmed?

4 Before it got to that point, whom could I call to help me find the resources I need?

How People Form Attachment Relationships to Things

There are three types of attachment relationships people can have with their things. (*Note:* A person can have more than one type of attachment relationship with the same item. Excellent work has been done by Randy Frost and Gail Steketee [2007] on describing saving patterns.)

1 Sentimental relationship. A sentimental relationship occurs when you use an item as a cue for an important emotional experience or time in your life, such as a job you were happy and proud of achieving. The item can be a reminder of a lost relationship with another person (e.g., spouse, parent, child, grandparent, or someone you admire). You comfort yourself thinking, *If I keep this thing, somehow I haven't really and finally lost the person or experience.* You convince yourself that what is important to you isn't really gone. The more things you keep as a reminder of the person, the more you buffer yourself from having to come to terms with the loss, that the person is not here in the physical sense any longer. The thing becomes a substitute, but it also becomes a barrier to accepting reality and to dealing in a healthy way with grief. Unresolved grief is an extremely destructive emotion.

Sometimes, when the object represents the loss of a person, there is a belief that the person's essence is somehow fused with the item, as if the person is actually "in" or part of the item, because he or she once touched it or held it. When you believe that an inanimate object can become fused with a person, letting go of the item is more difficult, because you have invested so much meaning in it. Keeping it buffers you against the loss you feel. The idea of parting with it feels like actually throwing away the person and dishonoring the relationship you shared.

The degree to which people form intensely sentimental relationships with so many of their things might increase concern for debilitating unresolved grief. In some cases, the person is not actually gone, but the item represents a special time in your relationship with the person; for example, after children have grown up and left home, you keep many of the items they used as a baby (e.g., their crib/mattress, baby wardrobe for potential grandchildren, perhaps decades away if at all). It is always a question of degree. How many things can you keep? There is no clear and easy answer. For example, what is the logic for keeping most of your children's baby clothes? Is this the best use of the storage space you have available? What condition will they be in if ever needed? How many other things do you apply this emotional thinking to? Is there enough storage space for your current and future life?

2   **Aesthetic relationship.** When you get a strong, immediate rush of adrenaline, which can happen during the stressful decision-making stage of whether to acquire something, or of dopamine, when you are attracted to a particular type of object and experience anticipatory pleasure, you may be exhibiting an aesthetic attachment relationship with the item. Even slight increases in dopamine can cause your memory to suffer; for example, not remembering that you don't want to acquire impulsively. You may not even have known that the item existed up to that point, but when you see it, you go from 0 to 100 in a flash and feel you have to have it. You may obsess about it. If you don't take it or buy it, you regret it. It calls to you. This relationship is about obsessions and compulsions, bordering on inability to delay gratification and self-regulate. It is simply "I have to have it *now*."

3   **Intrinsic relationship.** With intrinsic attachment relationships, the item itself is seen to have significant or potential importance. You have the strong inviolable belief in avoiding waste. I see this attachment with many people who have what I call "the engineer's brain." They don't necessarily have to be trained engineers. They are often highly capable, crafty, handy, or frugal people. The key element of an intrinsic relationship with objects is that you see the importance and transferable use in a disproportionate number of things and feel it is your duty to use objects in any other possible way. Sometimes people feel that the degree to which they can demonstrate an item's transferable usefulness demonstrates how worthy, capable, and resourceful they are or how right they are. The problem that often arises from the number of kept things is that they don't actually get recycled. That nth number of widgets is seen as important, so it is kept. The problem is that the more you keep, the less likely you are to find items when you actually need them. There is a failure to accept reality that the collections will, in fact, not end up being useful, especially in the numbers accumulated. Collections can also be impossible to maintain and keep in the condition needed for future use.

Characteristics of Good Support

If you want to support someone who hoards, be sure that you review the "Dos and Don'ts for Coaches in Hoarding Situations" (resource 16.6) *before* you start the process. This information will help you avoid starting out on the wrong foot when trying to help someone who hoards.

Common Misconceptions about Hoarding

Let's take a look at some of the common beliefs that people have about hoarding and about people who hoard.

MISCONCEPTION 1:

Hoarding is associated with either having gone through the Great Depression or having parents who went through the Great Depression and passed on the effects of deprivation.

Not so: Many millions of people who don't hoard lived through the Depression or had parents who did. In fact, the vast majority of these generations don't hoard.

Two concepts about hoarding are important to understand.

1 There is such a thing as *adaptive hoarding.* Adaptive hoarding is when people acquire and keep a supply of items because they know, based on their personal history, that they will use them. For example, people may stock up when something is on sale or is available for free, but they do actually use them in their daily lives, before the items reach the expiration date or otherwise deteriorate.

Why are they able to keep a supply of items and actually use them in time?

- *They may have personal values or a commitment not to waste.*
- *They may have strong environmental beliefs and be committed to intensive recycling.*
- *They may have a desire to be efficient by using things for their alternate uses.*
- *There may be other personal or practical reasons for their acquiring behavior, but their pattern of behavior is that things get used in the numbers acquired and supplies rotate regularly.*

The point is that people who hoard adaptively honor the things and their own values and beliefs by carrying out the purpose for which they acquired or kept the items in the first place. They carry out their intent.

Remember that every person who clutters does not necessarily go on to hoard. But conversely, in the 17 years I have worked with people who hoard, every single person has told me that they started out by creating clutter. The fact that you are reading this book may mean that it is time for you to decide where you are on the continuum.

2 *Maladaptive*, or *compulsive*, *hoarding* is what I am discussing in this book. Whatever the perceived intent of acquiring or saving the items, that purpose or intent breaks down and creates a hoarded environment. There are many reasons that this happens and many accompanying complicating factors that make "not hoarding" even harder.

From this point on, the terms *hoarding* and *hoarder* refer to maladaptive or compulsive hoarding behavior unless otherwise stated.

MISCONCEPTION 2:
Hoarding is caused by experiencing significant loss.

Not necessarily so: Loss is part of life, and we all attribute our own meaning to the things that happen to us. When life takes a downturn, most people experience a sense of loss, but most of us don't hoard as a result. Those who do might have a lower threshold for feelings of loss or might assign overwhelming meaning to situations involving loss. My clinical working hypothesis is consistent with a point made in a study outlined in the *American Journal of Psychiatry*: "It is possible that traumatic experiences or other environmental risk factors interact with particular genes to precipitate compulsive hoarding" (Iervolino et al. 2009, 1159–60).

Some people who hoard have experienced loss, and some haven't.

Sometimes the debilitating effect of the loss or setback is a measure of how significant it was personally. Sometimes a series of smaller losses occur within a compressed period, which doesn't allow enough time to restabilize ourselves before the next loss or setback happens.

Remember the "Three Paths to Hoarding" earlier in this chapter? I have seen people on Path 3, those who are chronically disorganized until they become vulnerable, become destabilized and overwhelmed as a result of multiple smaller losses and setbacks. Sometimes they report this period of their lives as when things began to build up. Items were not processed regularly. This situation can go on to create a hoard. *We can only deal with what we feel competent and adequately resourced to deal with.* When we are overwhelmed, denial, distraction, and avoidance are common coping strategies. If denial, distraction, or avoidance go on long enough, the accumulation can feel insurmountable and become overwhelming.

Whether or not you hoard, when you first realize that you are becoming overwhelmed, *reach out right away for help you trust to deal with the problems weighing you down.*

MISCONCEPTION 3:
Hoarded environments mean the person *must* be a compulsive hoarder.

Not so: There are situations in which the person with no discernible risk factors for compulsive hoarding has a hoarded environment.

Two types of situations stand out in my experience.

1. **Aging with mobility issues.** I have had numerous requests for help from people with no measurable or observable psychological factors related to the environment being hoarded. The problem for most of these people would turn out to be mobility limitations related to aging or being physically less abled. In addition, they were extremely reluctant to call for help because they were afraid someone would determine that they should not be living independently. The hoarded environment was the by-product of those two factors. I can personally relate to this perspective. I have (only half-jokingly) told my family that when I am old, the only way I am leaving my house is in a pine box. Anyone who tries to put me in "the home" is out of the will.

2. **Managing inherited items while grieving.** When people inherit items after the death of a person close to them, while in the state of acute grief, they sometimes can't see any other option than to bring excessive numbers of things into their own environment and thereby create a hoard. Quite often I have been told by people grieving that they don't necessarily even *like* or *want* many of the things bequeathed, but they cannot physically or emotionally make the necessary decisions to sort and dispose. The other person's things are still symbolic of the person and the relationship they shared. They are not ready to let go yet, and in their grief, they fail to consider other options that would avoid creating a hoarded environment. When this happens for a brief time, the hoarded environment may be the by-product of a natural grief reaction, feelings of excessive responsibility for too many things, and being temporarily destabilized by these feelings and the situation. In this temporary state, they may have created a hoard and need help developing and implementing a more appropriate and suitable plan. Read the story of Debbie and Mike in chapter 9 to see recommendations for supporting people in this situation.

A person who hoards must be crazy or they wouldn't live like that.

Not so: The term "crazy" depicts attributes I have rarely encountered in the people I have worked with. The fact is, mental health and wellness is a continuum that, on an especially bad day, none of us may score terribly high on. We all move up and down that continuum.

The better question to ask ourselves is, How well are we managing our physical and mental health needs?

Life is a like a cup. We are all walking around with our cups already partially full. What would it take for each of us to upset the balance and overload ourselves? In other words, what would it take for us to become overwhelmed to the extent that we become indecisive for a prolonged period, and what would we create as a result?

What we carry inside our cups must be continually kept in a manageable balance. Too much or too little of anything can upset the wellness balance. Choose consciously what you add to your cup and how much, as well as what you allow to drain its contents, so that the cup that holds your life stays in balance.

As you can see in the following photos, at both ends of the extremes, you are in serious trouble. The fill of our cup is the mix of positive and negative influences in our life. In "Running on Empty," you don't have enough of either positive or negative. In "Just Enough in the Tank to Manage," you have just enough mix of positive and negative but no surplus you can draw on when life deals you a setback. While "Life's Good" looks like you have more weight on your shoulders, you have some spare energy, focus, and positives to draw on to offset the balance of negatives. But continuing to add even more positives and negatives puts you in a state of being overwhelmed and stuck, because you have too many balls in the air ("At Your Limit"). This closes the circle back to a negative state ("Totally Overwhelmed").

With each decision you make, begin by asking yourself:

- Does this fill my cup? *or* Does it empty my cup?
- What does this choice mean for my physical and emotional wellness balance?

These questions are just a practical way to make choices consciously and give yourself permission to set the boundaries and limits you need before you find yourself overwhelmed at one extreme or the other.

Those who create a hoarded environment (and the act of hoarding itself) must be messy and dirty.

Not so: Sometimes the hoarded environment is meticulously clean, tidy, and well organized.

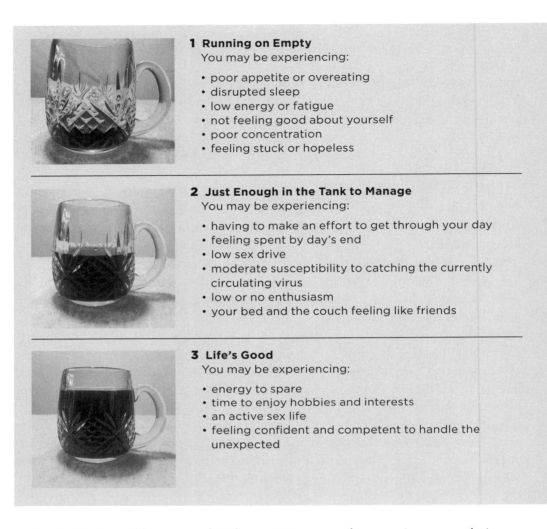

1 Running on Empty

You may be experiencing:

- poor appetite or overeating
- disrupted sleep
- low energy or fatigue
- not feeling good about yourself
- poor concentration
- feeling stuck or hopeless

2 Just Enough in the Tank to Manage

You may be experiencing:

- having to make an effort to get through your day
- feeling spent by day's end
- low sex drive
- moderate susceptibility to catching the currently circulating virus
- low or no enthusiasm
- your bed and the couch feeling like friends

3 Life's Good

You may be experiencing:

- energy to spare
- time to enjoy hobbies and interests
- an active sex life
- feeling confident and competent to handle the unexpected

So what's the problem, you ask? The main issues are the excessive accumulation and the failure to let go in a way that maintains a safe environment. Hoarding interferes with access to spaces intended for particular daily living use and activities. The fire fuel load is just as much an issue in a neat and clean hoarded environment. You and your hoarded environment may not create the crisis that results in a fire, but your excessive fuel load will make the fire spread faster. This reality will greatly lessen the precious time needed for you, your family members or roommates, and your pets to escape safely.

MISCONCEPTION 6:

People who hoard can't discard.

Not necessarily so: Some people who hoard can discard just fine. What they never do is balance the volume of what they acquire with what they discard. A bottleneck

4 At Your Limit
You may be experiencing:

- life feeling out of control
- seriously overscheduled days
- trouble mustering the focus and energy to finish tasks
- chronic severe stress every day
- chronic impatience and frustration
- small things and noise bothering you to an unusual degree
- an inability to face any more challenges

5 Totally Overwhelmed
You may be experiencing:

- emotional outbursts
- temper outbursts
- underlying irritation and anger most of each day
- mood fluctuations
- suicidal thoughts
- problems at school, at work, with family, and in social relationships
- low or no sex drive
- trouble initiating and following through with tasks
- an inability to make decisions
- difficulty getting out of bed
- the sense that you are running as fast as you can but getting nowhere
- a zoned-out feeling
- your feelings of being overwhelmed and stuck spreading into many other areas of your life with significantly negative results

is created, which produces the hoard. The only difference from the experiences of those who have trouble discarding is the length of time it takes for the environment to become hoarded.

Yes, some people who hoard can discard.

The pattern of acquiring, saving, and discarding varies from person to person, affecting how much time it takes for a hoarding problem to develop over a person's lifetime, what I refer to as a *hoarding life cycle pattern*.

A person able to regularly decide whether to discard items develops a hoarding problem through extreme acquiring (see the story of a compulsive shopper in chapter 8). A hoarded environment may be brought under temporary control only to recur with the next arrival of acquisitions. There is an ebb and flow to the level of hoarding, depending on the number of accumulated items arriving and leaving at any point. When acquiring *adaptively* (to meet an actual need for the item, such as toothpaste, without generalizing the act of acquisition to everything else that looks interesting while shopping for toothpaste), the person is able to let go with no impulse to fill the void with a replacement.

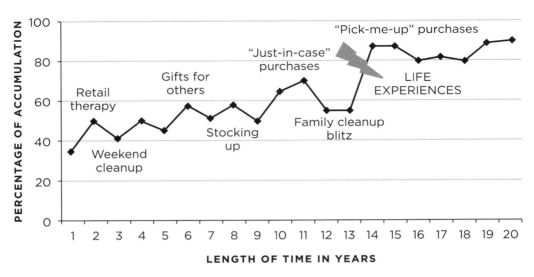

Hoarding life cycle pattern 1: Extreme accumulation and regular discarding over time

Sometimes in these hoarding situations, the person does not have difficulty discarding as long as the items go to a place that reflects the person's values or beliefs. They find it acceptable to discard if they know the item is going to someone who can use it, appreciate it, and take good care of it.

Whether or not your environment is hoarded, the following events can put you and others at risk. Any level of hoarding elevates that risk.

- *If an electrical or gas heat–producing appliance malfunctions, fire is a real possibility.* The malfunction does not even have to be in the hoarded environment; it can be in an adjoining property, especially if the properties are close or attached. A hoarded environment increases the fuel load and (depending on where the accumulation is located) decreases the options for a safe exit in case of an emergency. Combustible items (items that will catch fire and burn) in the hoarded environment add to the speed at which the fire will spread and consume the environment and anything inside it. There is a combined risk, as described below, when firefighters hose down the inside of a building, unaware that a hoarded environment exists. Responders can also be injured or perish as floors collapse under the weight of wet items (as has actually happened).
- *If flooding occurs (whether your unit caused the flood or not):*
    - *nonabsorbent items, such as televisions and electrical appliances, will be destroyed;*
    - *absorbent items, such as boxes, papers, and furniture, will hold the fluid, and the accumulation of wet items will weigh far more than it did when dry; and*
    - *depending on the volume of items, the structural integrity of floors may fail, causing them to collapse, taking possessions and occupants with them.*

- *A destabilizing setback can upset the "checks and balance" strategy of discarding regularly.* Setbacks in life are inevitable. They happen to all of us. Will the crisis require increased "retail therapy" to provide a pick-me-up? Old habits die hard. It won't take long to become overwhelmed again.

A second hoarding life cycle pattern is to offset infrequent discarding by acquiring fewer things less frequently over time. This pattern takes longer to develop into a hoarded environment, but it has the same potential to lead to an extreme hoarding situation. I have worked with many people who started out this way.

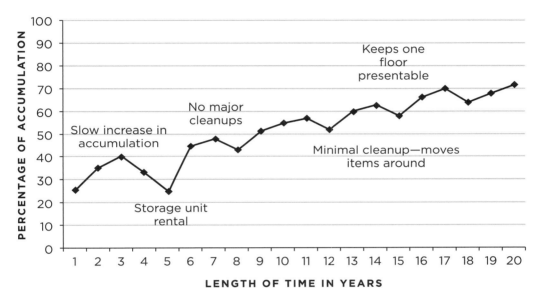

Hoarding life cycle pattern 2: Moderate accumulation and infrequent discarding over time

This pattern of accumulation involves acquiring, rigid saving, and using. People want to get value from each item, so they ask themselves, "How much did I spend on it?" If they feel that they haven't gotten enough use or value from the item, they may not be willing to let it go yet. They mistakenly believe that by holding on to the item, they somehow retain the money they spent on it or its ideal value, even if the item proves not to be as useful as anticipated. Keeping items is a way to get their money's worth.

Discarding happens differently as well. They tell themselves that they are too busy to spend the time it takes to discard, and they may have genuinely busy lives. They tend to overcommit their time and energy and are chronically overscheduled (see Lucinda's story in chapter 9).

People who engage in this pattern of accumulation and discarding need to reflect on why they keep themselves so busy. None of us is indispensable. At its core, keeping busy may distract from and help them avoid the priority tasks they need to do to address their hoarding disorder and to keep their environment safe and healthy. They are vulnerable to the risks that all hoarders face: fire, flood, and increased accumulation when having to cope with life's inevitable setbacks.

A third pattern of hoarding involves accumulating not much more than the average person accumulates, but never discarding anything. *Not one thing* that enters the environment, ever leaves it. Perhaps the person has an elaborate recycling system, but the items never actually make it out to the recycling bin for pickup. Perhaps the person is saving and storing items for others, such as old children's clothes and toys for a younger sibling's children, even though the sibling doesn't have a partner yet and does not expect to have children in the foreseeable future, if ever. This pattern offers a "noble" way to keep everything. The situation will probably take a while to develop into an extreme hoarding environment, but given enough time, and if nothing intervenes, extreme hoarding will occur. It never gets easier to deal with accumulation.

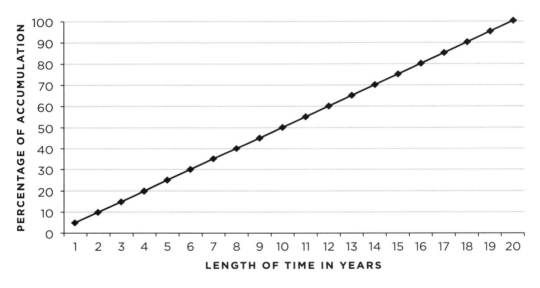

Hoarding life cycle pattern 3: Mild (average) accumulation but nothing leaves over time

If you see yourself or someone close to you anywhere on this continuum, please reach out for hoarding-informed help sooner rather than later (even if you have to access it through remote or internet technologies).

MISCONCEPTION 7:

There is no good reason that you can't "just do it," just get organized and clean up a little every day.

Not so: People who hoard have difficulty addressing the problem for many good reasons. One of my clients, Cathy, reminded me of the old saying, "Denial is not just a river in Egypt."† Thanks, Cathy! We only ask ourselves the questions we feel able to accept or deal with. If the answers are too difficult, avoidance and distraction can feel like allies. Denial and procrastination buffer us from bigger fears.

Being overwhelmed interferes with the mental tools we need the most (our executive functions, that is, the way our brains put things in a workable order) to help us

- sort things out;
- think things through to arrive at better options;
- decide on and develop a plan;
- follow the plan through step by step to conclusion; and
- problem solve along the way when hiccups happen, as they will—life is like that for all of us.

---

† Original source unknown.

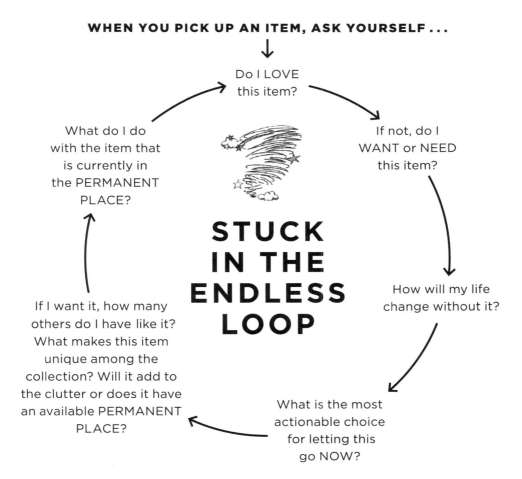

WHEN YOU PICK UP AN ITEM, ASK YOURSELF...

Do I LOVE this item?

What do I do with the item that is currently in the PERMANENT PLACE?

If not, do I WANT or NEED this item?

STUCK IN THE ENDLESS LOOP

If I want it, how many others do I have like it? What makes this item unique among the collection? Will it add to the clutter or does it have an available PERMANENT PLACE?

How will my life change without it?

What is the most actionable choice for letting this go NOW?

Stuck in the endless loop: How the questions we ask ourselves while processing our things can lead to endless questioning if we have no answers

Slow down. Take a few deep breaths. The more frustrated and overwhelmed we get, the worse the problem seems to become. It can feel like you are walking through mud up to your hips while trying to make progress.

Many clients tell me that every day, they start to work on the piles, but by the time they pick up the third or fourth item, they are overwhelmed because they can't figure out what to do with it. They get blocked and give up.

They get caught in a loop of asking themselves questions that only lead to more and more questions.

This pattern repeats itself, going around and around, with nothing resolved, not because the questions are the wrong ones to ask but because the person doesn't have enough guidance in how to answer them. If you are at this point, you probably feel deflated, frustrated, and maybe overwhelmed. You might be in a fog, feeling like your head is spinning. Perhaps you are feeling increasingly worse about yourself. You promise yourself that you will try again tomorrow. And you do try, but with the same results.

When you are in a blind maze and you want to get out, slow down, take a deep breath, and *get a guide*. Reach out for hoarding-informed help.

MISCONCEPTION 8:

I'm not a hoarder because I'm not as bad as the people on the TV shows. I'm a collector, not a hoarder.

Perhaps not: Hoarding is just a word. Some of the loveliest people I have ever met hoard.

Review the *DSM-5* definition or the working definition. Take the quiz earlier in this chapter. If you meet the criteria, then what you are doing is hoarding, regardless of the perceived value of the collection, or the price tag on the items. But being overwhelmed by your piles of things does not define you. *You* are more than your hoarding or any other problems you have.

The difference between hoarding and collecting is that collections usually have a social aspect to them. We are usually proud of our collections. They give us pleasure, and we often want to display them and share them with people who will also appreciate them. We are likely to want to include others in admiring them. We take care of them and maintain them. We may also invest in insuring them. They are part of our private *and* social life.

So when you consider this, what is your accumulation closer to? Is it a collection, or is it a hoard?

Now that you have had a closer look at what hoarding is and have done a self-assessment about your things, chapter 2 will help you take a closer look at the clutter in your environment and how your environment is affecting your activities of daily living. Chapter 2 also provides a self-assessment to determine the level of depression, anxiety, and isolation you are living with at present.

CHAPTER 2

Environmental and Self-Assessment

THE BEST PLANS ARE BASED ON THE BEST ASSESSMENTS. This chapter includes both an environmental assessment and a self-assessment.

Environmental Assessment

Let's take a closer look at the clutter in your environment by completing the "Clutter Checklist" (table 2.1). This assessment tool will help you determine the specific areas in your home that require attention so that you can prioritize the areas to work on first. To perform an accurate assessment, be sure you have already completed the "Five Red Flags of Possible Hoarding" checklist in chapter 1 and the quiz "Are You a Hoarder in the Making?" (table 1.1), as well as reviewing the *DSM-5* definition of hoarding disorder (resource 16.3) or the working definition of hoarding in chapter 1.

Please note, *this checklist is not a report card*. There is no score sheet attached to the checklist. You (or the person you are trying to help) already know there is a problem and do not need to be graded. The checklist is meant to provide information to help you develop a plan to move forward.

You may also wish to revisit this checklist later to track the decluttering progress you are making in your home.

TABLE 2.1

Clutter Checklist

LOCATION	DETAILS	YES	NO
Entryway	Door opens all the way		
	Accumulation stored behind the door		
	Clear passage to other rooms*		
	Smoke detector in place and working		
Kitchen	Clear passage to other rooms*		
	Items prone to falling out of cupboards		
	Countertops covered		
	Items stored on top of stove		
	Items stored in front of stove		
	Permanent use of extension cords		
	Clear ventilation around the refrigerator		
	Spaces usable for intended purposes		
Living room	Clear passage to other rooms*		
	Clear passage to rear exit/entry, if applicable*		
	Spaces usable for intended purpose		
	Permanent use of extension cords		
	Items stored on top of heat vent		
Bedrooms	Items hanging from the door		
	Door opens all the way		
	Items stored behind the door		
	Items stored on top of heat vent		
	Spaces usable for intended purpose		
	Clear access to the closet		
	Permanent use of extension cords		

LOCATION	DETAILS	YES	NO
Bathroom	Items hanging from the door		
	Door opens all the way		
	Items stored behind the door		
	Spaces usable for intended purpose		
	Items stored in the bathtub		
Basement or storage space	Clear access to the electrical panel*		
	Items prone to falling down (tipping, falling off shelving, etc.)		
Garage	Clear sight of the floor		
	Items in garage not related to outdoor use		
	Permanent use of extension cords		
	Clear access to the doors*		
	Spaces usable for intended purpose		
Balcony/patio	Clear sight of the floor		
	Items on balcony not related to outdoor use		
	Permanent use of extension cords		
	Clear access to the entrance door*		

Comments:

A reproducible version of this checklist is available from the Birchall Consulting website (www.hoarding.ca) should you wish to share it with someone else.

* A clear passage should be a minimum of 33 inches wide.

TABLE 2.2
Activities of Daily Living Assessment

DAILY LIFE TASKS	EASILY (0)	WITH A LITTLE DIFFICULTY (1)	WITH MODERATE DIFFICULTY (2)	WITH GREAT DIFFICULTY (3)	UNABLE TO DO (4)	N/A
Use clear counterspace to prepare food.						
Walk to the refrigerator.						
Use food in the refrigerator before the expiration date is reached.						
Walk to the stove.						
Maintain clear stove surface between cooking times with minimal effort.						
Maintain faucets in functional order with potable water (Are you comfortable having services in when maintenance is needed? Have you spent necessary funds on acquiring items?).						
Use the kitchen sink easily.						
Eat at a table intended for meals.						
Maintain clear access (e.g., pathways) for moving around inside the house.						
Maintain two clear doorways to enter and exit the home quickly in case of emergency.						
Use a toilet that flushes (see note for faucets).						
Maintain bath/shower: clear and available for use (see note for faucets).						
Maintain bathroom sink: clear and available for use.						

Item						
Maintain a clear, accessible route to answer the door quickly per local fire code requirements.						
Provide seating (sofa, chairs) for yourself and guests.						
Maintain completely clear bed surface available for sleeping.						
Maintain bedroom floor spaces, keeping them clear enough to allow for emergency exit should the need arise.						
Keep clothing stored so that it does not present a tripping hazard and remains wearable.						
Do laundry, keeping dirty laundry stored away from heat sources (furnaces, hot water tanks, etc.) according to local fire code requirements.						
Keep all hallways clear and accessible according to local fire code requirements.						
Keep all staircases clear and accessible according to local fire code requirements.						
Use bare light bulbs away from combustible items and make sure they are unable to fall onto combustible items.						
Functional use of rooms does not require permanent use of extension cords, and temporary use is not a tripping hazard.						
Keep taxes current (not in arrears because documents are missing in the clutter).						
Find important things (such as bills, tax forms, documents for eligibility purposes, etc.)						
TOTAL					_____ /100	

Now that you have assessed the location and type of clutter in your environment, the "Activities of Daily Living Assessment" (table 2.2) will help you take a realistic look at the ways in which your clutter is affecting how you live in your spaces. Clutter can involve inanimate objects, animals, or a combination. You may still be able to manage, but sometimes the clutter buildup requires people to make adaptations in how they function. Often these adaptations begin to feel normal. A closer look can help you make a more conscious choice about how you will move forward out of the clutter.

As you complete the "Activities of Daily Living Assessment" on pages 46–47, consider only whether the degree of difficulty is due to clutter.

What Is Your Level of Risk?

Gail Steketee and Randy O. Frost, in their *Compulsive Hoarding and Acquiring: Workbook* (2007), have defined five levels of risk based on accumulation in an environment. The weight of the accumulation and the amount of combustible materials can affect the fuel load (i.e., the available fuel for a fire). If combustible material catches fire, the fire will spread more quickly. In addition, when a large accumulation is hosed down, it weighs even more, which can affect the structural integrity of the building and increase the potential safety risk to firefighters, other first responders, occupants, pets, and neighbors.

This section looks at six potential levels of hidden safety risk *not* based on accumulation in an environment, where Risk Level 0 represents no risk, and Risk Level 5 represents the highest possible risk. A high accumulation can, in fact, have a relatively low level of safety risk due to fire, infestation, and contamination. Conversely, a low accumulation may still carry a higher level of safety risk. What do each of these six risk levels actually look like? The "What Is Your Level of Risk?" tables that follow include photographs illustrating various risk levels in three areas: near heat sources; around entrances/exits, pathways, and stairs; and in specific rooms.

With these examples of risks in mind, fill out the "Environmental Risk Assessment Checklist" for a summary of the key factors that determine the level of risk for you and anyone living with you or nearby. Take the results seriously.

Environmental Risk Assessment Checklist

Assess the risk your clutter presents:

    ☐ to you
    ☐ to other residents
    ☐ to pets
    ☐ to responders

Part 1. Environmental Risks around Heat Sources

RISK	EXAMPLE PHOTOS	DESCRIPTION OF RISK

Hot water tank

Level 0		• *The area around the hot water tank (gas and propane) is absolutely clear of clutter up to 3 feet (check your local fire safety regulations).*

Level 5		• *There must be 33–36 inches clear (check your local fire safety regulations) around any heat source, including gas and propane hot water tanks. It is also a good practice with electrical hot water tanks.* • *In this photo, the combustible materials surround the hot water tank too closely.* **Note:** *Take care with materials that are not combustible but can conduct heat. A prospective client called me after her house burned down because a metal shelf conducted heat to combustible items. This situation went unnoticed as the items smoldered. They caught fire, burning down the house.*

Flammables stored close to heat sources

Level 0		• *Flammables and combustible material must be stored 33–36 inches away from any heat source (see your local fire safety regulations).* • *Except for totes (Level 1), this is an easy fix. Three sides have ideal conditions, and the stacked totes could be easily moved farther away.*

RISK	EXAMPLE PHOTOS	DESCRIPTION OF RISK
Level 0		• *The area around the furnace is clear to at least 3 feet (check your local fire safety regulations).*
Level 1		• *A lot of combustible material is stored here, but the closest equipment is a water softener. Plastic totes would produce toxic off-gases if this area caught fire and they were not 3–4 feet away from heat sources.*
Level 2–3		• *Paint cans contain flammable material. Although the cans are not close to the electric hot water tank (not the same level of risk as a propane or gas hot water tank), they block access to the electrical panel, which requires completely free access at all times.*
Level 5		• *Combustibles too close to furnace and hot water tank.* • *See local fire safety requirements for allowable clear space around heat sources, especially when heat source is gas or propane.*

Clear path to electrical panel

Level 0		• *Even though the basement is relatively full, the pathway to the electrical panel is free and clear for access within the guidelines of 33–36 inches.*

RISK	EXAMPLE PHOTOS	DESCRIPTION OF RISK

Level 5

- *The pathway to the electrical panel must be absolutely free of obstructions and provide clear mobility for a firefighter in full gear.*
- *This area is a Risk Level 5 because the pathway is blocked by the small chest freezer.*
- *The closeup pictures illustrate how a Risk Level 0 can be compromised by a small amount of combustible material being left too close to the panel (i.e., cardboard boxes on the floor under the panel), increasing the risk level.*
- *The paint cans would be an obvious concern, but they are stored a safe distance from the electrical panel.*

Kitchen stovetop: Levels 4–5

- *Smooth-top stoves are not necessarily safer. They create an additional work space that, if not clear, can represent a significant risk.*
- *In this photo*
  - » *A metal container is on the stove. If the stove was left turned on, the metal container would conduct heat to the large glass jar immediately beside it, potentially causing the glass jar to shatter. Flying glass might injure anyone close by, or someone, including pets, might walk on the shards of glass.*
  - » *The saucepan on the stove would also conduct heat, burning anything left in it. If the contents contain oil, a smoke hazard or ignition is possible.*
  - » *The plastic storage container would melt, as would the plastic bowl that contains butter.*
  - » *The cardboard box would ignite, as would the oven mitts left beside the burners.*
  - » *Once the oven mitts catch fire, the counter and immediately adjacent cupboards are at risk.*
  - » *Should this fire begin with smoldering, and ignite when no one is close by, the fire would spread quickly, placing the home, pets, and neighbors at risk.*

Part 2. Entrances/Exits, Pathways, and Stairs

RISK	EXAMPLE PHOTOS	DESCRIPTION OF RISK

Doorway entrance/exit

Level 0		• *Space is entirely clear and accessible.*
Level 1		• *Clutter is left in place immediately after use, including items not needed but put down "just for now" by those entering and leaving (a change of clothes, indoor/outdoor shoes, umbrellas, lunch bag items), rather than taking the time to put the items in their permanent place.* • *Other items not normally used at the entrance/exit are left here too.*
Level 2		• *Items that were recently used and those previously left in the entrance/exit area have combined to leave less floor space clear.* • *The space can be accessed safely only by moving some items out of the walking area. These items are a tripping hazard.*
Level 3		• *The path to exit and enter is becoming continually obstructed.* • *Some spaces are obstructed short term, for example, garbage bags on their way out and shoes currently in use.* • *Other items are more likely left "just for now" and then left longer term—days, weeks, months.*

RISK	EXAMPLE PHOTOS	DESCRIPTION OF RISK

- *This is a Level 3 because a 3-foot pathway (see local fire safety regulations) to the entrance and exit does not remain in place.*

Level 4

- *Some items may be placed in this location short term (such as garbage bags for hours or days), but so many bags located in an entry/exit area longer than very short term creates a high risk should an emergency exit be required before the bags are removed.*
- *Even though other entrance or exit options may be available, when you reduce the number of choices, you increase the risk because the blocked option may be the best/ only option given the type and seriousness of the emergency.*
- *Notice that accumulation piles have started. This adds to the risk level because dealing with the piles is more than a one-step action.*
- *Notice that the ability to fully open the door to enter or exit is reduced by the type of items in the way. The stool will reduce the space, as will the garbage bags, as they will slide when someone tries to open the door.*
- *The mop handle in the far left corner of the space might also fall into the door opening near the hinge when the door opens. This blocks the occupant's ability to fully open and close the door during an emergency.*
- *This is a Level 4 because of the amount of accumulation/storage in the area surrounding the entrance/exit.*

Level 5

- *While the number of items blocking access is not as high as you might think is required for Level 5 (maximum) risk, the types of items create a Level 5 risk because they are:*
  - » *completely blocking access to entry/exit;*
  - » *piled chaotically and therefore unstable; and*
  - » *varied in nature—cat carriers, cleaning products, garbage bags, a tote, a stool, a sewing machine, a turkey—all brought inside but left, probably "just for now," and then forgotten.*

RISK	EXAMPLE PHOTOS	DESCRIPTION OF RISK
Clear pathway to entrance/ exit		• *Using a harm reduction model, this entrance/ exit path meets the minimum criteria for being a safe egress route. The clear pathway meets the 33-inch width required in the jurisdiction where this residence is located.* • *While there are piles on either side of the route, they are not yet at a level where toppling is likely. Note: A toppling risk occurs when the pile is high enough to injure the person if the pile falls in on them, not if the pile falls in on the pathway.*

Pathways between rooms

Level 3		• *The creation of clear and maintained pathways, 33–36 inches wide, between highly cluttered rooms reduces the risk to a Level 3 from Levels 4–5.* • *The pathways must remain entirely clear as per local fire safety regulations.* • *If pathways do not consistently and reliably meet what the local fire code requires, this area will become a Level 5 risk.*
Level 5		• *The same space shown in the previous photograph now has an almost complete blockage in one area of the pathway.* • *This space is now classified as a Level 5 risk, even though the other areas of the pathway remain the same as in the Level 3 example.*

Stairs

Level 0		• *The stairway is completely clear and unobstructed.* • *Stairs are safe to walk on and climb.*
Level 1		• *Items are beginning to be placed on the stairs temporarily, often to be taken up and put away on the next trip upstairs.* • *Usually items are placed on one side of the stairs, limiting mobility up and down.*

RISK	EXAMPLE PHOTOS	DESCRIPTION OF RISK
		• Stairs that have a wedge design as they turn (versus a landing) must be kept absolutely clear because accumulation on these types of stairs leave inadequate space to be safe for an emergency exit.
Level 2		• More items begin to be placed on the stairs. • The items are usually restricted to one side but left longer. • The accessible space is narrowed, increasing the risk when anyone uses the stairs, even nonurgent use.
Level 3		• Access to the stairway has become mostly obstructed. • Items are being left long term and creating a tripping or falling hazard. Emergency exits are risky.
Level 4		• Access to safe passage on Level 4 stairs is risky. The clear footing area is narrowed almost completely, and items are significantly piled, representing a toppling hazard when bumped.
Level 5		• Stairs are blocked by items stored chaotically. • Passage is obstructed and only possible by moving many items. Having to step on or over items creates an even greater risk of tripping, losing one's balance, or falling.

Part 3. Environmental Risks in Specific Rooms

RISK	EXAMPLE PHOTOS	DESCRIPTION OF RISK
Front hall: Levels 2–3		• Outerwear is hung in multiples, covering more than one season. • Outer bags have no place to hang, and nonessential items (such as nail polish) take up space where carry bags could be stored. This leaves only the floor area available to store them. • In a Level 2, the storage unit/organizer is used to hold various types of "like" items together for easier placement and retrieval. • In a Level 3, at the end of the hall, combination hoarding/storage has started. • The mixed nature of the accumulation indicates that permanent places for many items are unidentified or inaccessible. • This combination of items might also indicate that the closet is full of nonpriority items, which might be reduced or stored long term until they are needed again.
Living room		
Level 1		• There is mild clutter left around the space. • Good to fair clear floor spaces make safe mobility possible. • While the clutter left in place is not ideal, this is not far off a normal state of clutter for a family.
Levels 4–5		• Clutter is chaotic and extreme. • Mobility in this area is only possible by climbing over piles and walking on high accumulation. • This room cannot be used at all for its intended purpose.

RISK	EXAMPLE PHOTOS	DESCRIPTION OF RISK

Kitchen floor and counters

Level 0		• *Everything that has been used in the kitchen has been put away.* • *Counters are kept clear except for small appliances.* • *Floors are swept of anything that might have fallen during meal preparation, resulting in no accumulation buildup.*
Floor: Levels 0–1 **Counters:** Levels 2–3		• *This picture demonstrates how flat surfaces become cluttered first.* • *This is also an excellent example of putting things down "just for now" and then not coming back to finish the job of putting things away.* • *Feeling overwhelmed happens quickly now that putting things away has become a much bigger job than it would have been with one item at a time during food preparation.* • *Better slogans than "Just for now" would be "Just do it now; it never gets easier" and "Don't put it down; put it away."*
Level 2		• *Considering the dishwasher and sinks are clear and accessible, the accumulation in this area is resolvable relatively easily.* • *According to the "Activities of Daily Living Assessment" method, this part of the kitchen is a cleanup area, where water is accessible and routine activities are entirely possible.* • *There is no fire safety risk because no heat source is close by.* • *As long as the accumulation remains short term, there is also minimal risk of attracting bugs and vermin.*
Floor: Level 0 **Counters:** Level 1 **Storage:** Level 2		• *The floor is completely clear of accumulation.* • *Items on the counters are in use.* • *The cupboards do not allow storage of larger items.* • *The potential to quickly take up all available space makes it impossible to use areas for their intended purpose. Spaces not being available consistently for their intended purpose is one of the three criteria for an environment to qualify as hoarded, but all three criteria must be present in a situation (even to a minimal degree). One criterion consistently met may mean that your environment is on its way to being hoarded.*

RISK	EXAMPLE PHOTOS	DESCRIPTION OF RISK

Dining room

| Level 4 |  | • *The space cannot be used for its intended purpose, such as personal or family meals.*
• *Minimal clear paths have been created for passage as needed, even though access to the adjoining living room is inadequate.*
• *In this home, a clear emergency entrance and exit option from the living room is reduced.* |

| Level 5 |  | • *Clutter entirely prevents the normal use of the dining room for personal or family meals.*
• *Accumulation has reached at least half the height of the room.* |

Bedroom

| Levels 1–2 |  | • *Level 0 would be a bed entirely clear of clutter.*
• *In this photo, the collection of items typical of "nesting" or "cocooning" has started.*
• *This nesting indicates not just a clutter buildup but use of the bed as an area where tasks are not completed (for example, the contents of a suitcase not put away).*
• *Two books remain on the bed, possibly for easy access.* |

| Level 3–4 |  | • *The risk increases as the clutter around and on the bed, while not an extreme amount, is starting to collect on the floor, creating a potential tripping hazard.*
• *More nonsleeping activities are happening in the bed, such as laptop use, which requires an extension cord as a power source. The use of an extension cord interferes with the path required to exit the bed and the room.* |

RISK	EXAMPLE PHOTOS	DESCRIPTION OF RISK
Level 5		• The closeup of the picture demonstrates a clear Risk Level 5 by highlighting additional cords and wires that complicate the person's mobility path into and out of the bed and bedroom. • This is a good example of how a low level of accumulation can give a person a false sense of security if unaware of the actual risk posed by other safety hazards in a low accumulation environment.
Office: Levels 4–5		• Usable office work space is a Level 5 because room to work and sit is unavailable without moving a high number of items. • The accumulation is piled up, and piles are chaotic. • Floor space could be considered Level 4 because there are clear areas; safe mobility is questionable.
Spare room (craft and play room): Levels 3–5		• All the items in the plastic storage containers are being used in this room, so they are appropriate to the space being used as intended (even though it looks like a great deal of accumulation). • The storage of future materials is limited to the remaining available space in the containers. • This space would normally be rated Level 2 to 3 except that additional items in containers are not yet sorted. Instead, they have started to pile on top of containers, which starts the chaotic cycle, making this space a clear Level 3. • On the floor, however, the creepage of items onto the pathways reduces safe mobility. At the front of the picture and near the back, where the sliding door opens to the outside, access space to enter this room is less than the amount required by the local fire code. Creepage has begun near the door area, and cords on the floor create a tripping hazard. The state of the floor makes this area a Level 5 risk. • The angle of this photo does not capture an exit pathway that is more than adequate.

RISK	EXAMPLE PHOTOS	DESCRIPTION OF RISK

Main bath

Level 0		• *All spaces are completely clear of clutter and accessible for the intended use of the space.*
Level 1		• *A few items currently being used have been left on the floor and window sill "just for now."* • *Mobility is safe.*
Level 2		• *Items have started to accumulate in excess of those currently in use. This creates a longer term accumulation.* • *Safe mobility is still possible with some care taken to step over or around items.*

RISK	EXAMPLE PHOTOS	DESCRIPTION OF RISK

Level 3

- *The accumulation of items includes combination hoarding, a mix of items normally used in a bathroom with those left in unusual places because of the lack of available space: nail polish on the floor, cosmetics around the sink apron, Epsom salts as a door stop, clothing not put away after use, a collection of newspapers in excess of immediate use, and soaps and shampoos on the floor at the entrance because the cupboards are no longer accessible.*

Level 4

- *Pathways to access fixtures are obstructed.*
- *Piling of the accumulation has progressed to create chaotic storage of items.*
- *Multiple uses of the bathroom space makes its intended use unsafe for humans and animals.*

Level 5

- *Toilet and other bathroom fixtures are not accessible without moving garbage bags to other, already highly cluttered spaces. This increases the risk of the space and its contents being unusable for their intended purpose.*
- *Floor space is highly obstructed. Use of other bathroom features, such as the closet, medicine chest, and so on, is not possible.*
- *Risk of falling, tripping, and injury is high because of the degree of accumulation buildup and the nature of items present.*

RISK	EXAMPLE PHOTOS	DESCRIPTION OF RISK
Garage: Level 5		• *This garage was previously outfitted with heavy-duty shelving on both sides. All "keep" items were identified and stored with like items.* • *Over time, the pathway between both sides has become filled with "just for now" storage, leading to complete blockage. This obstruction makes it impossible to put things in their identified permanent place.*
Laundry area: Levels 4–5		• *Space is limited by the design of the laundry area in the home. This reality is a given.* • *Organization of usable space does not easily lend itself to adequate space for the laundry needs of an average young family.* **Note:** We reorganized the area to better meet laundry needs.

CLEANING PRODUCTS	FOLDING TABLE
	FIVE LAUNDRY BASKETS
STACKED WASHER & DRYER	FREE SPACE

Flat surfaces: Level 5		This photo shows the effects of chronic disorganization on flat surfaces. **On the table:** • *Some clear spaces remain available, but the majority of surface space contains items.* • *Items are not stacked.* • *Flat surface can be cleared relatively easily when needed.* **On the buffet behind the table (Level 3):** • *No clear spaces remain available* • *Stacking and large-volume storage strategies, such as buckets and baskets, are being used to manage the volume.* • *Combination hoarding is occurring. The area contains knickknacks, papers, and utensil storage containers. Miscellaneous items are put there and left.*
Complete apartment: Level 5		• *No area of the unit is accessible without climbing over piles 1–3 feet high, and in some cases higher. Any area of the environment that has an accumulation level similar to this situation is at a Risk Level 5.* • *Activities of daily living, such as cooking and socializing, cannot be carried out.* • *Sleeping and bathing can be done only if items are moved and then restored in the original spaces.*

Are there blocked entrances or exits
- ☐ to your home? You must have two clear (entirely unobstructed) ways to enter or exit your residence in case of an emergency.
- ☐ to any rooms, especially where rooms are in current and regular use?

Is there accumulation near ignition sources?
- ☐ furnaces
- ☐ stoves
- ☐ space heaters
- ☐ baseboard heaters
- ☐ portable heaters
- ☐ water heaters
- ☐ uncovered light bulbs
- ☐ other combustible items (things that will conduct heat or burn)
- ☐ electrical panel (circuit breaker or fuse box): if wiring is old, check amperage of all fuses regularly and take blown fuses seriously (take proactive action to prevent)

Are any extension cords in semipermanent or permanent use?
- ☐ Ideally rooms should be reorganized so that all electrical devices can be plugged directly into wall outlets (check the integrity of all cords).
- ☐ Extension cords should not be used in place of an adequate number of permanently wired electrical outlets connected to the main electrical panel. All electrical work should be done by qualified electricians.
- ☐ Electrical cords are a serious tripping hazard and vulnerable to vermin chewing them and starting fires.

Do you have
- ☐ nonfunctional or too few smoke detectors? (Consult your local fire department for enforceable standards in your area.)
- ☐ nonfunctional or too few carbon monoxide detectors, where legislated, given heat sources and degree of accumulation?

Remember:
- ☐ Accumulation must be removed from all heat and ignition sources.
- ☐ Blocked or obstructed stairs must be cleared.
- ☐ Consider whether an expert needs to assess the situation based on what you are seeing.

The bottom line is, you must
- ☐ consult your local fire department for enforceable standards in your area;
- ☐ have two clear (entirely unobstructed) ways to enter or exit your residence in case of emergency;

- [ ] ensure clear routes into and out of each room;
- [ ] make sure all areas near heat and ignition sources (e.g., furnaces, stoves, portable heaters, baseboard heaters, water heaters, and uncovered light bulbs) are clear (entirely unobstructed) of combustible items (i.e., things that will conduct heat or burn);
- [ ] avoid using extension cords in place of an adequate number of permanently wired electrical outlets connected to the main electrical panel; and
- [ ] confirm that smoke detectors are functioning and that you have enough of them placed correctly (consult your local fire department about smoke detector requirements in your area).

If you would like to know the actual percentage of risk your environment represents, complete the "Calculating Environmental Risk" tool in the supplemental online material (jhupbooks.press.jhu.edu/title/conquer-clutter). This tool is designed to help you calculate your risk quantitatively according to known risk factors found in hoarding situations that have a high probability of causing or worsening fire and other safety crises. Generally, though, the more boxes checked in the "Environmental Risk Assessment Checklist" above, the higher the risk in your environment.

Self-Assessment

Safety always comes first. Now that we have established how safe your environment is, it is time to do a self-assessment.

The very first step I take in my practice is to complete an assessment of the level of depression, anxiety, and isolation the client is living with at present. There is an excellent series of tools developed by Dr. David Burns in his *Ten Days to Self-Esteem*: the "Burns Depression Checklist," "Burns Anxiety Inventory," and "Relationship Satisfaction Scale" (Burns 1999). These tools are portable, user-friendly, and nonthreatening. Though written in everyday language, they are statistically valid assessments.

If you are troubled by the same problem or type of problem recurring and would like to decode why, take some time to answer the questions in the "Checking in with Yourself on Danger Signs" tool provided on the next page.

The questions help assess:

- what is happening right now;
- whether the current problem is a repeat of old problems;
- why it is important enough to bother you;
- what thoughts, beliefs, or fears automatically influence your reactions to the

Checking in with Yourself on Danger Signs

QUESTIONS TO ASK YOURSELF	EXAMPLE ANSWERS
What is the problem or event?	To be well informed, I need to buy newspapers.
How did it develop?	The people I have admired in the past, whom I consider well informed, read and referred to many newspapers.
When did it develop? What keeps it going? What prevents me from resolving it?	Throughout my childhood, I refused to explore other information sources or online tools such as Google searches, keyword searches, RSS feeds, bulletin boards, and so on.
What thoughts, ideas, beliefs, and values do I have that support it?	I am not good with computers. I can't afford a computer. All information online is suspect. It is easier just to buy a newspaper.
What meaning or reactions do I assign the problem or event? How do I translate through my behavior the meaning I assign: ☐ *emotionally*—What feelings do I invest? ☐ *behaviorally*—How do I choose to act? ☐ *physically, i.e., bodily reactions*— How do my physical choices and reactions add power to my assigned meaning?	• *Using a computer will always be beyond me. I am what I am, and it will never change. I enjoy the experience of reading the hard-copy newspaper. I buy numerous newspapers because I believe that is the best way to reconcile competing opinions.* • *Emotionally I feel secure with my choice.* • *I have a routine that I believe works for me.* • *I find it satisfying and comforting to sit with and read my newspapers, even just partially. I feel good knowing that I have them as a reference source and can read and reread them at my leisure.*
What outcome do I create?	Because I restrict myself to hard-copy news sources, with no expectation that I need to finish reading my newspapers and no deadlines for discarding old copies, I create piles of paper that limit my safe mobility throughout my rooms and increase the fuel load, creating a fire hazard.

problem (for example, when someone disagrees with you, and you automatically assume that they don't like you, don't understand how right you are, or aren't as intelligent and well-informed as you are, etc.); and

- what other choices you have to handle the problem (other than repeating the same thing over and over, achieving the same results) to get a more satisfactory outcome this time

Note: Many cognitive behavioral therapy (CBT) books ask similar questions. I developed this tool using generic CBT terms and concepts, but many other similar questions achieve the same purpose.

If you wish to delve deeper into what might be underlying influences on your vulnerability to hoarding disorder, complete "Building Your Conceptual Model of Hoarding" in the supplemental online material (jhupbooks.press.jhu.edu/title/conquer-clutter). You can also perform additional self-assessment by answering the questions outlined in "Figuring It Out" below.

Figuring It Out

ASK YOURSELF:

- *Do I comfort myself with things?*

- *Do I keep everything because I'm afraid of losing or not having something I might need?*

- *Do I find making decisions about sorting my things so difficult that I postpone doing or finishing it?*

- *Do I fall in love with things as if they were people?*

- *Do I recycle so intensely that I live with boxes, bags, and piles in my living space?*

- *Do I have two clear ways in and out of my home? Is there a 33- to 36-inch clear path around any heat source (e.g., furnace, hot water tank, electrical panel)? (Check your local fire codes.)*

- *Do I use extension cords as a permanent solution?*

CHAPTER 3

Goals

IN THE LAST CHAPTER, YOU IDENTIFIED the cluttered areas in your home that require work to improve safety and make them usable for everyday activities. Information on the risk levels that may be present in various areas should help you prioritize where to start. Now it is time to set goals for yourself to actually complete the work. You can increase the likelihood that you will achieve your goals by making SMART goals (Doran 1981).

On the following pages, I provide examples of how to create goals that meet these criteria. The goals you make should help you fulfill the basic needs you have. According to Tony Robbins (2018), humans have six major needs:

1   **Certainty:** assurance that you can avoid pain and gain pleasure
2   **Uncertainty/variety:** the need for the unknown, change, new stimuli
3   **Significance:** feeling unique, important, special, or needed
4   **Connection/love:** a strong feeling of closeness or union with someone or something
5   **Growth:** an expansion of capacity, capability, or understanding
6   **Contribution:** a sense of service and focus on helping, giving to, and supporting others

One way to decide on a goal is to focus decluttering efforts on an area of your environment that is really bothering *you*, and to tie the motivation to a reason that is really important to *you*. For example:

Today I will spend 15 minutes decluttering (e.g., my front entryway). This is a priority because I would like to have my best friend visit me in two weeks to show me how to knit hats and booties for premature babies in our local hospital, and so that

What Are SMART Goals?

SMART is an acronym in which the letters represent five key qualities of achievable goals.

S = Specific: Be precise. What exactly do you want to do?

M = Measurable: How much, how often, and when will you know you have done it?

A = Achievable: What is involved in achieving this goal? Is the goal something where:
- *you have previous experience doing it?*
- *you have done something similar in the past?*
- *you know where to go and what to do to learn it?*
- *you know how to get the help you need to do it?*

R = Relevant: Is your goal important enough to make it a priority and to apply the required effort to achieve it?

T = Time frame: By what date do you want to have reached your goal?

I can be safe in my home. If after my first 15-minute decluttering period, I feel up to another 15-minute decluttering period, I can go ahead. But if I commit to that second 15-minute decluttering period, then I must complete it and no more.

The reason I want you to plan your decluttering time in this way is that I want you to learn how to make a conscious plan you can commit to, and then carry out that plan, not go off the plan and make it drudgery you will not want to return to the next day. Trust me. Don't improvise.

Types of Goals

There's more to life than decluttering goals. I recommend that my clients make three goals for each period we are setting goals for.

Goal 1 relates to hoarding.
Goal 2 relates to increasing non-hoarding-related play, pleasure, and joy.
Goal 3 relates to making progress to learn or do something they have always wanted to learn or do.

Examples of the Three Types of Goals

GOAL 1 (hoarding related): Each day, I will

- ✔ take one pile, 2 inches deep (gradually increase), and
- ✔ sort using the 1–10 scaling process and permanent place system (as described in chapter 4).

Remember: Starting is the *hardest part.* Do the thing that you *least* want to do *first* and get it out of the way.

GOAL 2 (play, pleasure, and joy related): I will, for a predetermined, manageable period each day,

- ✔ read a book or magazine and dream, play a CD and sing or dance along, or do both (go wild!);
- ✔ do a puzzle and congratulate myself for each part I solve;
- ✔ call a friend and not complain or listen to complaints;
- ✔ go for a coffee or tea; and
- ✔ sit in the park, close my eyes, feel the breeze on my face, and breathe in the fresh air.

GOAL 3 (learning or doing something I have always wanted to do): I will

- ✔ take up knitting; and
- ✔ learn to play chess.

Setting Goals

Using the "My Goals Worksheet" that follows, set out goals for yourself or, if you are supporting another person, help that person set goals. Keep the following tips in mind:

- **S = Specific:** Be as precise as possible when choosing your goal.
  - ○ *Determine the specific steps and tasks needed to achieve your goal.*
  - ○ *Use the words "I will" because these words express action and commitment, not wishful thinking.*
- **M = Measurable:** Set a specific amount of time to put into your goal each day or week and describe what achieving the goal looks like.
  - ○ *How many hours per day, or how many days per week for how many hours each day?*
  - ○ *How will you know when you have reached your goal?*

A = Achievable: Make sure your goal is within reach using your current abilities and experience.

- *Be realistic about your time frame and how much time and energy you will be able and willing to give to your goal.*
- *Make sure you know how to access any resources you may need to achieve your goal.*

R = Relevant: Ask yourself if this goal is important enough to actually motivate you to do it.

T = Time frame: Decide on an overall length of time to put toward your goal.

- *How long will it take you to achieve this goal?*
- *Use the format "from this date, until this date" so that you have a firm time frame for beginning and ending.*

My Goals Worksheet

Between ___ / ___ / _____ / and ___ / ___ / _____ (dates) I will do the following:

1 Hoarding related: I will _____

_____

_____

_____

_____

_____

2 Play, pleasure, and joy related: I will _____

_____

_____

_____

_____

3 Learning or doing something I have always wanted to do: I will _____

_____

_____

_____

_____

_____

CHAPTER 4

Take Back Your Life

WHETHER YOU LIVE WITH HOARDING DISORDER, care for someone who does, or work as a mental health professional with people who hoard, you might find it helpful to read this chapter before you start to declutter the environment. I explain the full process and the underlying reasoning behind the steps to take back your life when your things are taking over. For helpers, the "Onsite Clutter Coaching Toolkit" worksheet is available online (jhupbooks.press.jhu.edu/title/conquer-clutter), although I also cover the worksheet topics in this chapter.

Unless the clutter in your environment violates local fire codes and ordinances, representing an immediate threat to your safety or the safety of others, consider starting your journey to uncluttered by getting help for the underlying reasons you hoard rather than making your sole focus a cleanup of the environment. The truth is that unless you focus on the two essential components for managing your disorder, the likelihood of having sustained success is low. Many people with hoarding disorder can attest that without addressing *both* components, repeated relapse waits in the wings, with demoralizing results.

The two essentials are

1   getting help for the underlying reason(s) you hoard; and
2   cleaning up and decluttering your environment.

When an individual with hoarding disorder is seeing a mental health professional for support with other life issues as well as receiving guidance from a hoarding-informed professional, working collaboratively to develop noncompeting priorities is important.

The condition of your spaces is the consequence of your disorder not being identified and treated effectively; that is, you aren't getting the help you need, in time, in a way that effectively manages your

- awareness of the problem at hand and readiness to deal with it;
- preferences about what should stay and what should go;
- ability to understand and adapt when your preferences are not wise choices; and
- pace for working at the tasks needed to regain a reasonably healthy and safe place to live.

If you are unsure whether your piles mean that you have hoarding disorder, go back to the definition in chapter 1 and decide if the three criteria fit. As you learn what experiences, beliefs, values, fears, and impulses influence your acquiring behavior, the next step is to seek hands-on decluttering support, gradually, with a trained, hoarding-informed clutter coach. Please choose this person wisely by reviewing the qualities of a good clutter coach outlined in chapter 16.

Over the years, I have learned from my clients that when it comes to decluttering, there is nothing they have to do. Even if the environment represents a serious hoarding situation, sometimes the choices people make demonstrate that they need to create a level of crisis that will result in enforced intervention. They may not be consciously aware of needing a heightened level of crisis to deal with the problem they have. If you are someone who cares about or coaches the person who is hoarding, trust and be guided by what they consistently do, not by what they say. Your role as their supporter may be to stand by them through the stress and turmoil to come. Better results are not gained by ramping up the emotion, stress, threat, and defense mechanisms that the person who hoards uses to cope. If you remain a consistent, supportive, and nonjudgmental influence (despite the person's unproductive choices), you will help him or her over time to an uncluttered mind and spaces.

Each person facing the heightened stress of an enforced intervention needs to ask:

- How much crisis and loss of control do I need to handle the clutter in my life?
- Do I really need the clutter to become so severe that enforcement agents from local fire, public health, bylaw or code compliance, Child Protective Services, or animal control departments must intervene to set and enforce limits for me, as well as monitor my life choices related to the risks caused by excess clutter in my environment?

If you do not want to give up that degree of control, please be willing to:

- get help for the underlying reason(s) you hoard;
- get hoarding-informed coaching to deal effectively with the clutter; and
- begin *today* saying two phrases to yourself and do your absolute best to act on them as well as you possibly can:
    - ✔ "Don't put it down; put it away" (or as close to "away" as possible).
    - ✔ "Just do it now; it never gets easier." Say this 20 times a day because if you let yourself put it down "just for now," when you eventually have to do it, you'll have three jobs rather than one. Just pick it up again and put it where it should have been in the first place.

If you start saying and following through on those last two statements today, you will be solving the clutter and pile problem from both ends: decluttering the piles you have already *and* preventing new ones. That is a winning combination with a real payoff.

Determine What Started the Accumulation

Imagine I am sitting with you now. Choose a space for us to look at first and consider:

1 What makes up the accumulation?
2 What influenced you to place each of these items and leave them where they are? (The reasons may be different for different types of things.)
3 What was the original plan for this area?
4 What were the ideas, needs, or vision behind that plan?
5 What events or choices prompted you to alter the plan?
    - *For now, let's accept that temporarily, these things are where they are. Did you begin to lose focus about the plan? If so, when?*
    - *Did something happen during the time frame when the buildup began?*
    - *Did you start to put the plan in place and encounter barriers to moving forward?*
    - *If so, what were/are those barriers?*
    - *When you look at the piles, do you see a collection of anything (for example, documents, unopened mail, bills, and receipts) with common dates? Are these dates associated with anything that happened at that time?*
    - *Was there some other reason that prompted you to change or abandon your plan?*
    - *Are you better at starting multiple things rather than finishing them?*
6 When was the last time you were able to assign *permanent places* for things?
7 Where would these things normally be kept and used?

If you can't figure out where you would normally keep an item, try the following system for determining each item's permanent place.

Problem Solving Using Cognitive Behavioral Therapy

Using these four questions about your thoughts, feelings, and beliefs will help you beat the feeling of being overwhelmed, get unstuck, and take back your life when your things are taking over.

Why is this happening to me (again)?

_____

_____

_____

Why is this happening now?

_____

_____

_____

Why won't the situation go away?

_____

_____

_____

What do I need to do to solve the problem?

_____

_____

_____

Decide the Permanent Place for Each Keep Item

Many people have found this technique helpful when deciding where their things should be kept. The gist is to hold or touch each item, then close your eyes and ask, "If I were looking for you, where would I look first?" The answer is its *permanent place.**

---

* I credit my lead clutter coach, Heather Wolfer, for this strategy. Thank you, Heather!

The item and its permanent place should meet the following criteria:

- ✔ The item must not be irreversibly contaminated.
- ✔ The place should be a dedicated spot where the item is normally used.
- ✔ The place must keep the item accessible; three deep on a shelf is not normally accessible (depending on the item).

As long as you are not creating a health or safety hazard, take each thing and, even if you can't put it where you have decided its permanent place is, put it as close to that spot as you can for the time being. It may feel like you are just moving piles, but as long as you are not creating a health or safety hazard, you will deal with it when you get to that area by using the scaling process described in this chapter.

Now, let's consider two questions.

What is causing the accumulation to be maintained?

Generally, something prompted your original plan for the area to be changed. You might have valid reasons for the change in plan and the clutter still being maintained.

The fundamental question is "What is maintaining this particular cluttered environment?"

What stops you from resolving the accumulation?

As you look at this space, the next question you must ask yourself is "What keeps me from resolving this situation?" Do your thoughts, fears, beliefs, or lifestyle habits prevent you from resolving the situation? Are you so overwhelmed by your clutter that you cannot move forward to uncluttered? Do you find making decisions to be more difficult than you can manage at the moment?

It is okay if you have to come back to this section more than once. These questions are like peeling an onion. Undoubtedly, there are multiple layers to progress. In the meantime, let's move on with what you know now. Let's consider how to approach this situation effectively at this point.

My guidelines are to:

- ✔ respect the attachment you feel;
- ✔ respect the relationship you have with your things, and therefore your preferences; and
- ✔ respect yourself by working at your pace.

To do this effectively, you need to understand:

- ✔ what you actually see when you look at an item;
- ✔ how you feel and what you say to yourself when you look at it; and
- ✔ what your relationship is to it and your need for it.

Scaling Process

I use a scaling process with categories from 1 to 10. I separate the 1 to 10 into three distinct levels, as shown in table 4.1.

Each category has a range because it is normal not to have the same feelings about everything within each category. By having some elasticity within each grouping, people find it easier to figure out for themselves where the boundaries are between the "I love it" group, the "I'd like to keep it if I can" group, and the "if something has to go, this is it" group.

Now let's look at how to use this scaling process to help you take back your life when your things are taking over. In addition to the material in this chapter, if it helps, you can use the "Onsite Clutter Coaching Toolkit" available online (jhupbooks.press. jhu.edu/title/conquer-clutter) to help you categorize the items into the three groups, and then further prioritize the items within each group.

Remember:

- Each thing that you keep must have a permanent place.
- The permanent place must be in the area where it is normally used, and it must remain accessible.
- Everything that you keep will require something of you—cleaning, dusting, maintenance, the dedicated use of limited space, perhaps the cost of insurance, and so on.

Start with the Easy Wins

This scaling process from 1 to 10 provides a flexible continuum to get you to where you need to be. The range within the three levels is important because even though you love 1s, 2s, and 3s, not all 1s, 2s, and 3s are equally precious to you. The same is true for the other two categories. If you are working with someone you trust, remember:

1 *Only you* get to say whether something is a 1, 2, 3 *or* a 4, 5, 6 *or* a 7, 8, 9, 10. *Note:* Some practitioners may use other priority scales if they choose, where 10 is the highest (top priority) and 1 is the lowest on the continuum. In this case, most important items would be 10, 9, 8, followed by 7, 6, 5, and least important at 4, 3, 2, 1. The reason I define the items you absolutely cannot live without as Category 1 is that they are your first and most important priority, and items that comparatively do not represent you as strongly are Category 10, your last priority.

2 The work must be done at *your* pace. Do not push yourself beyond your true limits. You can get on a high once you start and turn your efforts into a marathon decluttering event. You may not fully realize just how tired you are until you stop. The likelihood that you will begin decluttering again the next time it occurs to you is often diminished because you haven't developed the skill of

TABLE 4.1
Scaling Process Levels

LEVEL	DESCRIPTION	NOTES
1, 2, 3	Ranking an item 1, 2, or 3 means that you have an *exceptionally* strong attachment to this particular item or type of item. Your internal response is almost protective, prompting a response that is something akin to "Absolutely no way it leaves. I *love* it! I *cannot imagine life without it.* It doesn't matter if no one else values this like I do. It is *extremely* important to me."	If you love it and • *it is not irreversibly contaminated* • *you already have a dedicated permanent place for it, or you can allocate a dedicated permanent place for it to reside where it would normally be used, then keep it.* I believe we should surround ourselves with things and people we love as much as possible, those that add joy and meaning to our lives.
4, 5, 6	Items ranked 4, 5, and 6 are where the more difficult decisions must be made. Your internal response is likely to be "I really like most of them, but not like I *love* the 1, 2, 3s," and "If I had enough space, it would be really nice to keep all or most of these things."	
7, 8, 9, 10	Items ranked at the other end of the spectrum (7, 8, 9, or 10) produce a very different internal reaction in you. Some of these items would be nice to keep in an ideal world, if only to save you the trouble of deciding about them, but truthfully, your internal response is, "It doesn't really matter," or "What's that silly thing still doing here? It can go." The internal energy these items produce is very, very different. There certainly isn't protectiveness, or the positive intensity of a 1, 2, 3 item.	*Note:* If something is irreversibly contaminated, do your best to let it go regardless of its ranking.

setting manageable personal limits, and you associate meaningful decluttering with feeling awful afterward. You have set your limit level too high and don't feel up to it on a normal day. In addition, you may be telling yourself that accomplishing less than last time is meaningless.

The 15 minutes every day that you do consistently will get you where you want to be and keep you there, not the marathon moments.

KEY QUALITIES OF THE SCALING PROCESS:

Nonthreatening: There is no right or wrong answer.

Respectful: Only *you* get to say to which category something belongs. If you have a coach, that person can ask for clarification or give you feedback about how consistently you are applying *your* criteria for something to belong to each category, but no one can tell you what the answer should be. *You* decide the category based on the intensity of your relationship or attachment to each item. If everything begins to feel precious, try taking a break; you may simply be tired.

At your own pace: Base your efforts on how much energy you have to give on a particular day, and what you need to do to let something go.

These are the principles to guide you:

1 Don't create a *void* or a *longing*. Sometimes letting go can be like a death or parting with a friend. Rituals can play an important part in creating the necessary emotional release to let something go rather than get rid of something. Honor the thing, your relationship with it, and perhaps the person or something else it represents as you say goodbye. Tell its story, even to yourself. Touch it. Feel it. Smell its scent. Develop and respect your own ways (rituals) to acknowledge its importance and to say goodbye.

  Some people have found that taking a picture to capture the qualities they value about the objects was enough to make it possible to part with the items. Although not for everyone, try this method if you believe it might help. Sometimes it is difficult to appreciate the progress you are making, so taking pictures of the space being cleared as you part with items creates a concrete record that you can use to reflect on your progress objectively.

2 Don't start with the most intense categories to let go of. These are what are known as the "owies"—the "biggies." They are usually found among the 1, 2, 3, 4s. Be gentle with yourself and keep going until you are approaching your limit. Take a short break and see if you can resume working on the piles. Always respect your true limit. Remember: 15 minutes plus one more 15-minute work period. *No more* at first.

3 Don't let the decluttering work become drudgery. Don't keep working at the piles past your limit. It really is the little bit you do regularly that will make the biggest difference and will help keep it done. Remember, *mountains are best moved one stone at a time.* If you make the work drudgery, you will make doing it something to dread, and eventually you will begin to avoid doing it.

Begin the Hands-On Phase

To begin, just sit and look at what you can see in the pile facing you. Consider what the composition of each pile is. Stop and give serious thought about what criteria make something a 1, 2, or 3.

What are the

- reasons;
- memories;
- needs;
- ideas;
- values;
- beliefs;
- aesthetic or tactile characteristics; and
- scent of the item, if this is important to you (if it is, be ok with it; scent is a powerful memory)?

Visualize and experience *your* truth and the intensity of these various factors until your visual, auditory, and kinesthetic internal experience is rich.

Now, with this internal experience fresh in your mind, remind yourself why something belongs in each category.

1, 2, 3: When you see it, it creates a protective response in you. You say something like "No matter what else has to go to declutter, this stays. I love it and can't imagine my life without it."

LIST EXAMPLES OF YOUR "LOVE" ITEMS HERE:	LIST EXAMPLES OF YOUR "NEED" ITEMS HERE:
_____	_____
_____	_____
_____	_____
_____	_____
_____	_____

4, 5, 6: "I like it, and if I have enough room for it to have its own permanent place in the area where I will use it, I'd like to keep it." But you realize that some things in this category may have to go.

LIST EXAMPLES OF YOUR "WANT" ITEMS (ALL ITEMS MUST HAVE A PERMANENT PLACE):

_____

_____

_____

_____

_____

_____

LIST THE PERMANENT PLACE FOR EACH "WANT" ITEM LISTED:

_____

_____

_____

_____

_____

_____

7, 8, 9, 10: "What's that silly thing still doing here? I don't really need it. If something has to go, that can go." Maybe it was a gift that doesn't fit your taste. Maybe it used to be something you liked, but it is just not you today, as you move forward.

LIST EXAMPLES OF ITEMS REMAINING THAT ARE *NOT* "LOVES," "NEEDS," OR "WANTS":

_____

_____

_____

_____

_____

_____

LIST WHAT YOU WILL DO WITH ALL REMAINING ITEMS (SUCH AS DISCARD, DONATE, REGIFT):

_____

_____

_____

_____

_____

_____

Depending on how much sorting space and energy you have, decide on the size of area you will work on. Whether it is a room or a pile, begin with the 7, 8, 9, and 10s, and as you proceed, if you come across items that influence you to feel more intense attachment, set them aside for further consideration later.

The reason you do this is that intensely attractive items can distract you. Highly valued items can be resolved more easily later. Dealing with them now will slow you down. What you need to do now is clear physical space to work and mental space to make decisions more easily. Making these easier decisions first allows you to practice and become comfortable with the decision-making process. If you temporarily remove items of high intrinsic or emotional value as you come across them, this will create additional space for staging and sorting. Remember: You decide each item's permanent place by asking yourself, "If I were looking for you, where would I look first?" That location is likely to be the item's logical permanent place.

Identify and Select the 7, 8, 9, 10s—The Easy Wins

Remember, don't start with the biggies, or what I call the "owies." These are the things with the highest importance and attachment.

Instead, start at the other end and see if there are any "easy wins," any definite 7, 8, 9, 10s. When you see them, you will say to yourself something like, "Oh, that can go," or "That's kind of worn out," "I don't really need that," or "If I really think about it, it isn't truly special, but for some unknown reason, I feel obliged to keep it."

THREE-AND-A-HALF BOXES

1. Remember the *keep* items are going to be put (as part of this decluttering work period) in or close to where they will be kept and used, so assign a space that is easy to access immediately after you finish sorting each target area within the allowable 15 minutes.

2. There are three main choices for items. Start by getting three boxes or bags for "donate," "discard," and "recycle." Get another, smaller, easily identifiable container that you can carry around with you for important items like check books, unpaid bills, documents, money, and so forth.

3. There are two other potential choices to help you resolve how to let go: (1) *regift* or (2) *sell*. Think *very* hard about using either of these options because they take a lot of extra time and effort and, more often than not, prove not worth the effort.
   - **Regift:** Items in good condition that are suitable for someone you personally know can be designated and set aside for gifting later. Choose a specific *limited* space on a shelf and store all items of this type in the same spot so that you can go there to retrieve the gift when you need it.
   - **Sell:** Think very hard about this choice. It is often another high-effort, low-benefit option. To let something go, sometimes people believe they need

Boxes to donate, discard, keep, sell, recycle, and regift, and a container for important items.

to try to sell it. When making this choice, set a time limit to sell the item; otherwise, there is no resolution, and the item(s) will remain a part of an ongoing clutter problem. If the market for these items actually exists, they will sell within that time limit. Also ask yourself how much you believe you will receive for the item and factor in that the purchaser will always want a bargain, so you will likely not get the amount you feel the item is worth. How will you feel if you have to let it go at less than you believe it is worth? Will this fact become a barrier to being able to let it go at that time?

BARRIERS AND AIDS TO LETTING GO

Another painful fact is that being old does not necessarily mean something is an antique. If you believe it is, find out if your assumption is a *fact* by checking out prices online or consulting antique dealers and appraisers. If you choose to use the services of appraisers, you want to be sure to get the *market value*, not just the *insurable value*. If you choose to auction the item, remember to factor in and deduct from the market value the costs associated with sending an item to auction.

Holding on to an assumption and not checking out the facts makes it easier to avoid making a different and perhaps more difficult decision about the item. Selling an item also takes a good deal of time, thereby reducing the time and energy you have for decluttering. In the end, only you can decide if it is time well spent, given the goals you have set for yourself. Try hard not to let these more intensive ways to dispose of items become reasons to avoid or delay making decisions.

A little hint: Make sure the departing 7, 8, 9, 10s leave as soon as possible. Factor in the time needed to remove them as part of each decluttering session. When I work with clients, I take all donations away at the end of each session. It is easy to fall into second-guessing your decisions if the items remain in the environment.

Does it seem strange to realize you have different relationships with various items or categories of things? Would it make letting go easier if you knew that items you don't really need were going to secondhand stores that fund causes you believe in? Then, the people who will choose these items will be people who need and appreciate them. This giving can be especially comforting if the items leaving were gifted to you as presents or legacies. The pity is that you need to take on faith the joy, pride, usefulness, and pleasure you are passing along.

Another barrier to letting go can be uncertainty whether a new home will be "good enough" for the items, which can prevent "letting-go" decisions and maintain the clutter. The strategy outlined above is an excellent one for getting useful, lovely, valued but not needed items to appreciative new homes. Work hard to stay focused on *your* priority goal, which is to declutter your environment and to be able to live in it safely, enjoying life.

To lessen delays, set a decision deadline for acting on these items. As these deadlines approach, I strongly encourage you to remind yourself of your clutter goals and make solving your clutter the priority.

Perhaps the items being considered for donation were gifts or belonged to someone else you cared about. You are under *no* obligation to keep them if they don't represent your taste or if you no longer need them—if they are not who you are today moving forward. If you need to, honor the object, perhaps by taking a photo of it. Acknowledge the importance it had for the giver. Consider sharing it with someone else who shares the giver's taste and appreciation for it. Don't make a barrier out of not knowing the new owner. Donate it if you can, and the appreciative new owner will come.

We apply the meaning and significance to things. The things are just things. When I work with people, I help them understand and come to terms with their relationships to their things. When we form healthier relationships to our things, they will hold the right balance in our lives. Things are never a good or adequate substitute for what we really need. That is why it usually takes so many items when we try to meet our needs and longings with things.

Working shoulder to shoulder together, my clients and I remove the 7, 8, 9, 10s the same day the items are ranked. My team has sought out one or two worthwhile not-for-profit organizations. With the client's agreement, we deliver the items, knowing that the money from the sale of their donations goes toward community programs such as children's breakfast clubs, house fire victims, food banks, no-kill animal shelters, and so forth. No matter what the cause, the donations help real people, right now, who are struggling with real problems.

Clients will occasionally say, "I want to let this go, but before I donate it, I want to check with someone I know, to see if they want it first." I encourage them to set deadlines for contacting the other person and for either delivering it or having it picked up by the person. This prevents delaying their decision to let go of the item. I ask my clients for their permission to check in with them periodically to see if what may have been a good idea to give something to a specific person actually worked out.

One of my clients, who had a considerable quantity of excessive, excellent quality furniture to pass on, asked friends if they could use her extras. Many people said yes and promised to come by to make sure the items would work in their spaces. We moved the pieces to her garage rather than donating them, session by session, only to find months later that despite the expressions of interest and reassurances, not one person had actually come by to pick up anything. In fact, one friend who had heard about the possible donations dropped off a huge TV because people were coming by to look at things, and if all else failed, my company was available to take it away. This person hoped someone else might be interested in it and thought it would be a shame to waste it. My client was too stunned to make her friend take it back. Finally, when she needed the garage space again for seasonal storage, she had to pay another company eight hundred dollars to have the items removed later.

If the idea to offer donations to specific people and places doesn't work as well as hoped, have a backup plan so that those things don't remain for an indeterminate length of time. Remember the rule in difficult situations is to put your own lifejacket on first, before trying to help another person. Otherwise, you are likely to suffer the consequences.

Identify and Select the 1, 2, 3s

With the 7, 8, 9, 10s solved in the area you are focusing on, the next step is to identify the next easiest group, the 1, 2, 3s. Remember, for something to be a 1, 2, or 3, your attachment and connection must be very strong. Focusing on this will make it much easier to identify the things you love and that give you joy.

Because you will keep as many 1s, 2s, and 3s as possible, you must decide on the permanent place for each item. Choose the highest-rated 1 item that you can find. Hold this item in your hands. Ask yourself aloud (so that every part of you can hear its importance), "What makes this item the *top* item of all the 1, 2, 3s?" What is it associated with in your mind?

If you feel like it, tell its stories, relive your memories, and re-experience the feelings you have for the item. Often people will tell me about the special person who gave it to them, and why it was special between them. Why has this item remained a touchstone in your life even today? Sometimes it is a symbol of an achievement or survival during a difficult period in your life. No matter what it is, it has always been this important, and it remains so. The interesting thing is that items like this almost never became important over time—from the outset they were especially important. Fill yourself with the experience of it. Hold it, smell it, touch it.

You can carry out this process with your clutter coach, dealing with one item at a time through the piles. It does not take a long time, and whatever time it takes is well spent.

Item by item, ask yourself, "How does *this* thing I am touching or holding compare in importance to the top number 1 thing that I have in my other hand?" The items experienced as exceptionally but not-as-intensely important rank as 2s and 3s.

Next, look at those same 1, 2, 3s and choose an item that represents and *feels like* the lowest intensity of this most important collection of things. You will use the range between these two items (the strongest connection and the lowest connection among loved items) to distinguish the "I love it" 1, 2, 3 grouping from the 4, 5, 6 grouping, which consists of the "I like them a lot and in a perfect world, I would like to keep as many as possible" items.

When you hold items outside this range in connection or intensity of feeling, your energy changes, and it becomes clear quickly that you have less connectedness and attachment. The reason for this different internal experience is that your relationship *is* different. Items outside this range will become the 4, 5, 6 pile.

WHAT TO DO WHEN EVERYTHING IS A 1, 2, 3

If you are someone for whom *everything* is a 1, 2, 3, I encourage you to seek additional, qualified mental health support to carry out a comprehensive assessment. There may be other disruptive mental health challenges or lifestyle issues competing for priority, which need support before you can effectively do the work needed to resolve your hoarding situation. This happens and is why I work holistically. You will come back to decluttering better armed to make "I can live with it" decisions at that point.

Normally, people start with their family doctor to get a referral and some guidance about how to proceed. If this does not result in a successful match to a psychiatrist, psychologist, or social worker, then go online and choose from a list of each professional group in your geographical area, for example, the lists provided by *Psychology Today*:

In the United States: https://www.psychologytoday.com/us/therapists
In Canada: https://www.psychologytoday.com/ca/therapists

Or do a Google search for "finding a therapist." Add your location after the word "therapist."

Choosing a therapist is like buying shoes. There must be a fit. If, after making your choice, the fit isn't quite there, keep looking until you find the right match. If not finding a comfortable fit becomes a pattern, however, also look to yourself and ask, "Is my vulnerability about this issue making me afraid to take a risk and trust anyone?" Discuss this as openly as you can with the professionals you meet.

Dealing with the 4, 5, 6s

Now take the lowest-rated 1, 2, 3 item and an item rated at the top of the 7, 8, 9, 10 range. Hold them up and pass them along, in front of and close to the remaining items—those 4, 5, and 6s that are yet to be decided. Ask yourself, item by item, does this item rate closer to the 3 item or to the 7 item? Consider whether you

- ✔ need it;
- ✔ have enough space for it; and
- ✔ feel that keeping it or letting it go moves you closer or further away from your goal to live in a satisfyingly uncluttered home

This sorting and scaling strategy moves choices and decisions along faster and more painlessly than you can imagine.

You will have identified the 4s that are

- ✔ really important
- ✔ not as important
- ✔ least important to you

You will have made decisions in a way that makes you feel safer, calmer, and confident that your preferences are respected. As the items leave to new destinations (in keeping with your values, feelings, and beliefs), you will experience more comfort and confidence letting go. You will not create a void or longing that you then fill with more acquisitions. You are now able to move forward *as you are today* and not remain overwhelmed *as you used to be*—overwhelmed by piles made up of the past.

Working the Process: Recommendations to Helpers, Clutter Coaches, and Other Professionals

Sometimes the person wants to completely resolve all types of items in a specific area and then move forward to another area. For about 75 percent of my clients who had high volumes of things and were cognitively intact, as they followed the scaling process, they more easily got to the point where they could carry on independently, area by area, between sessions, regardless of the types of items they encountered as they decluttered. People get to the point where they have bagged or boxed items ready to leave even before I arrive for the next session. We are striving to touch things only an absolute minimum number of times.

For 25 percent of my clients, the clutter is resolved layer by layer. They need help to revisit areas systematically. As the accumulation is thinned throughout the home, they find it more comfortable and useful to have a fuller appreciation for the entire complement of what they have before moving forward to redefine what makes something a 1, 2, 3, a 4, 5, 6, or a 7, 8, 9, 10. Deciding how many of each type of item is reasonable for them to keep also helps them significantly.

Some people make decisions to part with things more easily in the moment. Others need to *process* before parting with their things. For the process people, I suggest that in between sessions, they lay out the items up for consideration to go and reflect on how those items fit within the scaling process so that by the next session, they have solidified their decisions. In some cases, this process takes extra time; often, however, it does not. It just adds an extra level of comfort to the decision. Perhaps from the start, at some level, they knew which decision was best for them. The time the processing takes is well spent because now, with that confidence in their "I can live with it" decisions, they have a minimal need to replace the items.

Whether decisions are made layer by layer or more completely the first time, area by area, *both* methods support individuals to develop a deeper understanding and insight into the underlying reasons and triggers for their collecting. They also reduce the need for unconscious acquiring.

Intensive Short-Term Cleanups

The intensive short-term "blitz" approach may sound like a good solution. Even if you consider doing it voluntarily, you may believe that if you could only get on top of the clutter, you could start fresh and keep it maintained. Yet, if the accumulation and buildup is serious enough to consider a blitz, the reasons it happened in the first place likely still exist and will cause it to happen again.

If a blitz happens involuntarily, because an outside party, such as an enforcement agency, requires it, when the door closes behind the cleanup crew, the hoard will likely happen all over again, often worse and faster than originally.

Intensive short-term cleanup blitzes are destabilizing, whether or not people want them. Their anxiety is intensified, and they often experience a feeling of disconnection and unfamiliarity with their new environment. For a considerable time after, they feel intense confusion and frustration because even though they may not have liked the hoarded environment, it was familiar, and now they feel that they can't find anything.

For this reason, unless extreme health or safety concerns necessitate a blitz, working systematically, session by session, is better. I combine counseling with hands-on decluttering, taking the time the person needs to develop insight and to integrate the learning. By doing this, less serious relapses become part of the process and can be addressed as they occur.

This method is respectful and effective. People have the time they need to learn during the process. They are also supported and guided to develop understanding and strategies tailored to their personal circumstances (strengths and limitations) and what works for them. Over time, they encounter and come to accept and like their authentic selves, which leads to asking, "What am I doing?" Their decisions fit with their values, beliefs, needs, and how they want to live their lives. By the time the work ends, they have developed effective ways to meet their needs, identify triggers, and lessen the chance of relapse.

It is important to acknowledge that sometimes a hoarding situation has gone unidentified and unaddressed for too long. These situations may represent an immediate threat to life for the person who hoards or others (including pets). In these cases, unfortunately, an intensive short-term cleanup, also commonly known as a *shovel-out*, may be required. Yet, even though the situation has progressed beyond what can be accomplished in the required time limit allowable, the shovel-out approach usually increases the negative impact on the individual and, with a high degree of certainty, will result in rehoarding more quickly and severely. Ongoing monitoring and management are important components of any aftercare program. Support should be qualified and offered immediately, perhaps incorporating additional treatment and services for comorbid issues on a session-by-session intervention plan. If nothing changes for the person generating the hoard, then nothing will change, and another hoard will soon be re-created.

Issues in a Severely Deteriorated Environment

If an item is rotten, expired, or irreversibly contaminated, and the person can't let it go, this is a warning sign of a more serious psychological or cognitive condition. This response may represent a more extreme mental health impairment and is reason to talk to the person (or a legal representative who has power of attorney) about obtaining an intensive psychiatric or mental health assessment. Build an understanding by looking at the items in question through the eyes of the people hoarding them, asking them what they see and believe about the items they assess as still edible or useful.

If an item is broken or contaminated, discuss the risks of keeping it. As an example, a client of mine had little else in her life besides her cats and a silk flower collection. When her physical and mental health deteriorated, she inadvertently put the flower collection in a non-climate-controlled storage space beside her apartment building. She thought she was storing the collection safely in boxes, but by the time I was called in, mice had accessed the containers and destroyed everything. Opening the first few boxes was extremely painful for her. It was also painful for the crew and me to witness her shock and grief. She and her now-deceased mother had created the collection together.

The current state of her collection was difficult for the client to accept. As she grieved the loss of it, I helped her transition through a continuum of stages of grief, responsibility, and denial to acceptance. It also helped her that my crew treated her collection with the sensitivity and importance her attachment warranted, as opposed to the value of its current condition. Everyone shared personal stories with her about times when we had a plan that didn't work as we had hoped. I helped her put her decision to store the flowers in the storage space in the context of what else had been going on in her life, which made this the best choice she had been capable of at the time. We discussed what was most important to *moving forward as she is today*. It was a heavy, sad price to pay, but she came to understand that she'd had good reasons for making the decision she had and that holding on to so much of the inventory she had shared with her mother had been a way to handle and lessen her grief. The storage space had been necessary because the three-bedroom apartment she and her mother had shared had been hoarded by both. As I helped her reduce her accumulation, I also recommended excellent community-based grief services for continued support.

 For grief counselors in your area, do a Google search on "grief therapist." Add your location after the word "therapist": for example, "grief therapist in New York City."

Pacing Yourself

Watch out for fatigue when working with the 4, 5, 6s. They can easily become 1, 2, 3s as you lose focus when you become overly tired. This process needs to be paced properly, and you need to be very aware of how much energy you have available coming into the process each time. Match the task at hand to the amount of energy you have on board each time you declutter. Respect your limits.

Another important factor in pacing is *always* to start each session with a check-in. Either you or your clutter coach can ask:

- Currently, are there any events happening that will increase or lessen my ability to work with the focus and energy needed?
- Is anything happening that affects my ability to be "present" that I should talk through with my coach before starting?
- What is working well about the plan to address the accumulation?
- What is not working well?
- What are the two most important things happening in my life right now?

I ask these questions to mentor and coach my clients in gauging how much fuel they have in their tank before deciding on goals for each decluttering session.

Whatever is happening in people's lives will be in the back of their mind, whether or not they want it to be, and it draws energy away from the work. If you are helping someone who hoards, you need to pace the process based on what the person has to give during the current counseling or work session.

Most of my clients tell me that even though they like me personally, they often do not look forward to my coming. Despite this initial negative reaction, however, they usually report that they feel a great deal better after the visit. The energy they expended focusing, processing, and deciding often makes them want to lie down after the session. Hoarding work drains people mentally, emotionally, and physically. As a supporter, or clutter coach, this may be true for you too.

If you are a clutter coach, you can help people learn to pace themselves by watching their breathing and their facial and neck coloring. Notice if they are "being present" by checking their eye focus. Watch if the certainty about their decisions changes. Notice if the certainty becomes increasingly fuzzy and they begin to default to "just for now" decisions.

Watch also if the opposite begins to happen, and they get to a point where they are quick to part with an unusually large number of items in a row. This is not what you are working to achieve. You want *conscious* decisions, without regret, a void, or longing setting in after the decision. It is far better to take a break and give people a chance to replenish their energy and focus than to push through and make the session about getting rid of as much as possible. Choices made under these conditions are not made consciously. You are not striving for compliance. The goal needs to be supporting conscious choices that minimize the chance for relapse.

We should not measure the success of our work as guides and coaches by how much or how far we can get people to go in parting with their things. Instead, our success is measured by choices being made that yield lasting, safe, and satisfying environments, where our clients can live the lives they want. *You never want to go into this process thinking that you are doing better the more you get them to throw out. The thinning of the accumulation will happen naturally and consistently if you follow the process outlined in this book.*

There is no average length of time for this process to take. It is determined by the needs of the person and the condition of the environment. Throughout the process, there is sharing, understanding, laughter, frustration, uncertainty, and sometimes tears.

Who Likes Homework?

In the beginning, I don't give homework. Unless the situation presents an immediate threat to life, or the fire department needs immediate access, I tell my clients that initially, I want them to take a break from the guilt and pressure caused by "shoulds." Almost certainly, they have looked at all the piles in their spaces every day and have probably judged themselves harshly. Usually the people hoarding are not the only ones judging them harshly.

Most people I have worked with have started many times and gotten defeated. To break the shame-blame cycle, I suggest, "Now, when you walk past something that has been bothering you, I want you to say to that pile, 'I have a plan for you. My clutter coach [or supporter] and I will get to you when the time is right.' And then go do something that replenishes your joy, fun, and play energy." A nonacquiring activity is a bonus.

I also tell them that if they see something really bothering them, and they *really* want to do something about it, to go ahead initially but to stop as soon as it feels like work. Quite often, when I return, people are happy to show me the sorting or decluttering they have completed. Hope and trust begin to return as they realize that what they dream of accomplishing can, and will, actually happen.

After as many as three or four sessions, I ask if they are ready to begin committing to working between sessions, and often they do. Sometimes the best they can manage is to commit to the scheduled session time as their dedicated work effort. Sometimes their homework is to do physically *nothing* concrete about the clutter, but to begin by focusing on an item that is a difficult decision—even though they know that keeping this item is not their best choice. I ask them to take this item and put it in a prominent place, such as on a countertop or table. Every day as they walk by it, they ask the item the following questions:

- What do you add to my life?
- What will it cost me if I keep you?
- If in the future, I discover that you are important, and I've let you go, how will my life change?

Remember, our relationship to our things is real. So even if the next strategy feels strange, try it. Sometimes for sentimental items, putting the object in a prominent place and talking to it every day when you walk by it honors the reality that you have a relationship with that thing. It helps you externalize the decision-making process, and you can hear for yourself what factors are playing out internally that influence your decision making. For example, you might say, "I'm sorry you might have to go. You were my children's toy. You made them so happy. I remember how much fun you gave us. But my life is in a different place now. I want to thank you for all those wonderful memories. I am going to donate you next week to a place where we can share that fun and joy with someone else, who will enjoy you as much as we have. I know that whoever picks you will really want you and enjoy you." In reality, you are not speaking to the item, you are speaking to your unconscious.

This process works. It honors the item itself, honors the importance it has for you, helps you become more self-aware, and respects you by working at your pace.

It is time to take back your life.

CHAPTER 5

Procrastination

BECAUSE PROCRASTINATION IS SUCH A COMMON BEHAVIOR in hoarding disorder, understanding what procrastination is, and how to manage it, is pivotal to achieving success. Perhaps you are procrastinating and have difficulty maintaining your initial enthusiasm to declutter. Perhaps getting started is where you get blocked.

I turned to Jane Burka, co-author with Lenora Yuen of *Procrastination: Why You Do It, What to Do about It Now* (2008), for her expertise on procrastination, including how some of our basic fears—fear of failure, of success, of authority—can influence us to procrastinate.

I was excited to have Dr. Burka as my guest on my weekly radio program, *Take Back Your Life When Your Things Are Taking Over*, on the VoiceAmerica Variety Channel, as she is an extraordinarily knowledgeable professional with specialized expertise in procrastination. This chapter provides a synopsis of the valuable information discussed on the show (Birchall 2016).

You may be like many of the listeners who feel puzzled and defeated. They say that they know what to do to clean up, but they just can't make themselves do it. The majority of people whom I see tell me that they struggle with and sometimes feel defeated by procrastination.

Doesn't Everyone Procrastinate?

According to Dr. Burka, everyone procrastinates on something because we are all so busy that we can't possibly do everything that we want or need to do. We can't possibly do everything that is expected of us. But sometimes procrastination gets in the way. Problem procrastination is what we are talking about here.

Whether procrastination is a problem for you really depends on the kinds of consequences you have suffered. If you put something off because you actually need more information, or you are not sure what to do, that's one thing that you can resolve. But if your procrastination is chronic, has been self-defeating for you, or if it happens around the most important things in your life, then it is a problem. The best approach is to think of the consequences of procrastination in your life.

There are two kinds of consequences:

1   *External consequences*, the price you pay for procrastination. Some examples:
    - You took too long to pay a parking ticket, and now you have to pay an additional fine.
    - You took too long to pay taxes, and now the government wants to talk to you.
    - You took so long to put up a fence in the backyard that now your wife is mad at you.
    - You took so long to submit an application that you were too late to be considered for the job.
2   *Internal consequences* include anxiety, stress, physical symptoms, and insomnia. These internal consequences may also be psychological if you feel you are a failure or that procrastination defines you. This leads you to lose confidence in yourself.

The more chronic and widespread these consequences are for you, the more procrastination is a problem.

Do Procrastinators Think or Approach Work Differently?

The first thing I do when a client is experiencing barriers is help them look at whether they have limiting beliefs or are doing something that is creating the barrier—in this case, procrastination. Cognitive behavioral therapy (CBT) is an excellent counseling method to drill down and discover these hidden thinking traps. You do not need to be a mental health professional to use CBT methods yourself. There are excellent self-help books available if you do not have access to a counselor. You can also use the worksheet "Problem Solving Using Cognitive Behavioral Therapy," available on page 74.

Dr. Burka notes that people who don't procrastinate don't understand it. They think, "Well, I know how long something takes to do. Why don't you?" But procrastinators approach work and time differently. For one thing, they tend to keep their goals in a vague state. They don't think concretely about them. They think, "Well, I'll do this tomorrow," rather than thinking about what they actually have to do tomorrow. Or "I can read *War and Peace* in one night." They are vague about what their situation is. They think in very optimistic ways—with a wishful thinking approach to work and a wishful thinking approach to how much time they have available.

Dr. Burka also stresses that procrastinators are usually perfectionists. They think, "If I'm not going to do it perfectly, it is not worth doing." When you ask procrastinators if they are perfectionists, they often say, "Oh no. I don't do anything perfectly." Note that perfectionism is actually an attitude; it is not really measured by results, how well you have done something, or how much you have done. Procrastinators who have a perfectionist approach are really setting themselves up for failure from the outset. Most people don't see themselves as perfectionists. They think of themselves as having high standards, which they think is a good idea. They think the high standards motivate them. Perfectionism is often *ego syntonic* (meaning thoughts and behaviors in line with one's ideal self-image), so people think it fits for them, but it is almost an invisible disease that the people afflicted with it are not aware of.

In our interview, Dr. Burka gave an example of writing an essay in high school and using the phrase "the most perfect." Her English teacher said, "You have to say 'the most nearly perfect' because there is no such thing as perfect, or most perfect." That really stayed with her because thinking you have to be perfect, or that you have to produce something perfect, creates a barrier for yourself. You make a mountain so high that sometimes you just don't feel like climbing it. It becomes overwhelming. Perfectionism is more self-defeating than motivating.

Main Causes of Procrastination

Low Self-Esteem

Most procrastination, according to Dr. Burka, is related to problems with self-esteem. People often misunderstand procrastination. They think of it as a problem of time management, or an issue with lack of willpower or motivation, and so they blame themselves. They get mad at themselves and think it is a weakness. But Dr. Burka and Dr. Yuen think that procrastination is a behavior that actually protects people in some way. While this seems contradictory to the consequences of procrastination, it really isn't. In some ways, it is more acceptable to feel that your problem is not getting to work on time than to consider other psychological issues, such as fear of failure, of success, and of feeling controlled.

Fear of Failure

In *Procrastination: Why You Do It, What to Do about It Now*, Dr. Burka and Dr. Yuen detail a complete list of causes, including how fear of failure is really anxiety about proving yourself. When people have a shaky sense of self-esteem or self-worth, they have a lot of anxiety about proving themselves and fear that if they do their very best, it still won't be good enough. Then they will feel like a failure again. Many procrastinators think that if you are not at the top, you are a failure. It is an all-or-nothing approach.

If you put off a task or a project but meet the deadline at the last minute, and you end up with a result that is not as good as you would have liked, then you can say to yourself, "Well, if I'd had more time, it would have been much better." This is sort of an out or a safety cushion. Ironically, it doesn't feel good or safe, but it does protect your self-esteem.

If you are determining your self-worth by what you produce, then producing something is like having a gun pointed at you every time. You feel that you as a person are being evaluated based on your results. A lot of people have unfortunately grown up with the feeling that their worth depends on what they do, how well they perform, and what they produce. If your worth is defined that way, then you really can't afford to do your best and see what happens. If it isn't good enough, you will lose self-esteem.

In my practice, I have observed how these fears create a very real trap for those suffering from hoarding disorder. Unconditional love and acceptance in childhood, which promotes self-worth, can be lacking in those who suffer from hoarding disorder. If my ability and self-worth hinge on the excellence of what I produce, unconditional love and acceptance can unfortunately become increasingly uncommon and the basis for a lot of internal anxiety. Anxieties disrupt most of my clients' lives and may be significant contributing factors to procrastination in their hoarding disorder.

Dr. Burka reflects that if you feel that your worth depends on something external, for example, all the things that you have, then your investment in those things is quite high. But ideally, our self-worth relates to our value as people, not what we have accumulated, or what we do.

Fear of Success

Fear of success seems contradictory because most people think that everybody wants success, that being successful will make you happy. According to Dr. Burka and Dr. Yuen, however, being successful brings along many new experiences, and some people are afraid of those experiences. For example, if you are promoted, and now you are the boss, then the buck stops with you. You have to make the decisions. You have the responsibility. You are in the spotlight. This adds to people's anxiety.

Another reason people are afraid of success is that they worry they will be expected to be increasingly more successful. They think of success as being like an escalator; once you step on, you can't get off. It feels like the pressure will just build and build. A good analogy is someone who is training to be a high jumper. Once the person clears the bar and sets a new record, the bar gets raised, so there is always a next level. Some people feel the need to avoid that kind of pressure.

In addition to the above reasons, some people feel they don't deserve success. They feel they are not worthy of success. It is easy to see how procrastination interferes with success, but it is not as easy to see the above reasons behind the procrastination.

Dr. Burka adds that people also fear being alone if they are successful, because they may be rejected by their group of friends or colleagues. If you are promoted above your colleagues, for example, then you are no longer part of that group. Success can also make people fearful of losing relationships. Having a spouse or partner who is not as successful as you are can be disruptive to your relationship. You have to rebalance things. You may come from a family that is not as successful as you have become. You may feel as if you have lost your family connection.

An example that Dr. Burka gives is when she was a counselor at the University of California at Berkeley, where she first started leading procrastination groups. She often met students who were the first people in their families to go to college. They were worried that if they did really well, they would move far beyond what their families had achieved. Their families didn't really understand college, their courses, how much work they had to do, and where they were headed. It was a barrier between them and their loved ones. Sometimes the students would not do very well, and some students even left school to go back home. Their fear of losing their connection with their families interfered with their ability to work.

I wonder how common this fear actually is, because I also know someone, a manager, who shared that getting the promotion felt good only for a short while, because afterward, he felt like he really didn't have any friends. The dynamic of the relationships in the workplace changed. Even though he wanted this job, with its higher salary and status, work became a lonely place to be.

Dr. Burka suggests that it can be even more complicated, because some people like the jobs they have or the people they work for, and when they get promoted, they don't enjoy their new situation at all. They may have to deal with a different boss or do work they did not expect or want. Getting promoted can mean going from loving a job to hating your work.

She adds that another aspect to loneliness and success is when people envy your success. Envy is a big issue. Today's workplace is so competitive that when someone succeeds above someone else, the envy can become a poison, making people treat the successful person badly and want to see him or her fail. People who are afraid of being envied sometimes procrastinate so that they will not be the one who got the A or the promotion.

Fear of Being Controlled

Procrastination is an indirect way of saying, "You can't make me do it," a way of not being controlled. You are doing things on your own time, on your own schedule, in your own way. "And for some people," according to Dr. Burka, "going along with what someone else expects is an insult to their self-esteem." For some people, their self-esteem depends on their sense of autonomy. In other words, "I am my own person. You can't tell me what to do." So if they do something on time and meet someone else's expectations, they feel like they have compromised themselves. They feel that they have given in or been taken over. So procrastinating, maintaining their separateness and their own control over what they are doing, makes them feel better. Cooperation feels like capitulation. These are people who probably grew up feeling highly controlled and micromanaged. They may have had someone hovering over them, judging them all the time. Now, by procrastinating, they can say, "I don't have to do what you want me to do."

HOW CAN YOU TELL IF YOU FEAR BEING CONTROLLED?

A key for Dr. Burka to determine whether people fear being controlled is to look at where they procrastinate. What are you *not* doing? You do some things every day—for example, brush your teeth twice a day—whereas you leave other things undone. Putting off things that someone else asks you to do is one sign that you fear being controlled. If you put off things that represent bureaucracy—if you don't do your taxes on time, pay parking tickets, or file paperwork when it is required—that is a sign that you don't want to be controlled. As I have noted, when I start working with individuals who hoard, I rarely find that their income tax has been submitted in the past four years. I wonder if this might indicate that a fear of being controlled is a common experience for those who hoard.

I asked Dr. Burka about something I encounter frequently with clients who are overwhelmed, feeling broken and flawed, and questioning their own competence. If the world doesn't feel like a safe, predictable place, can people be left feeling that they are not up to managing it? If the fear of control is part of their fundamental beliefs, how would this play out in the form of procrastination?

Dr. Burka responded that many people don't feel safe in the world. That feeling starts at birth, then expands in the family, in school, in the workplace environment, and in the world as a whole. In certain ways we are *not* safe, but when people don't have a core sense of security, then everything they do is much more highly charged. They are genuinely worried about how they will manage. They don't have the foundation—the ground under their feet—to fall back on when they take chances. When you feel like you don't know how to manage or don't feel competent, then you don't have the confidence to take risks. *Procrastination is an antirisk behavior.* You do, of course, risk experiencing the consequences of procrastination, and you risk upsetting people, but you don't risk your own value. I think that when people don't feel safe, they find ways of hiding. Procrastination is a way of hiding who you really are and protecting yourself from the ultimate failure: accepting that you have limits.

In reality, most people are average, but nobody wants to feel average. Dr. Burka thinks that procrastination protects people from putting themselves to the test (whatever that test might be).

Procrastination and Relationships

Day-to-day life involves the workplace, our personal lives, and mundane activities like going to the store—just the business of life. In many everyday situations, we have to cooperate with other people.

Dr. Burka observes that procrastination plays out poorly in relationships. For one thing, people simply don't like it when you promise them something and then procrastinate for whatever reason. You may have a boss or colleague who is angry with you. If you don't turn in the data that they need for a report, for example, then they can't do their own work well. People to whom you report or who rely on your work will get quite irritated.

In personal relationships, if one person is a procrastinator and the other isn't, a gulf of misunderstanding develops because everybody has a different relationship to time. This is true in workplace relationships as well as in intimate or family relationships. People have a subjective sense of time. We used to say that there is no such thing as a procrastination gene, but biologically, we do all have *clock genes*. These are cells that regulate our biorhythms and our relationship to time. For some people, their subjective sense of time is close to what the clock and calendar say. For others, biologically, their subjective sense of time is different. Time moves more slowly for them, or more rapidly. People who are able to tie themselves to the clock and the calendar don't have any understanding of what life is like for people who are wired differently. This is part of a basic problem in relationships, when people do not "get" each other.

In addition, some people have anxiety about performing, but the way they deal with that anxiety is to work really hard; they don't understand why someone else who has anxiety about performing would not perform. This shows a real lack of understanding between people who procrastinate and those who don't.

How to Stop Procrastinating

Dr. Burka suggests that it helps to understand why you are procrastinating. Because then you realize that the issue is not really how you are working or not working. The issue is some kind of anxiety and the way you are protecting yourself. Why you are procrastinating is the first thing to identify. Then, you can try specific things that will help, whether or not you understand your anxiety.

Step 1: Do a little bit at a time. Most procrastinators wait a long time to start, and then they feel that they need all the time it takes to do the project. None of us ever has all the time that we need to get something done from beginning to end, so the most important shift in thinking is to recognize that you can work on something for a short time—even 15 minutes. Dr. Burka suggests setting a clock or phone app for 15 minutes, then working for that amount of time on whatever you have been putting off. Most of us can stand to do anything for 15 minutes.

Step 2: Think about your project in very specific ways. Do not keep things vague. For example, what is the deadline for the paper that you are not working on? Most of Dr. Burka's students would say, "I don't know." Be very specific about what your goal is and when it needs to be done. One thing that procrastinators do is say to themselves, "I have to get organized," or "I have to write a report." That kind of global description really doesn't help. What helps is to think in terms of a concrete act that you will do, that will mean progress toward your goal. The concrete act might be something that you could even take a picture of yourself doing. Instead of saying, "I have to get organized," you might say, "I am going to spend 30 minutes filing the papers on my desk." This is a goal you can do. Another example is "I will measure the backyard to see how much lumber I need to build the fence." Or "I'm going to write four emails." Whatever it is, it should be specific.

When Dr. Burka and Dr. Yuen did their procrastination groups, they found that people could help one another make their goals specific. In other words, you may have the skill to do a project but have trouble being specific. It might help to work with someone else to get clear about what the project goals and time frames actually are.

The Cycle of Procrastination

Chronic procrastinators will recognize the cyclical pattern described in Burka and Yuen (2008).

Phase 1. It starts out with great optimism—the "I can do that" idea. People think, "I don't have to start now because I have plenty of time, but I can do that."

Phase 2. The next thing that happens is that people don't do it. Anxiety builds up. "Well, I better get started. I have to start soon." There is an awareness that they haven't gotten anywhere, but there is still confidence. As things move along, and they are still not doing anything, they begin to question, "What if I don't start?"

Phase 3. It dawns on them that maybe they will not actually get this done, which is the beginning of a paralyzing time. They start to get mad at themselves. They don't trust themselves. They start to second-guess and say, "I should have started back at the beginning." They may run around doing things to keep themselves busy, but they are still not working on the project. If they start, they feel burdened and anxious. They feel that they should not go out to have any fun because they are not working on the project. As they sink, and time gets closer to the deadline, the anxiety builds up.

Phase 4. They must face the music of the deadline. They have a choice: to either break through and complete the project or let it go. When they let it go, they feel really bad about themselves. If they break through and do it, they may say, "Well, this isn't so bad. Why didn't I start sooner?"

Another important point about the cycle of procrastination is that when you finally do start to make that push at the end, you can't be a perfectionist. You have time only to get it done. You throw your perfectionism and your optimistic goals out the window and just *do it*. At this point, you say to yourself, "Why didn't I just do it sooner?" Then you say to yourself, "Well, next time, I will get started right away." But that doesn't always happen the next time.

Accepting "Good Enough"

Dr. Burka stresses that nobody likes to feel mediocre, yet not everyone can be at the top all the time. If you have perfectionistic standards, then you have contempt for anything you do that is average or just "good enough." And then you have self-contempt. This attitude is common in some high-achieving families that put a lot of pressure on children to succeed. They question, "Why did you get an A-?" The contempt that goes along with this attitude really harms a child's self-esteem. If you get a B and your father is disappointed, or your mother cries at your C mark, you understand that anything not perfect is contemptible. This has a devastating effect on self-esteem. You never have the feeling that good enough is okay.

If you feel like everything must be done at 100 percent effort and 100 percent success, you may have difficulty differentiating between what is important and what isn't. It is hard to set priorities about the 20 percent of things that matter and the 80 percent that don't matter if you feel like everything must be done perfectly. Everything must also be done by you. You can't delegate if you are a perfectionist and feel like you are the only one who knows how to do it right. Then you have too much to do. Then you are overwhelmed. Then you procrastinate.

The Need to Go It Alone

In my practice, I have observed that many people want to do it alone. They are fearful, or reluctant, or can't accept help. I asked Dr. Burka about this tendency, and she replied that because individuals who procrastinate feel that they are the only ones who can do something the way they want it done, they end up trying to go it alone, which ends in procrastination. Dr. Burka also clarified that after being treated as though they have to do everything perfectly, they don't really have faith that other people will accept them. They don't believe that someone will help them. They may be much more worried that somebody will judge them. *Doing things alone is a way of avoiding dealing with someone who might be critical.* Usually, the other people are not the ones being critical; self-criticism makes the person afraid that somebody else will judge them as they judge themselves. But most people are kinder to us than we are to ourselves.

Believing in One Correct Choice

The perfectionist's attitude is often based on the belief that they must make the right choice, and they worry about making the wrong choice. Dr. Burka draws a distinction here, that to the perfectionist, there is only *one* right choice. An example she gives: "If you have to decide whether to move to Texas or Arizona, and you research these two places all the time but then can't make up your mind, it is because you sense there is one right answer. One of these choices will make your life better, make you happy, and solve everything. So if you waffle on a decision that has to be right, then you can put off making the choice because there is a chance you will make the wrong one. If you think there is only one right way, then everything else is wrong. So procrastination helps you avoid confronting that."

Fixed Mindset versus Growth

The concept of fixed and growth mindsets was made popular by Carol S. Dweck (2007) and others. If you have a *fixed mindset*, you believe there is only one right way. There is always a rational and objective answer, a linear perspective, and choices that are either good or bad. From this perspective, any mistake you make is the result of not being good enough. If you have a *growth mindset*, you look at everything that comes your way as an opportunity for learning. So if you try your best and don't reach your goal, then you try again. There isn't the judgment that comes with viewing everything as either a success or a failure.

A growth mindset is much more focused on the process: if you are trying and learning, that is good enough. Often when people have the attitude of "I'm just going to do this as an experiment to see how I do, and I will learn from it," they actually end up doing better than expected. Dr. Burka gives an example of someone whose boss would tell her specifically what she did wrong, and she would say, "Oh, thank you for pointing that out." This is a very different response than feeling humiliated and thinking that no one likes you or that you are a failure.

How to Adopt a Growth Mindset vs. a Fixed Mindset

Having compassion for yourself and seeing everything as a learning opportunity is, according to Dr. Burka, the best way to begin developing a growth mindset when you have been operating from a fixed one. If what you are trying to achieve in your life is growth (which means moving from where you are to the next place, not to the end point), you can always take one step in the next good direction. That is a growth mindset.

When Dr. Burka pointed this out, I agreed and said, "I love that. I tell my clients all the time to be gentle with themselves. You are not perfect. You are not supposed to be perfect. Even those moments when you think you are perfect will probably last a very short time because the next experience is coming."

Jane Burka and Lenora Yuen's *Procrastination: Why You Do It, What to Do about It Now* is divided into two parts. Part 1 helps sufferers understand what this vastly misunderstood behavior called procrastination actually is. Part 2 helps them overcome this debilitating behavior choice.

In part 1, "Understanding Procrastination," readers learn about the fears that undermine success, such as the fear of failure, of success, of losing a perceived competitive struggle, or of intimacy, which leaves people feeling misunderstood and alone. Another important idea is that people who procrastinate may have a different concept of time than those who don't. This book deals with the current neuroscience behind procrastination. It is important to know how our brains are working for us and against us. The book also helps people understand how they became procrastinators, which for many can relieve the shame and blame that this behavior choice produces.

Part 2 helps people overcome procrastination by taking a personal inventory of their vulnerabilities so that they can build an action plan based on their personal needs. It helps people set goals that they can actually achieve and teaches them how to live on the same time clock as the rest of the world. It helps them learn when and how to say *yes* to competing priorities. If you live on the continuum of ADD or are not part of mainstream culture, this book has information for you as well. It teaches you how to live with and manage procrastination in your life. The rest of this chapter is adapted, with permission, from *Procrastination*.

Knowing Yourself, Part 1: Feelings

Knowing yourself requires knowing your feelings.

- Avoiding feelings leaves you vulnerable.
- Knowing what you feel and why you feel it increases confidence, your sense of solidity, and your ease with yourself, while strengthening your ability to proceed with things in a timely way, without needing to procrastinate.

List below what you are feeling right now about your level of confidence.

HOW CONFIDENT ARE YOU ABOUT	100% (All of the time)	75% (Most of the time)	50% (It depends on the day)	25% (Sometimes)	5% (Rarely)
yourself as a person?					
how at ease you are with yourself?					
your personal relationships?					
the work you do?					
your past achievements?					
your present achievements?					
your ability to reliably finish things in a timely way?					

Respond to the questions in tables 5.1–5.6 (pages 105 to 113) to gain understanding of your specific fears, hopes, dreams, doubts, pressures, and memories.

TABLE 5.1

Fears

WHAT ARE YOUR FEARS?	QUESTIONS TO ASK YOURSELF	EXAMPLES FROM YOUR LIFE
Success	Do you feel anxious when receiving recognition? When making good progress, are you tempted to switch to another task or slow down?	
Failure	Do you believe that if something is not done perfectly (or right), it is not worth doing, and so you don't do it? Do you believe that if you are good at something, it should come easily? Are you a gracious loser?	
Being controlled	Generally, do rules apply to you, or do you think that an exception should be made for your needs? What is your tolerance for limits set by authorities?	
Intimacy	Does commitment make you anxious? Do you anticipate failure in relationships based on past relationships that haven't worked out? Do you leave a relationship because you fear being left?	
Trust	Do you need to do things alone because you can't rely on others? Do you prefer to work on projects privately to avoid others interfering with your ideas? Do you fear being controlled or manipulated?	

Abandonment	Do you believe that you can manage on your own? Do you need others to agree with you before you believe in your own ideas?	
Conflict	Do you have a strong need to be liked? Do you see conflict as a fight that creates winners and losers?	
Being exposed	Do you fear being exposed as "not good enough" or at fault for a mistake? Do you feel that your performance demonstrates your personal worth?	
Being unacceptable or inherently flawed in some way	Do you feel that you are broken and fundamentally flawed?	
Other	Are there other ways in which fears or insecurities disrupt your ability to finish projects that need to be done?	

Adapted from Jane Burka, and Lenora Yuen, *Procrastination: Why You Do It, What to Do about It* (Cambridge, MA: Da Capo Press, 2008)

TABLE 5.2
Hopes

What are your hopes?	
What five hopes would you put on your bucket list?	
What do you say to yourself about each item on your bucket list?	
Are you permanently dismissing any items on your bucket list because they seem out of reach?	
What prevents you from making these hoped-for items and experiences happen?	
If you had a coach, what would he or she suggest you do to overcome these barriers?	
Are you thinking inside or outside the box to find possibilities?	

List three things you hope to do within the next three months.	
List five other things you hope to do within the next year.	
Give your best friend two sealed letters, each containing your response to one of the last two questions, addressed to yourself, to be given to you as these dates approach (i.e., at three months and at one year).	

Adapted from Jane Burka, and Lenora Yuen, *Procrastination: Why You Do It, What to Do about It* (Cambridge, MA: Da Capo Press, 2008)

TABLE 5.3
Dreams

What are your dreams?	
What five dreams would you put on your bucket list?	

What do you say to yourself about each item on your bucket list?

Are you permanently dismissing any dreams on your bucket list because they seem out of reach?

What prevents you from making these dreams come true?

If you had a coach, what would he or she suggest you do to overcome these barriers?

Are you thinking inside or outside the box to find possibilities?

List three things you have dreamed of doing that are appropriate for the next three months.

List five other things you have dreamed of doing that are appropriate for the next year.	
Give your best friend two sealed letters, each containing your response to one of the last two questions, addressed to yourself, to be given to you as these dates approach (i.e., at three months and at one year).	

Adapted from Jane Burka, and Lenora Yuen, *Procrastination: Why You Do It, What to Do about It* (Cambridge, MA: Da Capo Press, 2008)

TABLE 5.4
Doubt

What are your doubts?	
Are you working from fear or fact?	
List your fears.	

List the facts that support your doubts.	
Given your fear and fact list, what is the evidence that your fears create actual barriers?	
What do you need to do to resolve these fear-based doubts?	

Adapted from Jane Burka, and Lenora Yuen, *Procrastination: Why You Do It, What to Do about It* (Cambridge, MA: Da Capo Press, 2008)

TABLE 5.5
Pressures

What are your pressures?	
What are your strengths?	

List your areas in need of growth or change.	
List the help you have asked for to manage the pressures preventing you from moving forward.	
Are there other types of help that you need?	
How willing are you to reconsider the belief that no good help is available to you?	

Adapted from Jane Burka, and Lenora Yuen, *Procrastination: Why You Do It, What to Do about It* (Cambridge, MA: Da Capo Press, 2008)

TABLE 5.6
Memories

List some supportive and unsupportive memories.	
When working to move forward on a task, are you recalling negative memories that reduce your ability to remain motivated? What are they?	

What alternative, positive memories that support you are you not considering?

What have you learned?

What have you changed?

How have those negative experiences helped you grow?

What can you say now to defend yourself against those negative thoughts?

List memories of past successes and the strengths and skills you learned that will help you succeed today.

Adapted from Jane Burka, and Lenora Yuen, *Procrastination: Why You Do It, What to Do about It* (Cambridge, MA: Da Capo Press, 2008)

Knowing Yourself, Part 2: Time

What Is Your Relationship with Time?

A *wishful thinking* approach to time is when we choose to apply subjective standards to our need to meet the requirements of scheduled events, such as school, work/meetings, religious services, time-sensitive social events, and personal commitments to friends and organizations. The questions to ask yourself are, "How frequently am I late for time-sensitive scheduled events? Do I feel entitled to be late? Does the same rule apply to me as to others who are attending these time-sensitive events? If not, why not? What prevents me from consistently being on time?"

Note: I am not suggesting a rigid level of perfection in timeliness; rather, is it truly the *exception* when you are late, rather than a *likely* occurrence? Write your response to this and subsequent questions in spaces below.

_____

_____

_____

_____

_____

_____

Conflicts with clock time: In the past month, what examples are there that you might be living in conflict with the reality of clock time in your arrival at time-sensitive events?

_____

_____

_____

_____

_____

_____

Difficulty anticipating deadlines: If you find it difficult to anticipate deadlines for projects, why do you think that is?

_____

_____

_____

_____

Difficulty working steadily toward a goal: In the past month, what evidence is there that you might have difficulty working steadily toward a goal? How many projects have you started but not yet finished? What prevents you from finishing a goal before you start another?

_____

_____

_____

_____

Difficulty predicting how much time you will need to finish a job: Do you find it difficult to predict how much time you will need to finish a job? Do you overestimate the time needed? Do you underestimate the time needed and are therefore unable to finish? Is your daily or weekly schedule overcommitted? Do you find that you are consistently left with not enough time to finish projects that you underestimated? What would it take for you to free up more time in your schedule between commitments? Have you had time-related problems in relationships, when you have lived on subjective time while others lived on clock time?

_____

_____

_____

_____

Knowing Yourself, Part 3: Your Roots

Family history: List the names of individuals in the family you grew up in who were likely to be on time, and those likely to be late, for scheduled events.

_____

_____

_____

_____

_____

Social relationships: List feedback you have received from friends, associates, acquaintances, and professionals concerning your tardiness.

_____

_____

_____

_____

_____

Your culture: Do you consider your culture to be a factor in your relationship with time?

_____

_____

_____

_____

_____

PART II

Moving Forward: Inspiration from Those Who Have Gone before You

CHAPTER 6

The Impact of Hoarding on Families

Her Pills Haven't Worked Yet

The human mind is a complicated place . . .
We hold onto things, images, words, ideas, histories
that we don't even know we're holding onto.

COREY ANN HAYDU

IN MY 17 YEARS OF WORKING WITH FAMILIES impacted by hoarding, I have learned that to be effective, you need to work holistically with individuals. This means addressing the other aspects of their lives that are overwhelming and distracting them from being able to deal with their hoarding disorder. Resolving a hoarding problem isn't just about cleaning up. Life is complex, and the many ways in which life breaks down are often compounded by mental health disorders and social dysfunction. For a family like Joan, Paul, and their sons, Timmy (age 8), Mike (age 3), and Gordie (age 2), there are no easy fixes.

Synopsis

Joan, Paul, Timmy, Mike, and Gordie's story is about a family trying valiantly to overcome complex, fragile, joint parental mental illness. Joan and Paul sincerely tried to persist in overcoming hoarding disorder. Their mutual hoarding disorders decimated their financial security, created severe health and safety hazards for all of them, and made them unavailable to meet parental responsibilities. As their most important goals evaded them, they finally had to redefine success.

Problem Overview

Most of the family home was 60–70 percent three-dimensionally full. The marriage had deteriorated into early stage physical aggression. The children were living in small corners of one to two rooms. Their school was calling home with concerns about them coming to school without lunch and snacks. Both fragile, mentally ill parents were not taking their prescribed medications because of financial mismanagement caused by compulsive buying.

Community Outreach Crisis Services had responded because of a violent outburst. Child Protective Services (CPS) was poised to apprehend all three children when Paul took the advice given and called me for help to reclaim their home and their lives.

Background

As Donna (my assistant) and I arrived on what turned out to be our last day, 8-year-old Timmy glanced up from the one clear spot on a heaped couch in a very cluttered living room. He continued clicking away on his video game while he explained, "It just looks like this because she hasn't been able to do very much. She hasn't taken her pills; she ran out. She was supposed to take the paper to the drug store yesterday and get them, but she didn't."

He added, "She got her pills this morning. Just not in time for them to work—to help her do anything."

His life and that of his younger brothers was so unpredictable, so filled with chaos. None of them could do many of the things that children loved to do. Here he was, squeezed into the only part of the sofa that wasn't heaped with clutter, playing his game and protecting his mom. I moved over beside him and asked him how he was doing and how he felt about things. "You mean around here? You mean the mess?" he asked. "I hate the mess," he replied and went back to his handheld distraction. Mike and Gordie were on the floor in the corner, searching amid the clutter, dust, and tracked-in sand for pieces of a toy they were sharing.

Today was unfolding to be the day that we had each, in our own way, worked hard to prevent. CPS was about to make a pivotal visit to the home to discuss how the environment continued to be insufficient for a child's needs. Although it was presented kindly and nonjudgmentally, with alternative options put forward, the facts were clearly outlined to Joan and Paul. Without continued support for addressing the reasons Mom and Dad hoarded, as well as additional decluttering work on the home, the chronic disorganization in their lives would quickly replace any clutter we removed. It would be no more than three weeks before CPS would have to recommend that all three children be removed to foster care.

Mom finally spoke up to the CPS worker: "Well, if you're going to take them sometime anyway, you might as well take them now. I can't stand it hanging over me. I'm doing my best, and it's just not good enough for you."

My heart sank as I heard the defeat and resignation in her voice. I felt sad for this valiant little family. I had worked with both Joan and Paul for the past year and a half, as they battled their individual hoarding disorders in their own way. I wanted to advocate for more time and financial help for the family to have a rapid cleanup, which I knew in my heart they were not ready to maintain.

I looked at Joan and saw the stress of dealing with her demons written on her face. Those demons were avoidance and procrastination. Her ADD (attention deficit disorder) locked her mind in endless spinning. Her OCD (obsessive-compulsive disorder) was her internal tyrant, making impossible demands, pulling her one way and then another, with impossible standards to achieve. The goals she set were never met, even if she stayed up and tried to work on them all day and night, which she sometimes did. No matter how hard she tried to quell the panic about the next visit from those of us who were trying to help and support her, she saw us as regular reminders of how she was failing, week after week, always inadequate. And the others too—the ones who had the power to take away her little guys—were a constant source of extreme distress. She told me that her internal voice kept taunting her, "Maybe once they are gone, they will never want to come back to this place . . . to me?"

I felt sad for her, knowing that she would miss tucking them in bed and kissing them good night. She would miss sitting with them when they came home from daycare and school, sharing a snack, and hearing about their day. She would miss hugging them, laughing, and teaching them all the important lessons in life. She would miss all of this. The weekend visits would be pale substitutes.

She was exhausted from the fight, from spinning and trying to stay ahead of the clutter in her severely hoarded home. She wasn't working for custody of her sons anymore; she was fighting for her own sanity.

Client's Initial Perspective

Joan believed that if everyone and everything just went away, she could do what was needed. Paul hoped that it was not too late to do what was needed to save their family and prevent the boys from being taken into foster care.

Therapeutic Plan

It was necessary to work strategically on areas of the home that were "activities of daily living" priorities. (See "Activities of Daily Living Assessment" in chapter 2.) Then, as enough free space was recovered, we planned intensive cleanups to reach the standards that the fire department and CPS required to support them as an intact family.

Intervention

Over the past year and a half, I had witnessed every week repeated examples of Joan's inability to make a plan and carry it out. Instead, the spinning in her head created chaotic piles that we would spend the next session trying to decode and undo.

She needed to go through all the garbage bags we collected in a session, item by item. After we cleaned up, nothing could be removed without her going through every single piece. Even if she had approved some bags to go, she would feel compelled to bring it all back in to be rechecked. The room we had set up as the boys' playroom was usually filled with garbage bags when we returned for the next session. It was very difficult to get her to feel that the checking was ever complete.

Joan also had rigid rules that punished her severely. Her rules made her feel that she was inadequate as a woman, wife, and mother if the unreachable high standards were not met.

As if that wasn't enough, Joan's ADD caused her to be constantly rushing and chronically disorganized. Under the pressure of a perceived crisis, Joan would dump all bags and items from the car, including the contents of her purse, on the floor to search frantically for something. The contents of the dumped purse would rarely get picked up and most likely would remain where they fell.

CPS was concerned that they were getting frequent calls about Timmy from his school, Mike by age 3 couldn't speak clearly, and Gordie seemed to be in a constant daze. Timmy got teased at school for not having a lunch and snacks like the other children and being chronically late for class. The school called home regularly and finally expressed their concern to CPS directly. The TV was the babysitter for the boys, especially when life at home became overwhelming.

I worked with Joan and Paul on their parenting skills, especially about the problem of allowing Timmy to watch TV in the morning before school, during the time when he needed to dress, eat, get his school things together, and be ready to leave on time. Paul and Joan's permissiveness was their way to compensate for their feelings of inadequacy as parents.

Joan was constantly rushing out the door late with Timmy, disheveled, not dressed for outdoors. She often had to return to the school later after receiving a call that Timmy didn't have a snack or lunch. Joan would rush home, and rush back to school a second, and sometimes a third, time with required items. Mornings were especially chaotic in the home.

Paul, to this day, remains a proud and loving dad who has fragile mental health due to bipolar disorder. He is frequently overwhelmed by the demands of managing his moods and medication. Bipolar disorder has left him with rapidly changing extreme ups and downs. He is ill equipped to compensate for Joan's challenges, or to be reliably available to take care of their boys on his own. When Paul is up, he is soaring, but when he is down, he is at rock bottom.

Paul has worked hard to maintain full-time employment because he knows his family depends on him. He has completed multiple postgraduate degrees and is an intelligent and educated man.

While Joan's hoarding created chaos, Paul also hoarded, but differently. Paul hoarded discriminately (see "Five Types of Hoarding" in chapter 1). His collections took over home spaces in a slightly more organized fashion. Paul had a massive music collection of both vinyl records and CDs. He also had bookcase after bookcase throughout many rooms, filled with books and magazines on specific topics. Bookcases became inadequate to hold his collections. The space in the home was no longer available for effective, organized storage and access. Moving around in the home was risky.

Everything Joan and Paul kept was absorbent and combustible, meaning it would burn and retain moisture; this meant that the fuel load was also large. Unplanned occurrences like a leak in the roof, a burst water pipe, or a mouse chewing on an electrical cord under a pile could have caused a disaster.

As has happened in other hoarding situations, floors can collapse under the weight of such a large, wet accumulation. If there was ever a fire, with so much stuff to fuel the fire, the family would have little time to get out.

Paul dreaded losing the boys. The thought of it propelled him to agree to accept support to sort through his collections. The process was grueling, but Paul was resolute. We developed criteria before beginning for what and how many of each item would be kept, and what that meant about what would go. For example, Paul would keep only the vinyl records he didn't yet have electronically stored and keep books on soccer strategies he saw used in winning World Cup games.

As he sorted through his music collection or his precious books, he said that he imagined Timmy, Mike, and Gordie's face on each item and reminded himself that while he loved his things, he loved and wanted them so much more. Sometimes the effort made it difficult for him to breathe. Many times, letting go of multiples of things he loved brought him to tears. Other times we had to rest and decompress as he fought panic. His clear vision of what he had to do for his sons, Joan, and himself to remain together and his determination to do what he needed to do was inspiring. He came to understand that sorting and letting go was usually extremely difficult only in the beginning. Once he learned to set the criteria for keeping and letting go, then put them into practice, he often said, "You know, I'm getting pretty good at this."

Having witnessed and supported Paul and Joan through the battle they waged with their things, I knew that even though CPS talked of a potential temporary care arrangement for Timmy, Mike, and Gordie, after the courts became involved, there would be no turning back.

Strategies

Even though as a social worker I am a mental health professional, I am a practical one, and I believe that sometimes you need to roll up your sleeves and help your client in practical ways while you counsel. We combined decluttering the home with building an understanding about what fueled their individual hoarding disorders.

One week we had an intensive cleanup. The crew worked for two straight days, clearing, cleaning, and sorting. But the clutter in the home was like the tides in the ocean. Things went out and spaces were cleared, but quickly chaos and other piles of things filled in the cleared space again. Week after week we all fought hard for less accumulation, less recluttering.

We did make progress; the house was probably 30 percent usable when we started; now it was closer to 70 percent clear. The kitchen (while disheveled and a struggle to maintain) was safe and usable, as were all staircases. The bathroom was family friendly again. Beds could be accessed from all sides. There were two clear paths into and out of the home. There were clear walking areas throughout the house. The furnace, hot water tank, and electrical panel were kept fully accessible. All these improvements were positive achievements from a health and safety standpoint.

Some rooms, such as the living room and dining room, were consistently only usable with extreme effort. Unfortunately, the living room is where all the living happens, and this room became chaotic and heavily reaccumulated easily. The part of the basement that was not near the furnace, hot water tank, or electrical panel was also a jumbled mass more than four feet high.

Laundry is a common problem in hoarded environments. It was not surprising that laundry was another major issue for the family. Both clean and soiled clothes were mixed and piled all over the house. Because floor space was covered, the clothes were a tripping hazard. Joan reported that there had been a mouse infestation in the basement laundry area two years earlier, and although it had been dealt with, Joan continued to feel that the area wasn't clean enough.

We brainstormed solutions. Paul, the crew, and I installed new flooring in the laundry area and basement powder room, disinfected the areas of the laundry floor that were reachable, retrieved a long table and made it into a sorting and folding surface. We also put laundry baskets in each bedroom and in the bathroom, so that as people undressed, they could put their soiled clothes directly into the laundry basket, not on the floor.

Additional life circumstances required specific interventions because they influenced the likelihood that Paul and Joan would make progress with their hoarding disorders. These same situations are often found with individuals and families where hoarding occurs.

These interventions were conducted during 1½ years of weekly 2-hour sessions working on:

- ✔ Joan and Paul's self-esteem, couple communication, setting boundaries and limits with the boys, setting reasonable expectations with themselves as individuals and as a couple;
- ✔ debriefing and problem solving numerous family and marital crises;
- ✔ overcoming noncompliance with medication due to spending and budgeting problems, which led to unregulated behaviors in both Joan and Paul: we worked on a budget, worked with their doctor to ensure that they were taking their medications reliably, and I negotiated with the family doctor to get samples of their medications as needed to tide them over during their budget shortfalls;
- ✔ building Joan and Paul's understanding and acceptance of their hoarding disorders;
- ✔ identifying and intervening with Mom not to model hoarding beliefs, values, and behaviors, which Timmy was developing;
- ✔ removing 40 percent of the accumulation on three floor levels;
- ✔ setting up a more functional layout of the kitchen and installing tools for easier maintenance;
- ✔ setting up a laundry area in the basement after cleaning and disinfecting the laundry area;
- ✔ setting up storage in the room that would become the boys' playroom;
- ✔ decluttering and setting up the living room as required;
- ✔ emptying one of their storage sheds;
- ✔ bringing inherited furniture into the residence and setting it up;
- ✔ decluttering and reclaiming 90 percent of the floor space in the master bedroom;
- ✔ decluttering the boys' bedrooms and setting up each room as their own space;
- ✔ reinforcing with Joan not to use the boys' spaces for her rechecking purposes;
- ✔ decluttering and setting up the family bathroom;
- ✔ decluttering and setting up the linen closet;
- ✔ decluttering all stairwells and keeping them clear;

- ✔ decluttering and maintaining limited storage use in all hallways;
- ✔ decluttering all cupboards in all rooms, including the kitchen, and setting them up with "keep" items;
- ✔ working constantly to maintain all spaces;
- ✔ clearing and reclearing two entrance and exit routes in the home;
- ✔ installing AB fire extinguishers and exit ladders for Timmy, Mike, and Gordie in their bedrooms;
- ✔ helping Paul and Joan understand and deal more effectively with their comorbid disorders;
- ✔ developing a budget and debt reduction plan, organizing their credit obligations, reducing their credit cards to two, and renegotiating an affordable mortgage at a better rate;
- ✔ getting Paul organized and feeling more assertive about collecting debts owed to him; and
- ✔ organizing a house-wide two-day blitz to intensively turn around areas in the home.

Outcomes

Joan still held on to the hope and belief that she could somehow manage if she could just be left alone to handle things. I knew that if support was withdrawn, or the need for accountability ended, there was no evidence at this point that she could handle family life on her own and manage her hoarding. The ongoing crises would result in all three boys being taken into temporary care.

Collaboration with Other Professionals

Community Crisis Outreach Service staff and the police department coattended and referred Joan and Paul to me for counseling and decluttering support for hoarding disorder.

- ✔ CPS and I worked closely to try to prevent Joan and Paul's boys from being taken into foster care.
- ✔ I also collaborated with their family physician to get prescription samples when

funds ran out and to advocate for specialized residential services for Joan to give her the time and resources to focus on re-establishing more stable mental health.

✔ Identifying and accessing other professional supports as needed, such as their psychiatrist and their financial planner.

✔ Identifying specialized resources for intensive treatment of Joan's ADD and OCD.

✔ Advocating for Joan to be given a chance to receive adequate and specialized help for her debilitating comorbid disorders.

Key Messages for Helpers and Professionals

Analyze the problem objectively.

- Make a commitment to yourself as a practitioner and to your clients to advocate on their behalf not for just *any* available care but for specialized care for complex comorbid factors.
- Research the key components in the available programs. What is their niche? How are they specific to this person's needs?
- Reflect on your network. Consider who you know who could help you find the right match.
- Make phone calls and speak to the liaison person at the institution to find out more about the program and confirm that it meets your client's specific needs.
- When on the call, don't expect that the person has the time for you to share your client's whole life history. Ask what he or she needs to know and provide the information as simply as possible.
- Get the help you need:
  - *The family doctor might be a valuable resource to help you accomplish a referral. Joan's family doctor was invaluable.*
  - *If the person you are helping has a psychiatrist, you should get them on board, or perhaps a family member could act on your behalf.*
  - *The way you engage the desired service or program is very important. Be professional, and be prepared with facts.*
- Be prepared:
  - *Lighten the family doctor's load by being prepared to do some of the legwork.*
  - *You can get a short list of the options for care.*
  - *Get the specifics of the programs.*
  - *Be an informed advocate.*

- *Do the groundwork and get all the information you possibly can to better assist the professional helping you and your loved one.*
- *Do not sit back and take a passive role. It is a partnership.*
- *If there are calls to make, papers to fill out and sign, don't expect the professional to do it; be prepared to do it yourself.*

- Stay focused. Keep your efforts specific to what the person needs and keep working at it.
- Prioritize. When there are several problems, and you don't know what the most important one is, ask yourself:
  - *What specific aspects of the problems are pivotal to progress? You are not looking for perfection or absolute healing in one step. You are looking for a level of stability that the person can maintain.*
  - *Which problems, if they got solved or improved, would be the catalyst for change and would be good enough to make a difference in the outcomes?*

Conclusion

As I prepared to leave the house the last day, it was clear that Paul did not agree with Joan's statement, "If you're going to take them sometime anyway, you might as well take them now."

Paul sat cross-legged on the floor with his head in his hands. He held his nose between his thumb and forefinger and wept, pleading, "I don't feel that way. I can't turn it around myself. You know that."

I crouched down beside him. "Please don't leave," he begged. "We can't do it without your support. Things won't be different without your help every week, and I will miss them so. They are good boys."

Paul smiled sadly as he thought about his sons and said, "They deserve a home they can live in, and parents who can cope. I've tried so hard." He continued, with a hint of anger in his voice, "I've worked so hard to let so many of my things go, and she won't even give up a magazine."

I assured him that I would persist in locating and acquiring specialized help for Joan for her nonhoarding issues and make myself available when Joan agreed in the future. I reminded Paul, "No matter how dark things look right now, you will always be Timmy, Mike, and Gordie's dad. A time will come when CPS's mandate will no longer apply. There will be time between now and then to make the changes necessary to succeed as a family and to learn how to manage your hoarding disorder."

The message from a poem, "The Weaver," by an unknown author, came to my mind.

"If you can think of life as a tapestry, Paul, even in the most beautiful pattern, there are dark threads. The final outcome depends on what you do with them. You are not alone, and this is not the end."

CHAPTER 7

The Impact of Grief

Drowning in Loss

> The reality is that you will grieve forever. You will not "get over" the loss of a loved one; you will learn to live with it. You will heal and you will rebuild yourself around the loss you have suffered. You will be whole again but you will never be the same. Nor should you be the same nor would you want to.
>
> **ELISABETH KÜBLER-ROSS**

SOME PEOPLE WHO HOARD GET STUCK in unresolved grief and loss. Things become powerful, poignant symbols and concrete reminders of happier times that sustained them. Sometimes the loss is of their health—mental, physical, or both. Often objects become evidence that in days gone by, they had pride and a meaningful role in life. They had a positive sense of self and achievement—something all of us need. The loss of those vital affirmations—whether love, relationships, career, financial success and security, status, or health—are often the tipping point into personal decline and the loss of identity. Things become touchstones, proving that their now diminished state was not always so. Objects become sentimental reminders and mementos of the what and whom they ache for. As long as they have these things, somehow they don't have to accept the loss as final. If the loss is of a meaningful role, people can also lose their identity, the sense of who they are and what defines them. For some people who hoard, the loss becomes a gaping wound that feels like a bottomless void calling out for "little jolts of joy"—proof that they can still feel something. Acquiring and saving things provides little pick-me-ups that lessen the bleakness and feelings of being overwhelmed that are often part of the lives of those who create a hoard. I have never met a person who hoards who hasn't described themselves as *overwhelmed*.

Synopsis

Katherine, a woman in her mid-sixties, needing what she thought was "just a little help with housekeeping" in her two-bedroom condominium, lived at Risk Levels 2–3. At first glance, her main problem appeared to be her reliance on "retail therapy" to provide a positive effect, with the purchases elevating low moods and temporarily soothing life's frustrations. As trust and rapport between us deepened, the true voids precipitated by profound trauma and loss, which had been eased by shopping and sentimental attachment, came to light. Katherine's willingness to share, while I served as a witness to the truth, helped us develop and implement lasting strategies to better meet her needs and help her maintain a safe, fuller life.

Problem Overview

Katherine's hoarding did not present a significant risk to others. The risk was that she would fall and further injure herself. There was urgency to complete our work because of needs arising from her deteriorating health. Together, she and I systematically used conventional onsite counseling and decluttering coaching techniques to re-establish safety.

Background

Katherine is a gracious, cultured, delightful woman who had a responsible, successful, detail-oriented career. She retired in her mid-60s to a comfortable condominium. In the first year of her retirement, her rheumatoid arthritis worsened significantly, and she was quickly facing limited mobility and the need for walking aides. The amount of clear floor space was now so limited that it created a serious safety hazard. Falling was a real prospect. Blocked exits contravened local fire codes. Emergency response personnel would not have been able to easily get to her if she needed them. Katherine loved to shop, especially from the Hammacher Schlemmer catalog.

Client's Initial Perspective

Katherine was proud of her home and its many cherished family heirlooms. At great effort and expense, she had brought her legacies with her when she had emigrated from overseas. As her health and mobility continued to deteriorate, a plan was developed for her sister to come to live with her and help her face whatever challenges lay ahead. Despite Katherine's belief that she just needed a "little help with housekeeping," it became clear that housekeeping help alone would not be adequate.

 As is often the case, people call community agencies for "a little housekeeping support" only to be told that the residence is more cluttered than the agency can deal with, and they are referred to me for counseling and declutter coaching.

Therapeutic Plan

My work with Katherine was to help her understand and deal with the underlying reasons she created excessive clutter and help her get the condominium ready for her sister's trial visit. If the visit went well, her sister would return home, resolve necessary business, and then live with Katherine permanently.

Intervention

Katherine's spirit and sense of fun, together with her charm and ready laughter, made her delightful to work with.

Unfortunately, Hammacher Schlemmer stocks rose healthily because of Katherine's patronage. The catalog featured all kinds of clever inventions, and Katherine felt the need for most of them. Her delight and mood buoyed when each new release of the catalog arrived.

 When there is such a complete loss of control in one's life, retail therapy can provide a short-term pick-me-up, for example, finding nice things at a great price, or purchasing the newest widget from the latest catalog.

At first, the problem appeared to be Katherine's habit of buying and keeping a few more things than she had space for. I suspected that she had always bought and held on to more than she needed but had been able to maintain clearer paths when she was more mobile. Now, the buildup of things had reached a risky level.

As is often the case, hoarded environments cannot be adequately maintained. Many minor fixes were needed. Her mobility problems, feelings of being overwhelmed, and, as I was to discover, her commitment to the vision of ideal standards was robbing her of her sense of pride in her home and things. There was a bottleneck of things leaving the condo because of her practical wish that things go to consignment.

 In my experience, sending things to consignment or yard sales can be a laborious and uncertain plan for freeing up needed space.

Strategies

Hoarding does not happen in isolation and it doesn't get better by itself, when the myriad of other pressures the person is living with are added into the mix. I believe in taking a holistic, "shoulder to shoulder" approach to supporting and counseling my clients.

I feel that my work often calls for me to roll up my sleeves and lend practical help as well. Usually being a therapist does not involve power tools, but from time to time, my crew and I add extra time to sessions at no cost and lend a helping hand to coordinate and solve simple house maintenance issues that the person cannot afford to have professionally addressed. Hoarding is not an inexpensive habit.

Hoarded environments are notoriously poorly maintained because access to the problem areas is not possible and funds can be scarce due to compulsive buying. I have been known to change light bulbs, install smoke detectors, change batteries, install blinds, help my crew rip up and lay flooring, help move furniture, and drive clients to shop for items for their home when those items will solve a problem. Mindsets change as the person feels the positive effect of moving forward.

The tour of Katherine's home on Day 1 revealed room after room of piles. The absolute priority was to clear a 3- to 4-foot path through her condo to provide two entrance and exit routes in case of an emergency (which no one ever believes will happen).

Her toilet did not work. A closer look showed a new part would fix it. We got the part and repaired it. The condominium also needed other small repairs. Though I am not a fix-it person, Katherine and I developed our therapeutic relationship, saving her money and tackling these small jobs together.

My crew did a bit of volunteer painting to freshen the condo, which was a big morale booster for Katherine. She had disconnected from her environment because she was too overwhelmed and in pain to handle the series of small issues that a little practical help would fix.

She had a second bedroom and a separate storage room in her condo. I kept suggesting that we use this space. I came to understand that Katherine had a keen ambition to acquire and retain materials to write children's books. This was not surprising given her past career, which had involved significant technical reference writing. It seemed the storage room was full of inspirational materials for different children's stories.

When Katherine wanted to hold on to something—something most people would want to keep—I would try to interest her in accessing, simplifying, and sorting the things in the storage area because cupboards were full, as were spaces under the beds.

Outcomes

Months passed as we systematically worked our way through the rooms. None of the "keeps" were going to the storage room. An obvious option was to reorganize the cupboards and identify any things that were not needed and were eligible for donation, regifting, discarding, or recycling. While trying to go through the cupboard, I reached up on one of the shelves and pulled down an old, worn, medium-sized suitcase.

When Katherine saw me struggling with it a little, she cautioned in a gentle but nervous tone, "*Oh!* Be careful with that."

It was clear that this suitcase was special, so I probed, "Can you tell me about this Katherine?"

Everything stopped.

I had been working with Katherine for several months at this point, and I recall that from time to time, Katherine would be a little lost, not quite present, having a little difficulty focusing. By the next session, however, things would be normal again, so I allowed for the possibility that this, too, might just be a momentary distraction. If it was more, I trusted that Katherine would tell me what she wanted me to know when she was ready. As everything stopped, I waited and knew this was the moment.

Katherine looked at the floor with a troubled look on her face, shook her head a little, and said, "Well, I probably should have told you this before, Elaine. The suitcase is full of newspaper clippings." The intensity of the moment made it clear that this was the missing piece. The importance of these clippings was palpable.

"Can you tell me about them?" I asked.

"Well," she began, "I used to be married before. I had two little boys. They were 4 and 5. One day they got out of the backyard. It was spring. We were never exactly sure how it happened, but they were both found drowned after an intensive search. I remember it like it was yesterday. The panic at them being gone, the helpless fear about where they were, the shock and numbness when the knock came on the door, the shaming pity in everyone's eyes when they saw me for years after. People would invite me to join in their activities, but I realized that they really only wanted to use the opportunity to learn all the morbid details, along with being voyeurs into my emotional response to them. I was very aware of the whispering when I walked down the street. 'That's the woman who lost her children. They drowned, you know.'

"My babies were gone; my husband and I parted. I couldn't get away from the morbid curiosity and pity of people."

For Katherine, life changed in an instant, forever. Each person tries to handle grief in his or her own way. When guilt is added to the equation, it complicates the recovery far more.

Katherine had understandably gone into a deep depression fueled by profound loss and guilt. In her small town, even when she was beginning to recover a little, and just get out of bed to face the morning that she wished wouldn't come, she was constantly identified as "that woman whose children drowned." Townspeople would stare and whisper. Some tried to be compassionate and caring, but they just kept talking about it. Sometimes she wanted to be able to take one breath and not have to remember that her sons were gone. Just one breath without feeling responsible that her supervision of them might have allowed them to go unnoticed long enough to get out of her sight. How they got out of the yard and found their way to the water remains a mystery.

By remaining in that community, she could not get out of her hole of grief because she was constantly reminded, and her only identity seemed to be "the mother who let her toddlers drown." This felt true no matter whether the onlookers were apparently well meaning or morbidly curious even two and three years later.

Grief took over her and her husband's lives, leaving no common ground for a marriage. Despite the end of their marriage, over the years, she tried to keep her most important role in life being a mother to her boys alive. They were gone, but her love for them didn't die. Fresh, fierce grief arrived with every one of their birthdays, every Christmas, every Easter. Every Halloween, when children came door to door for candy, it left a fresh wound. When she saw people putting out Easter eggs for their children, she remembered and grieved more. In September, she imagined what it would have been like to walk them to school, and she grieved. In June, she imagined what their graduation would have been like, and she grieved. On Mother's Day, she ached.

Her strategy to deal with her profound loss was to collect materials and inspirational items to write children's stories someday. She said she wanted to use her considerable writing skills to write the stories she would have wanted to read to her boys. The problem became that the collection of things was as large as the grief she felt, and so she stored the things until she could recover enough to begin her writing.

Those were the things taking up all the space in the storage room, leaving inadequate space for the items from her current life. My work with her was to respect her choices, work at her pace, and help her change her relationship to enough things from both eras to make it possible to live safely and healthily (mentally and physically) in her current home, and make room for her sister and her sister's life there too.

Slowly and methodically we worked on one area at a time, with minor relapses when the next issue of the Hammacher Schlemmer catalog arrived or she spotted some attractive little item that would make the home cozier.

Katherine reoutfitted her condo and decluttered. Paths were opened up.

We made room for a writing area; we organized the materials and itemized them so that she could move forward with her writing.

Her sister did return and live with her.

I think about Katherine often and smile every time I drive by her condo. I also think of her and send her positive thoughts at Christmas, Easter, Halloween, and Mother's Day—from one mother to another.

Collaboration with Other Professionals

Working collaboratively with other professionals was also important. When other issues of physical health as well as mental health are so severe that they disrupt progress, the treatment for hoarding disorder can be much more effective if a psychiatrist, psychologist, social worker, or physician treats the comorbid issues, while I treat for the hoarding disorder.

Key Messages

1 Continue to ask for the help you need. Do not allow clutter to make you uncertain about calling for help when you need it. Accidents happen even in mild to moderately hoarded environments.

2 The crisis you face may not be caused by your hoarded environment. Your neighbor may have a fire, flood, or infestation, and your environment may become affected by it. The effect on you if your environment is hoarded will be far more severe.

3 An accumulation that becomes wet weighs far more than it did dry, often with hazardous outcomes.

4 An accumulated environment (even if you did not cause the fire) will provide excessive fuel to a fire, greatly reducing the time and chance you will have to escape, often with hazardous outcomes for you and anyone or anything else living with you.

5 Hoarded environments (even just cluttered ones) are havens for "visitors," for example, mice, bedbugs, other bugs, mold, and so forth. Mouse scat can be very harmful to a person's respiratory system many years after contact.

6 If traumatic events have occurred in your life and they remain unresolved, please seek specialized expert support to take back that part of your life and functioning. These supports can coexist with hoarding-informed treatment.

Conclusion

Does grief and loss cause hoarding? No one knows for sure. The answer is almost certainly complex. No one who works in the specialized area of hoarding can deny, however, that loss is an underlying theme in a great number of hoarding situations. I believe loss may provide a tipping point, activating vulnerabilities that have been latent up to that point. A loss of control in maintaining balance in life results in the creation of a hoarded environment and puts that person undeniably on the continuum of hoarding disorder. Some research has been done with inconclusive results. Better research is needed to establish if the apparent correlation is fact or impression.

Katherine's life serves as a reminder that life is like a backpack. Everything we don't deal with effectively, like grief, anger, and resentment, becomes a boulder that gets added to our backpack until we can't carry it anymore and still stay healthy mentally or physically. What is the cost to us to carry these burdens with us all the time? The heavier we make our load, sometimes through excessive numbers of possessions, the more we look for something to make us feel better. Those who hoard substitute things for solutions.

We would be better off unloading the weight of the boulders rather than settling for substitutes to what we really want and need to build the life we deserve. Some boulders are heavier than others and much harder to unpack.

What are you carrying in *your* backpack?
What would it take to knock you off balance?
What would you use for *your* solutions?

CHAPTER 8

Impulse Shopping

Can't Buy Happiness

Compulsive acquiring is like being lost at sea without adequate fresh water to quench your thirst. You are surrounded by water, but no matter how much you consume, it will never, and can never, meet your need because it is the wrong thing. Continuing to use this strategy to meet your need can, and will, harm you. No matter how many nice, useful things you get, those things will never meet your needs or make up for the void you feel.

ELAINE BIRCHALL

IMPULSE OR COMPULSIVE BUYING CAN TAKE MANY FORMS. Rachel's story is a montage of many people who look to shopping to restabilize their mood and give themselves relief from their lives. Today, the increase in, and convenience of, the number of online shopping options can compound the compulsions for many individuals. In this chapter I discuss strategies you can use to make conscious choices about what and how much you purchase or acquire. If online shopping is a particular vulnerability of yours, I recommend that you familiarize yourself with the specific tools and intervention strategies detailed in this chapter, including the resource "Online Impulsive Shopping (Problematic and Pathological)."

Synopsis

Rachel, a woman in her midforties, had extreme compulsive shopping behavior that put her financial security at risk. She suffered from extreme hoarding disorder as well as a combination of other comorbid factors. Her family background involved addiction and multiple types of abuse. She contacted me wanting to make a fresh start. Throughout the 2½ years I worked with her, we used various tools and strategies, such as the *conscious acquiring process*, to help her deal with her compulsions and the rituals she used to self-soothe. At the same time, we addressed the Risk Levels 3 through 5 in her home, which put Rachel and those who lived near her in imminent peril. At times, we had to revert to a harm-reduction approach to take into account life crises as they arose. In the end, Rachel and I established progress in her environment, creating a safe welcoming place for her to live at Risk Levels 0 to 2. Rachel reached a point where she proved to herself that she could manage her environment independently long term and has continued to do so.

Problem Overview

Rachel was hooked. She had a $1,200-a-day buying habit, on credit. The credit she used was the collateral she had worked hard to establish in her home, as well as her credit cards. Day 1 was a buying spree. Day 2, she returned at least $800 of it so that on Day 3, she could repeat Day 1.

When I began working with her, this pattern of behavior had been the only way Rachel could quell her overwhelming feelings of anxiety, emptiness, and feelings of futility about her life. She was hooked in a loop of compulsions and rituals in attempts to self-soothe. The loop that Rachel was caught in was the compulsion to acquire. The ritual was to shop. The attempt to self-soothe was the moment of acquisition. In her depressed, anxious, compulsive state of mind, Rachel had fended off many other impulses, including self-harm, by frantically looking for things that would lessen the extreme pain she was in. The amount she acquired and the frequency at which she acquired things, matched the amount of extreme pain and anxiety she was in and how overwhelmed she felt. Rachel's need was extreme; so was her compulsive shopping.

Rachel compared her life now with the past, when she remembered being outwardly successful. She had a great job, making good money. She had friends and plans. Retail therapy was a source of entertainment. Sure, she shopped, but she remembered also being good with her money. She remembered feeling vulnerable, and at times shaky, especially when she felt compared to others. But she had friends, and a girls' day out of shopping, a new outfit, and a new hairdo always did the trick.

Even when she didn't quite feel in control, she knew how to take charge again. It had always worked in the past. Rachel knew who was in charge now—the compulsions.

Even on days when she had no intention of shopping, when in fact she knew she was on the brink of exceeding her credit limit, she would start out to buy bread or milk at the corner store and end up at stores with products that best soothed her compulsions—not clearly remembering how she got there. She said it felt like her mind went into a trance. She reported what resembled a dissociative state, not even being fully aware that she had arrived in the parking lot.

Rachel's first moment of awareness was the sense of elation she got as she began to put items in her basket. She could feel the excitement, but it was as if she were watching from outside herself as her hands, legs, and mind operated.

Only as she approached her car after leaving the store with her packages did she begin to come out of the fog. When she more fully realized what she had done, profound regret, panic, and dread began to set in. The anticipation of the shame at knowing that she would have to return most of the purchases crept in and was lessened only by the hope that if she chose a different time of day to return things, the same staff wouldn't be working to witness her shame.

The equity in her home was almost gone because of compulsive shopping. Her stress felt like a vise.

Background

Rachel's mother and father had divorced when she was a baby. Her mother lived with addiction, and her moods swung back and forth randomly during Rachel's life. Their relationship alternated between enmeshed, manipulative, dependent, histrionic, and, for brief times, happy.

Rachel's mother demanded a lot from her and was frequently dissatisfied with Rachel's efforts to be a good, loving, and supportive daughter. Growing up, there had just been the three of them: Rachel, her mother, and her younger sister, Louise.

Her father, now deceased, had been a "mean drunk." Rachel's mother had tried as best she could to protect them, but with her erratic mental health, she couldn't prevent Rachel's father from targeting his oldest daughter innumerable times for verbal, emotional, and sexual abuse. He ridiculed her as a weak, stupid girl who would amount to nothing. Rachel thought that Louise had escaped the abuse, but years later, Louise fatally overdosed, and Rachel discovered the truth in her sister's journal. From the age of 5, Louise had suffered the same fate as her sister. Their mother died the same year as Louise.

In the dead of winter and in a parking lot, Rachel found a container with a litter of six newborn kittens. She formed an immediate and intense attachment to them, bonding to the kittens so strongly and immediately that they became her main emotional touchstone. This immediate, intense relationship to animals paralleled her immediate, intense relationship to inanimate objects. Her increased vulnerability was stronger than her ability to control her impulses.

Client's Initial Perspective

When Rachel called me, it was because she wanted a fresh start. She was focused on how to store everything more efficiently so that she could keep everything. She realized she had too much but was strongly committed to better storage as the solution. She could not give up anything. The fact that she had multiples of things that she rarely used was not important to her. She was not interested at all in sharing, selling, or donating the surplus. She was resolute. She was stuck.

Therapeutic Plan

My work with Rachel was twofold: (1) to help her set boundaries and establish livable limits, and (2) to help her deal with the ever-growing pathways and piles.

Intervention

As in all situations where flooding is involved, we decided to focus on the challenges that the physical environment presented. Rachel's basement had flooded, which provided her with an opportunity to remain in denial. Rather than the accumulation being about her acquiring behavior and the clutter being the by-product of that behavior, all clutter and the risks associated with it were attributed to the flood. To add to the chaos, some of the items in the basement had become moldy. In an attempt to salvage as many things as possible, she had strewn the contents all over, chaotically, in an attempt to dry them. She was unable to discard the ruined items and felt that the cost to rewash and dry them was too expensive. The result was chaos and an extreme risk to anyone or anything a fire would affect. The basement was three-dimensionally 80 percent filled. There was not enough clearance around heat sources like the gas furnace and hot water tank. She also had no clear path to the electrical panel. This situation violated local fire safety codes and represented an imminent fire hazard—a Risk Level 5. (For a real-life representation of what all levels of risk look like, please refer to "What Is Your Level of Risk?" in chapter 2.)

During my initial visit, I had to reschedule my later appointments so that I could remain onsite to help Rachel remove enough items to a storage unit to clear a 3-foot path around the furnace, hot water tank, and electrical panel, reducing the immediate fire risk. In subsequent sessions, Rachel and I worked in the basement, as she had finally agreed to wash and dry unspoiled items. We repacked them and stacked the boxes a safe distance from all heat sources to create adequate paths. Coming to terms with the obvious fact that she would have to part with ruined, moldy items was painful and produced anxiety in Rachel, and she accomplished it only with great difficulty and much emotional processing and coaching.

 I counsel clients that safety is the number one priority and to take it very seriously. Health is a close second priority. If you are injured or perish because of an unsafe situation, it won't matter how healthy you were. The third important priority is happiness, which I define as things being the way we want and need them to be.

At every session, I checked the condition of the basement because Rachel had a habit of churning through the basement piles and reproducing the chaos. Each week we discussed the risk she was re-creating by doing this. Each week I reminded her that if it continued or worsened, I would be obliged to call both the fire department's inspection branch and the Animal Welfare Society about the potential risk to her, her pets, and her neighbors. I assured her that I would not make the calls without having her with me. I wanted her to know that the information discussed in the calls would not be derogatory or judgmental.

My goal was to add fire services and animal well-being expertise to the treatment plan and to increase her level of accountability before something happened that she would regret forever. Rachel lived in a two-level condo, with other units beside and partially below her. The risk she created was shared by anyone living close to her, neighbors and pets alike. The additional risk others had was that they didn't know about the risks they were living with, and so they didn't know to prepare for them.

Where accountability is concerned, I use the Rule of 3. The first time something happens is an accident, because the person may not have good information. The second time it happens is a coincidence, because habits are hard to break, and slipups happen. The third time it happens is a pattern, and we must deal with it.

The third time Rachel churned the basement, leaving items randomly and chaotically placed, that area became the highest priority. Combustible items were lying on top of the gas furnace and hot water tank. I advised Rachel, "There have been three sessions in a row where you have undone the safety our work created. This time there are combustible materials *on*, not close to, but *on* a heat source. You have a pilot light on your furnace, and this is January. It's time to make the calls. I want you to stand beside me while I call, and I want you to hear what I say to the fire department and Animal Welfare Society. I am going to ask them to come and do an inspection."

Rachel was upset, but she knew what I was saying was true.

Although the basement was the highest safety priority, other areas of the home were also of concern and would be included in the inspections. Multiple areas in the house represented a risk of tripping, toppling, or becoming shelter to bugs and mice.

Every room in the house was overfilled in the range of Risk Levels 3–4. Some, mostly unused rooms, were blocked with excess furniture.

The halls were crowded with stacks of things. Clothing lay in heaps on all railings. The stairs were narrowed by a combination of items on their way upstairs and down. The piles had become confused and mixed. The bathrooms were crowded and hard to access because the floors and vanities were covered with personal care and cleaning products, as well as other items used, forgotten, and left in place. There were three bedrooms. Only the powder room off Rachel's bedroom was passable, and then only with great difficulty.

Strategies

At this point, our counseling and decluttering work took an important turn. We agreed to remove all items that she did not use often to a storage unit and set the house up with what remained. Most of the items in the basement were boxed; all excess furniture, anything being held on to "just in case," and all off-season clothing went to storage. All items that were kept "just in case" were stored at the front of the unit, where Rachel could access them if she found that she needed them. All boxes were labeled and itemized. Rachel was given a manifest list. We developed a map of the unit showing where each numbered box was located. This was done to provide Rachel assurance that if she needed anything specific, she would know what box it was in and where in the unit the box was located. The boxes were stored in rows, with access between each row.

 My clients have named the process of intensive, rapid 2- to 4-day environmental turnaround the blitz. I sparingly use this process as a harm-reduction strategy when absolutely essential, for example, to prevent homelessness or to allow the individual to return home for health and safety reasons.

The blitz accomplishes the following:

- It temporarily solves the excessive accumulation problem.
- It eliminates the risks.
- It makes "keep" items accessible.
- It provides an opportunity to do sorting for items to be discarded and donated as we remove things.

- The size of the unit is dictated by how much the person is willing to fund and therefore provides a self-imposed way to set limits.
- It removes some of the immobilizing pressure.

In this situation:

- It removed the denial factor that the flood had provided.
- It gave us adequate room to use as a staging area in each part of the condo.
- It gave Rachel a sense of optimism and manageability about her home.
- She could now feel comfortable inviting friends to her home, which enriched her social network.
- It improved her ability to see the clutter. When someone's environment is extremely cluttered, they often have to turn themselves off. I believe we can only afford to look at and acknowledge what we feel able to deal with. Rachel felt more able to maintain her environment when it was more manageable. She could see the places where first-stage clutter was recurring.
- She was able to begin to use my feedback as a hoarding behavior and declutter specialist.

The calls for input from enforcement agencies and having my support and the help of my declutter crew provided the two essentials for change:

1 Understanding the *importance* of the tasks to be done
2 Understanding her *capability* to do it (right *time*, right *tools*, right *support*)

Rachel and I moved to Phase 2 of our work together.

She soon became nervous about her credit card balance, which was out of control because of her impulse buying, even though the amount of shopping was significantly less than before.

Rachel and I discussed how best to take a temporary complete break from shopping. She agreed to try and was successful for about three weeks. I recommended a complete break for a month so she could experience the stresses and triggers that impulsive/compulsive shopping relieved. During this time, we discussed what these stresses and triggers were; for example, one of her triggers was when anyone walked away in anger during an unresolved conflict. At the point that her resolve was weakening, we agreed to switch to a harm-reduction approach for her shopping behavior.

Conscious Acquiring Process

The *conscious acquiring process* is a step-by-step checklist to turn back impulse buying. This is a harm-reduction strategy I developed and have used with many clients who struggle with compulsive acquiring.

Included in this chapter is a handy cheat sheet for on-the-go buying decisions. I highly recommend that you familiarize yourself with the more detailed resource 16.2, "Conscious Acquiring Process."

This process is meant to:

- ✔ slow you down;
- ✔ break the rush of excitement and urgency that fuels impulsive acquisition;
- ✔ support you to develop other options;
- ✔ give you time to rationally consider other alternatives without the influence of the roller-coaster rush of adrenaline, serotonin, or dopamine coursing through your body, influencing a rash, impulsive decision you may regret;
- ✔ support you to make decisions you won't regret later; and
- ✔ help you avoid digging the rut of hoarding even deeper.

Rachel agreed and used the conscious acquiring process successfully.

I have also developed a laminated checklist the size of a business card, which clients can carry in their wallets to help with decision making, such as determining whether to buy something while shopping ("Should I bring this home?") or whether to let something go from the home ("Should I let this go?"). The checklists are also available online at jhupbooks.press.jhu.edu/title/conquer-clutter.

Should I bring this home?

- Do I need it now or in the near future?
- Do I have others like it I can use instead?
- What makes this item special and unlike anything I already have?
- How would my life change without it?
- If I'm acquiring an item for someone else, have I asked them first if they want it?
- Have I previously gotten things for other people and not delivered them?
- Can I find and give those items as gifts the next time I would give a gift instead of acquiring new?
- As I rediscover items "too good to discard or donate," could I create a gift box or shelf that I can choose from the next time I need a gift for someone?
- Does acquiring this item today move me closer or further away from my goal of taking back my life when my things are taking over?

Conscious Acquiring
On-the-Go Cheat Sheet

1 Take a break from shopping by delegating to trusted people or, if you must shop yourself, always shop from a list and stick to it.

2 On the way to the cash register, pull over and compare your purchases to the list and then try one or more of the following steps:
   a *Put extras back.*
   b *Buy some time, break the rush, change your mindset:*
      » Remind yourself of your goals.
      » Leave the store.
      » Practice relaxation breathing as described in resources 16.1, "Breathing to Destress."
      » Remind yourself of your actual needs versus wants.
      » Focus your self-talk, recognizing that tomorrow is another day with possibly another list if the items are in fact important.
      » Remember it's not a "deal" if you are paying with credit.
   c *Call a trusted friend to remind you of what you want and need most or, if you have time, complete a pros and cons list for whether or not to buy.*
   d *Convince yourself to sleep on it.*

3 Make your choice consciously, and congratulate yourself if you resisted acting impulsively.

- What is the best decision I can make today?

Should I let this go?
- Do I love this? If *yes*, and you have an available permanent place where it would be used, *keep it.*
- Is this item *me* going forward? Is this item *me* as I used to be? Am I better living in the present or staying in the past?
- Do I use this often? Could I get it elsewhere if I needed it, such as by borrowing, renting, sharing, or buying used?
- Am I keeping this because I miss someone and they liked it? Do I love it? If I donated it, would it comfort me if someone else who also loved it—as the person I miss did—had it, used it, and loved it?

Outcomes

If Rachel (unavoidably) had to shop, she agreed to create a list before leaving the house. I advised her to look at her basket before she went to check out. If items not on her list were in her basket, she would try to make herself put them back. If this proved too difficult, she could call me on my cell phone. If I wasn't free, she would make her decision, and we could discuss it at our next session.

One day my phone rang, and it was Rachel, feeling very distressed. She was waiting near the cash register in the store, and she needed extra support because even though she had previously agreed not to go into a store, an unavoidable urgent situation had occurred. Options to delay buying or to delegate to a friend were not possible. As often happened, Rachel saw many other things in the store that in the moment, she realized she needed or wanted.

As soon as I picked up the call, she started apologizing. She hadn't wanted to go to the store, but she had absolutely had to and was now panicking.

I reassured her. "We agreed that if this ever happened, calling me was okay. Have you got your list?"

"Yes," she replied.

"Okay, and are you looking at the basket?" I asked.

"Yes," she repeated tentatively.

"So how are you doing?"

"Not so good," she whispered.

"Rachel, do we need to discuss anything?" I probed. "Did anything happen before you went shopping to explain your current stress level?"

Rachel replied, "I want to do what we discussed, but I don't seem able to."

I reassured her. "Every day, Rachel, whether any of us is ready or not, all we can do is our best. You're an adult. It's not my right to tell you what's the right or wrong decision. I know *you* know, though, and I believe that if you can put yourself 'on pause' and give yourself a chance to gain distance from the things that influence you to make decisions you will regret, you can do what you need to do today."

I continued. "Find a quiet place and give yourself permission to do whatever *you* need to do, and you will make today's best decision. Ask yourself this—of the things that are in the basket that are not on the list, is there anything that is absolutely essential, and what makes it essential?"

She thought about it for a minute. With uncertainty in her voice, she replied, "Umm."

Together we reviewed the "Should I bring this home?" questions.

I suggested she ask a teller to hold her basket while she went to the restroom and did some relaxation breathing (see "Breathing to Destress" in chapter 16) and consider, when she returned home, what she would be happy she had done.

I reassured her that I was there if she needed more processing after she reconsidered the basket contents (which I deliberately did not ask her to disclose).

I paused for a minute and said, "Ask yourself, what is the best decision you can make right now? Call me back if you need to."

We hung up.

About 10 minutes later, I got a second call from Rachel.

"Hello," I said.

"Hi," she said, with excitement in her voice.

"How did it go?" I asked.

"Great! I put the barbecue back," she announced triumphantly.

I congratulated Rachel for giving herself the time, space, and permission to do what she would be proud of, to combat the impulsive urge and let it pass.

The barbecue, as it turned out, was not an entirely impulsive and frivolous idea for Rachel, but the point was that the barbecue wasn't a *need* that day, and she decided it wasn't something that would move her forward in managing her hoarding disorder. That simple barbecue, and the tools and other supplies that she put back, were a triumph in taking control of her anxious impulses and taking a huge step forward on many fronts:

- Handling unplanned, anxiety-producing demands of the day
- Asking for the right help when needed even though she was uneasy asking
- Making a plan and following the plan
- Holding on to her self-worth even though she was overwhelmed, discouraged, and uncertain
- Doing her absolute best even when she feared she couldn't
- Accepting acknowledgment from others and owning it
- Managing her expectations of herself within manageable periods—one day, one hour, one minute—whatever she felt capable of to start but starting *anyway* (Courage is being afraid or uncertain and doing it anyway. Allow courage into your life, and be proud of yourself, one decision at a time.)
- Accepting that she would not excel every day, and the sun would still come up; next time she could continue to work her plan

This feeling of accomplishment gave Rachel immense feelings of self-worth and satisfaction.

She and I continued to work together for another 18 months. During that time, in collaboration with her psychiatrist, we helped her learn to manage her extreme anxiety, grief, and shame. We helped her to develop the confidence to make more friends. We supported her in learning for the first time in her life to set boundaries and limits and not to feel she had to justify her needs. She and I created a home for her where she could reclaim her center and reestablish a sense of peace and self-control.

She made decisions in counseling sessions about vast amounts of important papers. She set up a filing system for herself. We went through every room in the condo, and I counseled and supported her to identify and process thoughts, feelings, fears, and impulses that were preventing her from managing her hoarding disorder. I had her ask herself four questions:

1 Why is this happening to me?
2 Why is this happening now?
3 Why won't the problem go away?
4 What do I need to do to resolve the problem?

We went through every drawer, cupboard, closet, and flat surface. Rachel established a sense of organization and ease living in her environment, and she felt a control that she said she had never felt before.

Rachel came to understand that as someone with hoarding disorder and a life history that perhaps had resulted in other coexisting mental health disorders, under sufficient stressors, her default behavior may always be to acquire excessively and hoard again. If you anticipate that you might have some of the same compulsions as Rachel, understand that you (like Rachel) need to:

- remain vigilant every day about how you are balancing your mental and physical health;
- identify early stage relapse (i.e., when you are slipping back), for each of your risk factors;
- proactively identify the best sources of current help and support, such as what has been useful to you in the past;
- reach out sooner for the help you need;
- with that support, make a plan you have faith in;
- work that plan;
- know that the best and worst life events never last forever;
- keep going in the direction that you believe is forward;
- if there are long stretches when things look and feel bleak, *remember to look for and take a minute to appreciate whatever gifts* (like my daily sunrises) might be sent to you that day; and
- *Use these gifts to fortify yourself*, because they are also present and available to you to use as you need to, even when things feel the darkest.

Do these gifts change the dark? Maybe not. But they do give you some positive strength to persevere until the next positive period. Given time, there will always be a better period ahead. Remember that the light at the end of the tunnel you are in is right ahead. Keep moving forward, even if you are only taking baby steps.

Like the sunrise, it is a certainty.

Collaboration with Other Professionals

When I met Rachel, she had been off work for some time. During that time, she had sought psychiatric help for depression and anxiety. Her psychiatrist told her he would leave the treatment for hoarding to me. He continued to treat her and manage her medications. At one point, she also attended a mental health day program and received various valuable mental health supports from other health disciplines.

During our work together, her psychiatrist retired, and she transferred to a new one who welcomed working collaboratively to form an open communication care team with Rachel and me. We defined the role each of her two therapists would assume. Her psychiatrist would treat the comorbid factors (other coexisting mental health challenges), and I would treat the hoarding disorder. All three of us would adopt an open communication system and share some sessions using conference calling. Rachel had to be present for all discussions. We both encouraged Rachel to try new things, like increasing and diversifying her social activities. Rachel attended a day program for mental health well-being and thrived. She made new friends in the group and used safe online methods to join groups based on mutual interests.

Key Messages

1 In my experience, the internal feeling of being compelled to acquire anything is a danger sign because it strongly influences you to ignore other options that you have but don't explore. These other options are to:
   ✔ not acquire;
   ✔ acquire only after you discard proportionately;
   ✔ use a harm-reduction approach and try acquiring less;
   ✔ make a list of things you really need and are looking for, and acquire only those things first—in other words, no impulse purchases; and
   ✔ share purchases with a close friend; also share the storage of them, for example, gardening equipment, kitchen equipment, snow blower, and so

forth. Clients of mine have actually started doing this with neighbors, and it works for them.

2 As you consider an item, ask yourself, is this item *you* today, as you move forward to your goal, or is this item *you* as you used to be?

3 What is the cost to you of carrying it forward as you work to reach and maintain your goals?

4 Is the item symbolic of another problem in your life that needs to be dealt with? For example, a client of mine recently discovered that much of her clutter was boxes from her parents, who were downsizing. She didn't know what was in the boxes, didn't have the time or space to figure it out, and even if she didn't want the items, she was afraid to make her parents angry by getting rid of the contents. She realized that she was living well without the items or even knowing what was in the boxes. The major issue was not being able to say no and having her choice respected. Interestingly, this was also true in her relationship with her husband, her in-laws, and her children. These issues in one area spill over to other areas of life. Because this is true, it is important to face or get help with problems as early as possible.

Conclusion

After I worked with Rachel for 18 months, we lengthened the intervals between sessions to once a month, then every 3 months, 6 months, and finally once per year at her request. Rachel said she wanted to see me once every year until she felt able to manage entirely independently, saying, "I will make decisions differently every day knowing that I will see you and we will discuss things at the end of each year." I agreed, realizing that this was a novel approach to personal accountability. When we met at the end of the year, Rachel decided that she was safe to manage her environment on her own.

Online Impulsive Shopping (Problematic and Pathological)

It may be very difficult for a person suffering from hoarding disorder to avoid the lure of late-night shopping channels or internet deals. The dizzying rush that you may feel from the instant availability of any item that attracts you is the same as a traditional in-store shopping impulse. "Great deals" lure you in and urge you to purchase now. The buyer's remorse and anxiety you feel the next day is also the same as the regret felt after in-store impulse shopping except that it is far more convenient. As such, a problematic online shopping habit requires different coping and treatment strategies to be successful.

According to a recent study (Trotzke et al. 2015) to determine how to categorize online pathological shopping and whether it is similar to impulse control disorders, obsessive-compulsive disorders, or gambling addiction, scientists investigated *cue reactivity* (excitability from shopping cues), which constitute the emotional and motivational basis for experiencing a craving (Drummond 2000; Franken 2003). A craving is commonly described as the irresistible desire to consume a substance and is associated with drug seeking and relapse (Drummond 2001). The cue reactivity and craving concept has been transferred to behavioral addictions such as gambling, online gaming, and cybersex use (Sodano and Wulfert 2010; Laier et al. 2013; Brand et al. 2011; Thalemann, Wölfling, and Grüsser 2007).

Factors That Make People Vulnerable to Online Shopping Addiction

The study found *three key factors* that made people especially vulnerable to an online shopping addiction (Wei 2015):

1 *Preferring to buy anonymously and avoid social interaction.* There is an overlap between pathological impulsive buying and anxiety, especially *social anxiety.* For people who don't comfortably tolerate crowded malls or the social interaction at the checkout counter, buying online may seem like the perfect solution, but it actually increases the incentive for an individual to avoid social interaction.

   People with pathological impulsive shopping behaviors often feel shame and regret about their shopping and seek to hide their online shopping habits. The anonymity and privacy of online shopping can make this worse.

2 *Enjoying a wide variety and constant availability of items.* It's not surprising that online shopping cultivates satisfaction in people who like a great deal of variety and want to have the latest model of what attracts them. Added to the attraction is the fact that online stores never close. This can lead to more frequent indulgence of a person's cravings for shopping.

3 *Seeking instant gratification.* People who seek immediate gratification are drawn to online shopping, where purchases are one click away. The quick satisfaction feeds into the cycle of cravings and rewards.

In addition to these factors, online shopping websites and shopping channel ads *are designed to compound the problem* in several ways:

- Online auction sites and television ads are designed to create a sense of urgency. Often the online site includes a countdown of the time left before the deal expires, or ads show a countdown of the number of items left at the unbelievable sale price.

This marketing strategy leads to anxiety and an overwhelming urge to purchase *now*, before you can take a breath and recognize that the best decision for you at this time is to move yourself forward toward the person you deserve to be.

- Sites cue induced craving (Trotzke et al. 2014). To cue you to increased craving, when you browse for a product online, targeted ads and sponsored ads start popping up in your browser soon after. Businesses try to capitalize on your initial interest by providing you with cues to get you to click for a closer look at their product. If your initial interest was based on a craving for the item, it can quickly turn into an irresistible urge to purchase.

- Robert LaRose and Matthew S. Eastin (2002) found that although online retail websites have features that encourage self-regulation (e.g., shopping carts to contain products before purchase and therefore allowing time to consider; search engine opportunities to find and evaluate information; and past purchase history to trigger awareness of buying behavior), these were outweighed by website features such as advertising pop-ups, timed discount offers, vivid interactive graphical displays of products, and "one click" purchases, all of which encourage purchasing and weaken self-regulation (see also Rose and Dhandayudham 2014).

Many of us enjoy the convenience and immediacy of online shopping, so how is pathological impulsive online buying different from the average shopper's behavior? According to Marlynn Wei (2015), people with pathological impulsive buying issues feel preoccupied with shopping and feel like they have no control over it, even if it leads to severe work or relationship problems or financial bankruptcy.

10 Signs of Compulsive Online Shopping

1. I feel like I can't stop online shopping even if I wanted to, or I have tried to stop without being able to.
2. Online shopping has hurt my relationships, work, or financial situation.
3. My partner, family members, or friends are concerned about my online shopping. I end up in arguments with them over it.
4. I think about online shopping all the time.
5. I get grumpy or upset if I can't shop online.
6. Online shopping is the only thing that helps me relax or feel better.
7. I hide things that I buy because I'm afraid other people will think it's unreasonable or a waste of money.
8. I often feel *guilty* after I go online shopping.
9. I spend less time doing other things that I enjoy because of the time and money spent online shopping.
10. I often buy things that I don't need or much more than I planned, even when I can't afford it.

If you think you may have a problem, Wei (2015) provides some additional tests for shopping addiction: the Compulsive Buying Scale (Valence, D'Astous, and Fortier 1988) and the Bergen Shopping Addiction Scale (Andreassen et al. 2015).

Pathological impulsive buying can also be tied to or worsened by other psychological issues, such as anxiety, depression, obsessive-compulsive disorder, hoarding, or mania. Treating the underlying issue can help improve the buying behavior if it stems from another disorder. For pathological impulsive buying itself, the standard treatment is cognitive behavioral therapy with a mental health professional.

Strategies to Deal with Online Shopping

There is no easy answer to online shopping habits because online shopping is numbingly easy and available. Marketing strategies are designed to make even the tawdriest bauble look like the crown jewels or a solution to your everyday life problems.

First, let's look at the obvious.

1 Why is the shopping channel or online retail websites your viewing choice of the day?

2 What is stopping you from turning off the TV or internet or at least changing the channel or website?

3 When you want a down-time activity, what other choices do you have? List these other choices and work yourself down the list to provide variety and get unstuck.

4 Who have you not connected with in a while? Turn off the TV or internet and try writing, calling, or emailing them instead. Nothing you see or purchase online from the shopping channel cares about you the way the people in your life do, even if relationships have drifted. Be sure to ask the people you contact how things are going for them first. Everyone has a story and needs someone to lighten the load by being a good listener. Then be willing to share with them.

5 Are you a night-owl shopper? Make a contract with yourself: No shopping after 7 p.m. or when you are bored, feeling down, or need something you can't identify.

6 No matter what the item, make a contract with yourself to take notes on it.
   - Put yourself on pause for 24–48 hours and then decide how handy or problem-solving the item really is. *Never* buy the same day you get excited about a new purchase if shopping has ever been a problem for you.
   - Ask yourself what the priority problems, frustrations, irritations, longings are for you at this moment in your life and do a pros and cons list of how these desired acquisitions will solve these issues for you.
   - Make a list of your problems, frustrations, irritations, and longings and spend your TV or internet time developing a list in the next column of what you can do about each. Use the "Figuring It Out" tool in chapter 2 to decide what you need to do to solve these issues and get the help you need to make the progress you desire.

- Remember, your willingness and ability to stay on pause is being deliberately tested by online shopping marketing strategies in the hopes that the suggestibility of their advertising will wear you down and you will buy or express greater interest by going online to further research details and eventually buy their products.
- Reread the "10 Signs of Compulsive Online Shopping." These signs are also true for problem shopping offline.

Remember you are worth not letting yourself get propelled by your feelings of impulsive necessity or possible usefulness. Be the driver and decide your own best path.

CHAPTER 9

The Sandwich Generation

Overwhelming Obligation

We need to find the courage to say no to the things
or people that are not serving us if we want to rediscover
ourselves and live our lives with authenticity.

BARBARA DE ANGELIS

TWO COMMON WAYS TO CREATE a hoarded environment are through intense feelings of obligation or responsibility for the things of others. I call these two mindsets the *curator* and the *clearinghouse*:

1 Accepting, or being appointed, the family's *curator*. This mindset is illustrated in this chapter by Lucinda, who becomes the curator of the lives, possessions, and properties of three families.

2 Appointing yourself the retainer of possessions and becoming a *clearinghouse*, with items "too important" to pass on to strangers because they *might* be needed by the next generation, so they are kept just in case. Many individuals from the *sandwich generation* are adults who store the possessions of their parents, while also storing possessions of their young adult children. Debbie and Mike are in this situation, suffocating under the weight of all these possessions in their basement.

Bequeathed Obligation—Lucinda

Synopsis

Lucinda's early beginnings were unpredictable, despite being cared for by two sets of committed, loving grandparents. Both families were in shock and profound grief at the time they coparented her. The rules and expectations in each home were distinctly different, and she learned to adapt by responding to the demands of each home. What she did not learn was to expect her grandparents to consider her needs as a child. Smiling brightly and "carrying on," she continued this learned behavior of excessive obligation into adulthood by regularly assuming responsibility when others bailed on projects. This profound sense of obligation and the failure to consider herself meant she did not ask, "Does this item meet my needs? Does this reflect *me* as I am today, moving forward, or is it an obligation from the past?"

Problem Overview

In Lucinda's adult life, she still has loving, committed relationships in which the other person is unavailable, leaving Lucinda to smile brightly, reassuring herself and others that she is "just fine" and has enough to cope with the void. The void gets filled with the latest fashion, the next interesting book, or the latest and finest of painting and sewing supplies. As stresses build up, so does the volume and variety of exciting "needed" items. Still, no one reliably meets many of her needs except for Lucinda herself, but she is not enough. Close, but not quite. Consequently, she faces an overwhelming schedule, piles of potential materials, and committees where she gets commandeered from her preexisting priorities. Lucinda is left with the ever-familiar internal sense of chaos, always running too fast toward impending deadlines.

Background

Lucinda is the curator of the three blended families she was born into. At 9 months of age, she lost her mother to suicide due to what was forensically assessed to be poorly managed postpartum depression. Only recently, in counseling, has she come to realize that she was not abandoned. Instead, she was left in the care of two sets of devoted and committed grandparents, who alternated taking care of her and who tried to meet her every need despite their own profound shock, grief, and guilt.

She came to realize that her father did not just disappear. Revisiting her history through adult eyes, she saw that he almost certainly had suffered a complete breakdown and been removed from her life for a long time, to recover and to begin to rebuild a life for both of them. Part of his recovery and rebuilding was to find a mother who could be present for his baby daughter.

Lucinda came to understand that her mother fought fiercely for 9 months to overcome the chemical and hormonal war battling within her, and that she fought a valiant fight to remain with her daughter—that is, until what is believed to have been an incorrect prescription upset her tentative balance and caused her to take her baby daughter to her own mother's house, retire to a room with her child, and take her own life.

In recent counseling, Lucinda also realized that her pattern of smiling too brightly and assuring all around her that she is fine is an old pattern of "passing" that may not serve her well any longer. Almost certainly during her nine months alone with her mother while her mother tried to regain equilibrium, there must have been times when her mother was unable to respond to Lucinda's needs because of postpartum depression. This was not a matter of not loving or caring about her enough; her mother was simply incapacitated, unable to respond to an infant needing care and reassurance. For Lucinda, no one came. Over and over, no one came.

When Lucinda was 7 years old, her father remarried. Her new stepmother turned out to be a controlling tyrant in the extreme. Lucinda's only role was to comply with her. Her kind, gentle, affectionate father, who tickled her and read her stories, bought peace by deferring to his new wife. Everyone deferred to her, so the pattern of verbal and emotional mistreatment continued. Lucinda learned to manage her life by smiling brightly and not making demands. Individual needs? What needs?

Seven-year-old Lucinda was left to comply with all expectations and carry on, deferring to her stepmother, thereby yielding unrestrained power to squash any chance Lucinda had to learn to be herself. To this day, despite her cheery demeanor and lovely manners, Lucinda interprets feedback defensively and often sees adaptation as capitulation.

The rules and expectations were quite different among each of the three homes. She needed to be a chameleon to survive. From 6 months to 7 years old, she alternated between her maternal and paternal grandparents' homes. As her father recovered, he became more present in her life. At age 7, during the week, she lived with her father and new stepmother. Alternating weekends, she was again with her maternal and paternal grandparents. One set of grandparents hoarded. Absolutely everything was stored on shelving in rows, filling the interior of the house, and leaving only pathways to navigate from area to area. The second set of grandparents lived with the Great Depression mindset and taught Lucinda that waste was a sin. They would not tolerate it. Yet, they didn't let their stock of reusable items accumulate. They kept things to use and stocked extras in safe, manageable ways. Her third family, made up of her father and stepmother, expected Lucinda to do exactly and only as she was told, and to be exactly and only what was expected of her. A rebelliousness began developing within her, which she expressed through passive resistance.

The influence of her strict grandparents demonstrates itself in her well-honed manners as well as in the things that make up her current hoarded environment. Being an only child and therefore first to inherit from all sides of the family explains the volume of things each side left to her. This fact does not explain, however, why so many of the things remain long after, especially those she doesn't particularly like. She sees herself as the curator of all these people's lives, and she feels an obligation of love, responsible for not wasting or squandering the beauty and value of the things that represent those lives.

Growing up with two sets of strict "thou shalt not waste" grandparents imprinted on her the importance of not wasting and of valuing things for their potential alternate use. There was no option to ask whether you liked something, whether it was *you*. Life could be uncertain, and you had to make yourself ready for it, so you did not give things away, in case you needed them in the future. It was a grievous personal deficiency not to be prepared.

Lucinda lives with varying degrees of depression and obsessive-compulsive personality disorder, or OCPD. She is delightfully charming unless you interfere with the way she wants to do something. She gets rattled easily when you don't use her plan. She is quite locked in to her own strategies, and these strategies typically comfort and soothe her.

Client's Initial Perspective

Lucinda's habit of generally overcommitting left her feeling overwhelmed, fatigued, and frazzled. As each set of loved ones died, Lucinda became the curator of their lives, properties, and possessions. Old, well-loved, and cared-for things became receptacles of memories, symbolic of the taste and values of the people who had been her haven in the maelstrom that was her infant and young life. She saw herself as the last living member of all three families, surrounded and obstructed by lovely things, almost never her taste, definitely too plentiful for one house. She repeatedly asked herself, "How can I part with this because it meant so much to them?"

Lucinda was smothered by her sense of duty, made worse by the fact she was alone to deal with it. In addition, there was the paperwork involved in settling three estates, including property rights. She was required to file final income tax returns for all three and hold on to documents for seven years according to tax law. Lucinda took this responsibility seriously.

Her burden was real and evident. Her response of holding on to things became generalized to more and more things, especially now that she was free to express her own taste and interests. All these vulnerabilities and choices were her path to a seriously hoarded environment, and it is not hard to understand, given her history.

Therapeutic Plan

In our sessions, she began to ask herself, with my help, who *she* really is and how all these things represent *who she is moving forward*. Are they her taste or someone else's, someone loved but gone? If the item is not her taste, is living with piles and pathways the best and only way to honor her loved ones and all that she shared with them? If the items are not truly her, then where are the homes and the people who will appreciate and value these things as their original owners did? Which items are so important that she wants them to have a place in her life today?

Intervention

When I began working with Lucinda, she was submerged in estate papers. She couldn't decide how to store them and yet keep them accessible for referring to without churning them and creating chaos when she needed to find something. They took up a great deal of space, more space than she could spare. Lucinda's legacy also involved all the china, crystal, furniture, and knickknacks of eight people: her mother, father, stepmother, two sets of grandparents, and an aunt. Lucinda attributes her hoarding somewhat laughingly to her OCPD as well as a trait of being distracted by a "bright and shiny thing" and needing to have all versions of the set of whatever has caught her fancy.

The hoard contained layers of obligatory legacies of eight lives, topped with the layer of her and her husband's life, work, and personal history. The unmanageable task had become to make room for the history and lives of ten people and still manage to live safely and functionally in their home.

Another factor hindering Lucinda was her difficulty self-starting. As a former teacher, she had learned to live by the bell. She had learned to make herself work to a deadline (be in class before the bell; get each lesson delivered in the 40 minutes allotted before the bell; wait to use the comfort facilities at school until the bell; get lessons planned, work marked, return parents' calls, take extra career development courses, and be back in class before the bell). Each 40-minute block in a day became a series of "crunch times," with looming deadlines for test results and report cards, then cramming to meet the deadlines (see chapter 5). She still uses this method to manage her life, but with my help, she is learning to set short- and long-term goals and deadlines, say no to competing activities, and resist the urge to rescue group projects in trouble and make them turn out "right"—the way they should be done.

She has learned that "opportunistic others" will always come, if you are making yourself indispensable and saving them from their own reluctance to finish work they took on. This is a surefire way to guarantee that you matter. Lucinda is getting quite proficient at using the strategies "Does this fill or empty my cup?" and "What will this choice do to my mental, physical, and spiritual balance given my other priority responsibilities?" Under excessive stress, she falls prey to old habits. But her progress is that she realizes it and corrects her course sooner.

Her hoarding impulse is fueled by her OCPD. The OCPD does not cause her hoarding disorder, but it does make it more complicated to deal with by adding another layer of complexity to implementing the processes and strategies that would resolve her hoarding.

In the past year Lucinda and I have begun to peel back the layers to allow room for the "real," authentic Lucinda to emerge and claim her space. This helps her give herself permission to acknowledge how she really feels, who she really is, and who she was meant to be with all her bumps, warts, and gifts, to make room to uncover and accept her authentic self and preferences. Allowing room for her authentic self also helps her figure out what items fit her current life and what items don't fit, as well as find acceptable strategies to deal with the rest.

Lucinda is a gifted artist, something she inherited from her birth mother. She has an extensive inventory of art materials of all kinds stored in the garage and studio, which can become chaotic and overwhelming if she does not remain vigilant. She is sorely tested by all three attachment patterns: sentimental, aesthetic, and intrinsic (see "How People Form Attachment Relationships to Things" in chapter 1). She definitely hoards discriminately while being charming, engaging, cheery, and extremely gifted.

One of the ways in which Lucinda gives herself validation and meaning is through her active social life, keeping herself overcommitted. When I met her, she couldn't say no to any request. Without realizing it, she used this choice as a distraction and a method to validate herself by making sure her participation or much appreciated rescue effort was carried out perfectly—at much cost to Lucinda's anxiety level. If she gave her word, no matter how off the rails the project had gone, she would keep her word and salvage it. The committee members' commitment to Lucinda, however, was never reciprocated. When she needs help, support, or another pair of hands to volunteer in a salvage project yet again, Lucinda is associated with people who never support her.

Outcome

Lucinda's story is still being written. She remains the family curator, still figuring out the true meaning of an abundance of family legacies. The things are often lovely and tempting, so we process them slowly, facing down such issues as procrastination and the need to fill the emptiness left by ruptured attachment with beautiful things. The emptiness, while less, remains. Lucinda has normalized the emptiness. She accepts relationships that repeat the pattern of no one coming to help her, and lovely things substitute for what she needs.

Collaboration with Other Professionals

Lucinda worked with additional professionals on other physical health issues.

Conclusion

Lucinda and I continue to work together. At present, physical health limitations are causing us to change our focus to counseling only. When she recovers, we will return to our normal counseling and hands-on clutter coaching.

Stuck in the Middle: Debbie and Mike

Synopsis

Debbie and Mike are typical middle-aged parents trying to balance the needs and demands of their parents and children. They inherited hand-me-downs from parents and accepted them with little thought of their own tastes. The problem arose when they attempted to bequeath these items to their own children, not realizing that the younger generation might have different tastes and expectations. It became clear to Debbie and Mike that they had inherited a generational value from their parents, that if something is free and it comes from a family member, it should stay in the family. Unfortunately, their children do not share this value.

Problem Overview

"Who in the world needs three dining room sets?" Debbie asked herself regularly, but she still could not make herself part with any of them unless someone in the family, who would value them, took them.

Background

The maple dining room set with its three leaves and six brocade chairs was their first purchase when they married 30 years ago. She remembered their first candlelight dinner as if it were yesterday.

Debbie had heard the story many times about how Grandma had brought the luxurious Italian limestone dining table all the way from England on a ship. Before Debbie's mother passed away, she had made Debbie promise that it would stay in the family. "Surely one of the kids will take it," Debbie mused.

This past summer, Debbie and Mike had helped his 78-year-old parents downsize from their large country home to a small duplex in town. All his brothers and sisters had decided that as the oldest son, Mike should keep the pine table that had been the location of many family dinners and wonderful memories in Mike's life.

So now there were three.

Debbie and Mike were using the maple dining set in their dining room, with the other two sets relegated to the basement. Debbie was proud of her home and kept the main floor neat and tidy, but the basement was starting to make her anxious. Every time she went down there, she saw that more and more things were piling up. She dreaded the day when a repair person might have to go down there to fix the washer or inspect the furnace.

Debbie was also storing furniture and appliances for the children. It was easier to keep these items "just for now" rather than decide what to do with them. She felt anxiety about making decisions to let useful things go. It felt so final, especially with the uncertainty that someone might need the items in the future. Debbie didn't dare throw anything out because sure enough, just when she thought that extra couch would never be needed, it was.

When Mike's parents downsized, his dad was positive that his grandsons would need his stuff once they got their own homes. Now Mike and Debbie's garage was starting to fill up as well, with shovels, rakes, hammers, other tools, an upright deep freezer, a weed whacker, a leaf blower, even a snow blower that "still works like a charm."

Debbie was starting to feel like she would suffocate from all the stuff, but she didn't know what to do. She felt stuck in this never-ending "just in case" phase, caught between the obligations she felt to her parents and to her children. Debbie and Mike had lost track of their own right as adults to have boundaries and set limits, even with those they loved. A family subculture of remaining adult children to their parents and "forever providers" to their children was an unspoken expectation, generation to generation. That is when she called me.

Client's Initial Perspective

Debbie and Mike felt stuck in the middle when we began working together. They questioned whether they actually met the diagnostic criteria for hoarding disorder or were just collectors of good reusable things. They *could* discard some things. Surely that was proof this wasn't hoarding. Doesn't everyone collect something?

Therapeutic Plan

The first step in working with Debbie and Mike was to separate the stigma of hoarding from their situation. The second step was to help them develop the insight that the stigma is an externally applied judgment often devoid of fact.

Getting them to set aside self-recrimination, I helped them compare their situation to the *DSM-5* definition of hoarding disorder to determine for themselves if a hoarded environment had developed.

I outlined the strategies we could use to help make decisions more comfortably.

They agreed, and we began working together.

Intervention

When in doubt, always refer to the *DSM-5* definition. See the working definition in chapter 1, and the full definition in chapter 16.

Here is how Debbie and Mike's situation compared to the *DSM-5* criteria.

DSM-5 DEFINITION FOR HOARDING DISORDER	DEBBIE AND MIKE'S ENVIRONMENT
Persistent difficulty discarding or parting with possessions, regardless of the actual value	Depending on how long they had been acting on the obligations they felt to their parents and children by making their home spaces a storage area, the answer might well be *yes*. In fact, a good rule of thumb is that if the accumulation has been excessive for 4–6 months with no active plan to resolve it, you almost certainly qualify as having started or added to a hoarding situation.
This difficulty is due to a perceived need to save the items and to feelings of distress associated with discarding them	Debbie *and* Mike both perceive a strong need to hold on to things, and although this is frustrating and distressing for them both, they have been unable to resolve it. See the summary at the end of this chapter for alternate ideas to resolve situations like Debbie and Mike's. The answer to this criterion is a definite *yes.*
The difficulty discarding possessions results in the accumulation of objects, which congests and clutters active living areas and substantially compromises their intended use; uncluttered living areas are the result of third-party interventions (e.g., family members, cleaners, authorities)	Even though the actual communal space where most activities of daily living happen isn't being used for storage, excessive use of the basement interferes with clear, adequate access to the furnace, hot water tank, and electrical panel. Added to this is the distress that Debbie feels at having anyone need to go into the basement. This makes the answer to this criterion a definite *yes.*
The hoarding causes clinically significant distress or impairment in social, occupational, or other important areas of functioning (including maintaining a safe environment for self and others)	Until an in-depth psychological assessment is completed, which is best done over a long term to ensure that the results do not represent a transitory phase of perception and need, it is difficult to determine with certainty if Debbie and Mike have clinical symptoms of hoarding disorder. Their social and occupational lives are not affected, but there certainly is impairment in functioning for their safety, with a basement filled with combustible items, especially because they interfere with any maintenance being carried out. Such a filled basement also lessens the likelihood that Debbie and Mike would realize maintenance is necessary in time to prevent a crisis. Again, the answer to this criterion is a definite *yes.*

DSM-5 DEFINITION FOR HOARDING DISORDER	DEBBIE AND MIKE'S ENVIRONMENT
The hoarding is not attributable to another medical condition (e.g., brain injury, cerebrovascular disease, Prader-Willi syndrome)	Any indications of other medical conditions would of course need to be followed up with appropriate assessment and treatment. Debbie and Mike do not have any other relevant health issues, so again, the answer to this criterion is a definite *yes*.
The hoarding is not better explained by the symptoms of another mental disorder (e.g., obsessions in obsessive-compulsive disorder, decreased energy in major depressive disorder, delusions in schizophrenia or another psychotic disorder, cognitive deficits in major neurocognitive disorder, or restricted interests in autism spectrum disorder)	Both Debbie and Mike demonstrate a slight tendency to seek "perfect" or "right" solutions. They do not, however, meet the clinical criteria for any of the other disorders that would disqualify hoarding disorder. Again, this criterion results in a *yes* rating.

Outcomes

Debbie and Mike do meet the clinical diagnostic criteria for hoarding disorder. If labels create a barrier for people, however, then they are unhelpful. There is no need to wear the label "hoarder." We are all more than the labels we qualify for at any given time. Mental health is a continuum, and we all move up and down that continuum regularly.

The fact is that what they have created over time is a hoarded environment. When helpful, focus on the condition of the environment being hoarded and not on applying a label to the person.

As Debbie, Mike, and I worked together, I introduced them to three questions we would use to make decisions:

1 What is *your* vision for your home spaces?
2 Is this item *you*, as you are today, moving forward, or is the item as you used to be, or as someone else sees you? As you move forward in your life, do you get more out of living in the present or in the past?
3 Are you keeping or acquiring this item for someone else? If so, have you asked first if that person wants it? Can you give up control and honor his or her choice if it means letting the object go? Can you set a deadline for its exit date? Can you honor the thing, and the person who gave it to you, by letting it go to someone who will choose it and appreciate it as much as the person did who gifted it to you?

Debbie, Mike, and I continued to work together sorting, getting to "I can live with it" decisions. Here are some of the alternative viewpoints they considered to challenge their status quo.

FOR SENTIMENTAL ATTACHMENT

- Consider that the gift of a memento or other things symbolic of better times is not the item itself; rather, the gift is that you were thought of highly enough to be given a gift. The thing to value is the positive relationship, and that will never change.
- Your importance to the person giving you the gift isn't temporary. They will always have felt the same about you. All possessions are temporary—they break, fade, get lost or stolen, or wear out. If *you* love it, and it gives you joy while fully expressing who you are, *keep it*. If, however, it isn't *you*, and you are treating it as symbolic, you are placing undue importance on the tangible item. Eventually one of the outcomes (breaking, fading, getting lost or stolen, or wearing out) will surely happen. Things are just things. Memories are forever. The memories are in you, and without this symbolic item, something else will trigger the memory and remind you.

FOR INTRINSIC ATTACHMENT

You may have what I call an "engineer's brain." You see possibilities and alternative uses for practically everything. You are the crafty folks. You love having projects, and while you go through your day, you see the possibility in everything and feel a strong need to acquire and keep them "just in case." The problem is you have an overwhelming impulse to gather materials well in advance of the many projects you would like to do.

Others with intrinsic attachment hold the belief that it is a sin to waste. You may hold this belief so strongly that discarding things makes you feel guilty. Given the reality of the limitations in your life (time, health, space, energy, ability to focus and complete tasks, the number of priorities you can juggle), it proves unrealistic to expect that you can effectively manage:

- such comprehensive recycling;
- finding the right home for your extras; and
- following through on handing things over to specific people you think may be a perfect fit for your extras, without creating piles you have to maneuver around daily.

FOR AESTHETIC ATTACHMENT

"Beauty is in the eye of the beholder," someone said.* To varying degrees, we are all attracted to things we find appealing. Those with aesthetic attachment feel an immediate and intense attraction to things that have particular characteristics. The attraction can be to things of no apparent value. Sometimes we hold on to our intense attraction to things even when they have become unsafe for health or safety reasons. Remember things change; that is a given. When the risk is irreversible, consider that jeopardizing your health and safety is too high a price to pay. Please consider putting yourself and anyone else who could be put at risk before any object, no matter how lovely or what that item has meant to you in the past. Consider taking a picture of each item that needs to go and making a collage that you can put somewhere visible, remembering it that way and keeping only the very best examples of the items you value most.

Collaboration with Other Professionals

Collaboration with other professionals was not necessary in Debbie and Mike's situation.

Key Messages

- *Before* accepting delivery of items, even cherished things, formerly belonging to someone else, ensure that they will *not* interfere with:
  - *the normal use of spaces needed for activities of daily living; or*
  - *the space needed for safe mobility, entrance and exit routes, or adequate clearance around heat sources.*

---

* Attributed to Margaret Wolfe Hungerford's book *Molly Bawn* (1878).

- Instead, *delay* bringing things into your environment until you have obtained advice and developed alternate strategies for preventing a hoarded environment.
- If for any reason you cannot turn down the opportunity, seriously consider adopting a harm-reduction strategy and temporarily put the items in external storage to prevent the risks associated with a hoarding situation.
- You can decide permanent places in your environment more slowly and strategically, making final selections between the new arrivals and existing items according to your proved (not perceived) need and available spaces where they would normally be used.
- Remember everything changes with time. Items may fade, break, wear out, get lost, be stolen, become less interesting to you eventually, or actually turn out to be a jewel and represent you, today, moving forward.
- Times when you are in pain, grieving, or overwhelmed may not be the best for making important decisions about what to do with your things.

If you are helping people decide about a legacy:

- The objective is to prevent, or at the very least reduce, the occurrence and level of accumulation.
- If people are determined to bring items into their environment despite other options being considered, try to determine how they can resolve the buildup. Are they "decide area by area" people *or* "decide one layer at a time" people? Work with who they are and don't try to change them to work in the other way.
- Help them to discover what their relationship is to each item and help that relationship become a healthier and more balanced one.
- Help them make "I can live with it" long-term decisions.
- Do not create a void that they will then fill with new things (often more of them, more quickly acquired, which they will be less open about having amassed).

Conclusion
- Consider giving yourself some time and space to make the best long-term decision you can make.
- Use some of the other strategies outlined in this book to let things go where they will be honored and appreciated by people who feel about them the way the original owner appreciated and felt about them.
- Be aware that in making "I can live with it" decisions, you may initially be frustrated by limiting beliefs associated with your thoughts, ideas, fears, values, and wishes that are not relevant to the situation you are immediately deciding about.
- The context of "who you are today, moving forward in your own life, toward your own goals" must take precedence. There are always strategies and solutions to the uncertainty you experience when making *today's* best decision.

CHAPTER 10

A Life Stored, Not Lived

Secondary Diogenes Syndrome in Seniors

People assume you aren't sick unless they see
the sickness on your skin like scars forming a
map of all the ways you're hurting.

EMM ROY

THIS IS A STORY ABOUT MARIO AND ANDRE, each of whom lived with secondary Diogenes syndrome complicated by different comorbid factors. In Mario's situation, the comorbidity was a blend of obsessive-compulsive personality disorder (OCPD) and obsessive-compulsive disorder (OCD). Andre's comorbidity was Asperger syndrome.

There are two forms of Diogenes syndrome (Huizen 2016):

1 Primary Diogenes syndrome is when the syndrome is not triggered by another preexisting medical condition.
2 Secondary Diogenes syndrome is the result of other mental health disorders.

Mario

Synopsis

Approximately 0.05 percent of the general population above age 60 live with Diogenes syndrome (Huizen 2016). Typically, people living with Diogenes syndrome demonstrate extreme self-neglect, domestic squalor, social isolation, apathy, compulsive hoarding (often of things better disposed of), and lack of concern about the conditions they have created and live in. They are often suspicious and feel paranoid about others, particularly authority figures and officials. Mario is atypical of Diogenes because of his ability to socialize and engage with others. As you will see, though, he engaged almost entirely on his own terms.

Problem Overview

Mario was in his eighties, recently postoperative from prostate cancer, with a prognosis of nine months to a year to live and an unrivaled zest for life, fueled by his single-mindedness and rampant obsessive-compulsive personality disorder, or OCPD. His chronic and unsuccessful pattern of dealing with people and life challenges was fueled by an excessive need for perfectionism as he defined it, including but not restricted to his environment. He demonstrated a preoccupation with details concerning his collections and an absolute inability to part with things of no use or value to him. While you might not describe him as miserly, he took frugality and repurposing to extremes. For example, things he might accidentally find on the street, such as damaged and dented canned and fresh food items dropped by someone else, Mario considered edible. During the time I worked with him, he was unable to develop any insight even into his social functioning, which alienated him from many people. This personality style was chronic with only minor situational variations.

He also demonstrated some symptoms of an anxiety disorder, obsessive-compulsive disorder, or OCD. He experienced recurrent obsessions with spending significant parts of each day acquiring and keeping complete sets of items of interest. He felt compelled to be authoritative and correct on all subjects, which in part fueled his ritual of storing vast numbers of things simply to have them "just in case" they might ever be needed. The ritual was to store his complete sets of items to have them, not necessarily to use them. He lacked the ability for insight, however. He carried out these behaviors because he believed himself to be unquestionably right. He had a strong need for others to conform to his way of doing things. His absolute belief that he was right and his obsessions, compulsions, and rituals (which occupied excessive hours of each day) consistently blurred the line between OCD and OCPD.

His first plan when back home was to get back up on the roof of his house to finish the skylight repair job he had started when he had fallen off approximately seven months before. He had been taken to the emergency department of his local hospital for orthopedic repair and received the surprise diagnosis of stage 4 cancer. Despite his terminal prognosis, given his determination to live, I thought he might just prove them wrong and live to be the last person on the face of the earth.

Background

Mario's nephew Salvatore called me because they had been living together after his surgery. Mario's home was extremely unsafe and unhygienic. The home was accessible by very narrow paths throughout, leaving nowhere to rest, recover, and carry out necessary activities of daily living.

Mario was a lonely and isolated but outwardly gregarious person, with a few friends who dropped in regularly to check on him and provide moral support. Everyone close to Mario knew about his extreme hoarding behavior and offered advice, but Mario was an immovable object. He had rules to live by, and live by them he did. His friends were left to love him and respect his wishes.

Client's Initial Perspective

It was clear from the outset that Mario's was an extreme hoarding situation. The risks were so extreme that I agreed to work with Mario only if he did not live in the house until we returned it to a safe status. He reluctantly agreed.

Therapeutic Plan

Mario had a brother, Tomas, and a sister, Louisa, who were very concerned but unavailable as they lived in Italy. Despite the distance and expense, they came to help Mario in any way he would let them. They stayed with Salvatore, and Mario agreed to join them. Tomas helped with the physical work needed for a while. The house was a beehive of activity when I arrived. Tomas's job was to help remove whatever Mario would allow him to remove, relocate, store, and discard. And Louisa's job was to coax Mario to return the house to "good enough" condition so that Mario could continue living comfortably in his own home.

Intervention

The pathways in the house were so narrow that at one point, I was having difficulty maneuvering through them, explaining that the space was not wide enough for emergency response or fire department equipment in case of emergency. He was unconcerned.

Tomas, Louisa, Mario, and I did an extensive assessment. We confirmed that all areas of the three-bedroom split-level home and property qualified as a Risk Level 5+ (according to the levels of risk for hoarding situations outlined in chapter 2).

Mario loved to tinker and kept everything that could possibly have transferable use—including the motor head and other car parts for his then-defunct Chevy Chevette. He also loved electronics, especially if an item needed fixing. Photography was a category unto its own.

His collections of magazines and periodicals contained every edition from the beginning of his awareness of the subject area. The collections were methodically stored, but they were inaccessible and unusable because of the volume of other acquisitions.

In the basement and crawl space, he had multiple appliances, four washing machines, and five dryers. This made the left side of the basement almost impassable. The right side of the basement, which contained the furnace, hot water tank, and electrical panel, was accessible with great difficulty. When walking through this part of the basement, you could easily get snagged on hanging metal car and appliance parts.

The upstairs and basement, including crawl space, were about 90 percent three-dimensionally full.

In ranking order of priority, safety concerns always come first, followed closely by health needs, and then the things about our home that are preferences and make us happy. By the conclusion of my assessment visit, I had noted so many, and such severe, safety hazards that I set as a condition for my involvement that Mario live elsewhere and not be in the house without someone there with him until pathways were at least 3 feet wide and no higher than his waist. After that, he could be at the house during the day but would sleep and have his meals somewhere else.

The kitchen's usable space was a pathway 18 inches wide. The room had significant toppling, tripping, and electrical hazards. Hoarded environments are notoriously poorly maintained, sometimes simply because needed areas can't be accessed. In addition, financial resources are often diverted to acquisitions. Access was clearly an issue at Mario's. His electrical service was also suspect, judging from the noticeable scorches on the wall at some outlet sites. Sometime later, while working together, we confirmed the severity of this risk when we tried to plug in a fan. At the moment of contact with the outlet, a giant spark torpedoed out of the wall, leaving a large burn mark on the wall around the outlet.

Mario meticulously managed his finances, however. His rule of thumb was to pursue the absolute least expensive homemade solution to a problem. This became a major issue as violations of various local codes became apparent.

The first issue to present itself as an unexpected code violation were his narrow, oddly angled back steps, which were 5 feet above grade. I repeatedly walked by them during sessions, and their peculiarity began to intrigue me. When I finally took a closer look at them, I realized that they were missing stringers and proper handrails. The handrails were more like doweling and looked precarious. I discovered that the steps weren't actually constructed. They were just stacked wood that Mario had positioned to look like steps.

Thus began the adventure of convincing Mario to get a building permit, construct or have someone else construct replacement steps, and submit to a building inspection of the finished product. Mario vehemently maintained that the cost of a permit and inspection was just a "bureaucratic cash grab," and any steps he built would be better than some "upstart's" sent to inspect and certify them.

The back steps provide an interesting example of how Mario thought. He loved to demonstrate how his solutions were always cheaper and better than anybody else's. He did have an engineering-type brain and was technically and mechanically capable. He loved to tinker, and so he had simply tinkered his back steps into existence.

When I raised the issue of the steps not being to code, he demonstrated their adequacy by scurrying out the back door (which was 5 feet above ground), taking hold of the handrail on both sides, raising himself up on his toes like an Olympic diver ready to do a triple flip (I hoped not), and swinging both feet out and over the steps. Eyes wide and stifling a gasp, I watched from below as he scampered down the steps on his toes, landing with both feet planted firmly at the bottom. If he'd been a competitive gymnast instead of an eighty-year-old do-it-yourselfer, he would have scored a 10 for his perfect dismount. With a twinkle in his eye, he said proudly, "I told you these steps are perfectly fine!" Tomas and Louisa looked at each other and rolled their eyes. They both looked over at me and shrugged their shoulders, turned, and got back to work with resigned faces.

In the months to follow, Mario continued to refuse to believe that the steps needed professional work, and he resisted all requests to get a building permit to build the steps correctly. In typical Mario fashion, he led me on a merry chase from the beginning to the conclusion of this project.

Other issues with the house were a strong musty smell that permeated throughout, a broken bedroom window, heat-bleeding ancient windows, and what appeared to be black mold growing in the corners of the bedrooms. The basement needed to be cleared, all stairwells and hallways needed to be cleared, two ways into and out of the house needed to be clear and passable, the area around all heat sources and the electrical panel needed to be clear and accessible, and the general level of combustible materials needed to be lessened. If Mario and I could not agree, the local fire inspection branch would need to approve the safety level of the house.

The backyard was also a bylaw concern. He had been cited and fined numerous times in the past. He had large piles of things under tarps in the yard, and neighbors were complaining. These kinds of accumulations were welcoming habitats for undomesticated animals like rats, mice, ground hogs, skunks, and raccoons.

Strategies

Mario and I agreed on a plan to deal with his accumulation, except for his collections stored in the basement. We worked that plan for 4 months, in three 2-hour sessions per week. The challenge was not to get into a power struggle with him. I suggested that we agree to disagree; to resolve issues, we would consult the "expert" (rule-based) source on the matter. This worked well in most situations. His friends stopped by regularly to encourage him and to try to speed up the process. Mario had his way of working with me, and I respected his needs and his pace. He debated everything, but we were making real progress. I would have preferred to continue at his pace, but Mario understandably began to get impatient to return home.

Mario had severe OCPD, and I suspected he had secondary Diogenes syndrome as well, because his behaviors and choices translated into squalor and other symptoms, although he was more social and energized than is usual. He could be endearing at times but also frequently lacked a filter, resulting in inappropriate and unnecessarily rude remarks. Being right trumped everything.

Parting with anything was agony. Yet he came to trust me enough that we could come to an agreement on the number of things that would be reasonable to keep, when his collections were too large to store everything.

We used the items at hand to make a bookcase. We shelved his vast vinyl LP collection in the bookcase. This is where Mario and I discovered we had something in common, a love of music. We played albums—swing, big band, blues, jazz, and rock—and talked while we worked. We reminisced about classical, soul, and the blues. Mario was an encyclopedia on the subject of music. We "met" around music, all types of music, including pan flute and fiddling, which I loved too. This meeting of the minds made the second bedroom, the bathroom, and the upstairs hallway easier to deal with and make progress on.

Finally, we arrived at the kitchen. We stuck to our strategy of using the accepted standard for "right." For example, for food, the acceptable standard was the "best before" date. Even though Mario maintained that "best before" dates were just a marketing ploy to increase sales, he realized that we had to use something, and he was becoming increasingly anxious to be home again.

I started by opening one cupboard in the corner. Mario quickly assured me that I didn't have to worry about anything in there. That was his medicine cupboard, and there was nothing in there older than six months. I reminded him that we had agreed to look at everything: "We did say we would check, so let's just be certain."

The first thing I picked up was a 500-tablet bottle of vitamin C. As I looked at it, I had another uneasy feeling, reminiscent of the back steps. The price was an incredible deal, and I wasn't certain if the pharmacy was still in business. Mario continued to reassure me that he had recently (no more than a few months ago) purchased those vitamins. I continued to inspect the bottle for more clarification. As I turned the bottle around and looked at the label on the back, I noticed that the expiration date was August 1986. Unfortunately, that day's date was in May 2008.

I think that Mario genuinely believed what he was saying. This was not my first encounter with people who hoard experiencing severe "time compressing." Clients are often startled by how much their sense of time has warped. As I discuss in chapter 5, there is such a thing as "clock time" versus "subjective, or wishful, time," according to Jane Burka and Lenora Yuen (2008). Mario couldn't believe the expiration date on the bottle and, with what appeared to be genuine confusion, said he had no idea how that had happened. This was only one of the many other expired items in that cupboard, which we continued to deal with by applying our agreed rule.

We continued working our way systematically around the kitchen. When we got to the refrigerator, I had a vague recollection of an indirect, inconsequential comment made at the outset by one of his friends: "Check the fridge." When the comment was made, we couldn't *see* the fridge. Three months later, Fridge Day had arrived.

I approached the fridge door with curiosity. Remember, Mario was not supposed to be living in the house, so when we opened the door, I was surprised to see fresh food and asked him to clarify. He said that the sandwich on a plate and the fresh fruit and veggies were from his nephew's house; they were his provisions for the day.

I looked beyond those items to the other contents in the refrigerator and became immediately concerned with the internal temperature of the fridge, because everything else was the same gray bluish-green color. Mario again attempted to reassure me that the fridge was "just fine."

I put my hand inside the fridge and realized it was not even cool. As the meaning of what I was seeing began to dawn on me, I added, "We also need to check the freezer." Mario made a face and flinched in dismay. I reached for the freezer door, wondering what we would find. On the left side, the freezer was filled with large stacked ice cream containers, front to back. On the right side was meat; the only variety still recognizable was a package of what I thought must be chicken, positioned right at the front.

There was dairy and meat in there, and the temperature wasn't any different from the warm fridge. As I reached for a container of ice cream, he reached across my path trying to block me, saying, "There's nothing to check. Everything is just fine."

By this time, I had the ice cream container in my hands, holding it by the sides, and Mario pressed his hands top and bottom. The pressure on the container caused the melted contents to collapse, and the fingers on my right hand slipped under the lid into a frothy, warm mass. The pressure Mario was putting on the container dislodged the top so that the inside became visible. Mario and I found ourselves looking into frothy green sludge. The smell was sickly sour.

I said, "Mario, look. It is *green*." With defiance in his eyes, he looked back at me and with a straight face said, "I don't know what is wrong with your eyes. It's not green. It's chocolate."

Green or chocolate, it all had to go—along with the mystery meats. When items are a health hazard because they are contaminated, a more intensive discussion is necessary until the situation can be resolved, especially if there is intent to consume these foods.

With the ground floor and garage greatly improved, the barrier preventing Mario from returning home was the untouched basement. On the subject of the basement, Mario and I were at an impasse. Mario felt that everything was essential. The basement, particularly the areas around the heat sources and electrical panel, were unquestionably violating local fire codes and therefore needed to be solved. He was digging in stubbornly, so I suggested we resort to the strategy that had served us well throughout. At this point, Tomas and Louisa had to return home to Italy.

Collaboration with Other Professionals

The local fire inspection branch agreed to come by just to provide an informational session for Mario's benefit and offer us expert advice about what remained to be done before the house was habitable. Mario reluctantly agreed. As much as he did not want their interference, he knew this solution would prevent a bigger problem. He had already had enough previous citations and fines.

When the officer came, he came as an ally. "Well, sir," he said to Mario, "in the kitchen here, you have things on the floor that could present a tripping hazard for you. When you're cooking at the stove, if there's a problem, when you move out of the way, you might trip over it. Before you know it, you have either scalded yourself or spread a fire."

"That would never happen," Mario responded. But most of the fires start either in the kitchen or around other heat sources, like the furnace, hot water tank, or electrical panel.

I suggested we have a look at the area of disagreement, the basement. At the bottom, pathways were tight, the routes to the electrical panel, furnace, and hot water tank were almost impassable. Wires, car parts, and cameras hung everywhere from the rafters, like claws trying to catch those who tried to pass.

The officer took a deep breath and informed Mario that at least 50 percent of the accumulation needed to be removed to make the area fire safe. Mario was unconvinced and unconcerned.

At that point, I stepped in and said, "Mario, this is where we listen, because whatever this inspector says is the way it has to be. We can accept his feedback today unofficially or do it anyway when it becomes official."

Although the officer had arrived as an ally wanting to offer a senior citizen in poor health help and guidance, he left as a concerned municipal official with a clear understanding of the risk that Mario put himself and others in because of his blind need to be right and not take expert advice when he was offered it.

As time advanced, Mario decided he wanted to return home soon. I recommended that my crew and I carry out a 2-day blitz and bring all the remaining areas to code. The dates were set. I told Mario that I would need an itemized list of everything, or categories of things, specifying the numbers that he felt absolutely had to be kept. The list had to be in his handwriting, signed by him, and witnessed by someone he trusted.

In all situations when the client is not going to be present while the intensive work is being done, I always get the client to list the 1, 2, 3 items and categories to be left onsite.

Working with his list, we would then know what, and how much, could be removed. No matter what we thought about what he put on the list, that is what would happen. I gave him my word. If, after the blitz was done following his list, the basement and backyard still contained an excessive accumulation, then we would have to ask the fire department and code enforcement to inspect and approve whether both met code requirements.

Day 1 of the blitz arrived. He had agreed to the plan and left a list of things to be kept. I saw that it was signed and witnessed, but as I read it, I was completely perplexed. Even though it seemed legitimate, it contained only two lines and no description.

I reminded the crew, "We all agreed that we would go by the list, so whether we agree with his wishes or not, we will do what he wanted. This list is so short that there almost certainly will be enough room remaining to set aside anything you discover that you believe might be important, valuable, or you know is a particular love of Mario's. We can determine how many can be kept when we know better how much storage space is left. Mario and I can make a final determination during our future sessions."

Outcomes

The work began. We tore up threadbare wall-to-wall carpets. We vacuumed hardwood floors. We sorted and removed broken and expired items. We cleaned and made the kitchen cupboards functional, reorganizing categories of things to be stored together: dishes with dishes, glasses with glasses, food with food. Everything was washed and cleaned.

We always put sticky notes on each cupboard and drawer so that we know where items are going to be relocated, and in this case, so Mario would be able to find things as he needed them. One of the most frustrating things about extreme cleanups to someone who hoards is that they feel they can't find anything after, combined with the fear that things have been mistakenly discarded.

Hours of work later, we were ready to deal with the basement.

We cleared paths in the basement to 4 feet wide, removing all hanging hazards and relocating some of Mario's cherished items, such as car parts, to his new "consider pile" of things we believed would be special to him and for which there was enough space given the minimal list we had been given to work from. We hauled away duplicates and nonfunctioning appliances, making sure the remaining ones worked. The furnace and work room were culled, cleaned, and set up to be functional and accessible, as was the hot water tank and electrical panel areas.

We then mowed the front lawn and filled his collection of unused flowerpots with plants we had all brought from our own gardens.

The next area to be resolved was the backyard. I threw back a tarp covering one of the large piles of yet unknown items and found myself face to face with an equally startled adult female raccoon that looked as big as a Smart car. It was a toss-up which of us was going to run first. I took a step back and yelled, "Critters!"

The raccoon turned tail and disappeared into the depths of the woodpile. We put our heads together about what to do that wouldn't harm it but would get it to move elsewhere. It was Sunday by now, and all services were closed. We opted for making enough noise to motivate it to leave. All of a sudden, six more heads popped out of the combined collection of piles, with mama reappearing with two large, fat adolescent young. Nine raccoons scampered across the yard in line like a wildlife version of *The Great Race*.

Using the size of the removal truck to gauge the volume of materials, we estimated that we had removed 9 tons from the house and 11 tons from the backyard—oh yes, and nine raccoons.

Extreme cleanups are destabilizing, and even if the person wants them done, they should be done only as an absolute last resort. This was the case for Mario as well. His home, while now to code (even with us having kept more of the things we knew he loved), was disorienting. Even though it was now habitable, it didn't feel like his home. He appreciated having his lovely hardwood floors to see and enjoy—and not having to move the furniture and remove the rugs that had covered them. The smell was gone. He really liked the labeling of the storage areas, for example, closets, cupboards, and drawers. He couldn't reconcile the loss, however, of his stored things in the basement, even though keeping them would have prevented him from returning home. The loss for him was tremendous.

Mario lived for another 18 months. I went to Mario's funeral mass and saw the affection and amazement so many people who knew him felt for this inwardly lonely, emotionally isolated man. I talked with his brother and sister, who now were left with the sad and overwhelming job of finally closing down the house. Going through his stored life was enormously painful for them. Their sadness was immense.

I still have the bottle of vitamin C in my office as a gift from Mario and a memento of his struggle. A person has the right to create the crisis that they know they need, albeit unconsciously, to get the help they know they need (again often unconsciously) to solve it. You need to have and demonstrate genuine respect for the people hoarding and their wishes, always working at their pace.

Mario's Secondary Diogenes Syndrome Existing Symptoms
- Poor insight or comprehension of public health or safety
- Distrust of society or strangers
- Paranoia or general suspiciousness
- Excessive hoarding or collecting of household items and waste
- Obsessive-compulsive tendencies
- Unsanitary or unsafe living conditions
- Poor nutrition or diet
- Unwillingness to accept outside help or intervention
- Hostility and aggression toward others
- A distorted concept of reality

Typical Secondary Diogenes Symptoms Not Present
- Aloofness or detachment (Mario did live his life almost entirely on his own terms and from his unique perspective, though)
- Extreme social anxiety (Mario did live with anxiety but not socially)
- Skin conditions due to uncleanliness (not present)
  (Huizen 2016)

Andre

Synopsis

Andre was a software engineer who had just taken early retirement at the age of 57 from a local IT company. He left work because of mental health and work relationship issues.

Andre's cognitive intactness was impaired, which added a layer of complexity, preventing him from fully understanding how deteriorated his living conditions were, and how at risk he was living in such conditions. His lack of engagement was less about willingness and more about his capacity to comprehend.

Problem Overview

The condition he was living in had been discovered when he called a community service agency providing discounted services to seniors. He told them that he felt he needed a "little bit of housekeeping" help. When the worker went in, she discovered a dangerous situation of senile squalor. She suggested that Andre call me.

Background

When I visited him to complete an assessment, I found the ground floor of his small detached home completely impassable, with piled furniture and newspapers. He lived mostly in the upstairs, accessible by a steep flight of stairs, also impassable, with litter, papers, books, and clothes. Upstairs, all floor areas were covered with books, newspapers, and other debris. It was necessary to climb over piles to maneuver through the home. The kitchen was badly deteriorated with grime and biodegradables. The washroom was strewn with untended personal hygiene byproducts. The toilet, sink, bathtub, floor, and walls were in squalid condition.

This was an extreme health and safety hazard.

Given the extreme condition of the house, I could not agree to work with him unless he agreed to stay with his sister, who lived elsewhere in town, until the house was returned to a safe and healthy condition. I explained my concerns about the lack of a 3-foot pathway throughout the house and sufficient open space around the furnace, hot water tank, and electrical panel. Once this was re-established there would have to be an inspection to verify the structural integrity and electrical safety of the premises, given possible damage to both during the time that such a heavy accumulation had existed. Andre understood, disagreed with my assessment of risk, but reluctantly agreed to make arrangements with his sister immediately.

Client's Initial Perspective

Andre had no clear appreciation of the true conditions he had been living in.

Therapeutic Plan

The work necessary was going to require the assistance of a trained crew.

Intervention

The downstairs level contained an impassible jumble of stored furniture that had to be sorted, allocated permanent places, made available for a friend, or donated to a local charity of his choosing. The dirt basement held his oil furnace. The kitchen was strewn with stale, rotting foods and other perishables. Dishes, bowls, cups, glassware, and silverware were coated with mold from deteriorated, caked-on food, which covered every flat surface, including the floor. The front room upstairs was piled knee deep with toppled piles of newspapers and flyers strewn everywhere. Soiled clothing and books added to the chaotic jumble. Navigating down the hall to his bedroom and bathroom meant stumbling and sliding on a floor covered in unstable piles, listing unsteadily against the walls.

The first room on the right was Andre's bedroom. It was in a similar condition. His mattress was made of carefully placed couch cushions from reclaimed throwaways he had obtained, I learned later, from other people's trash. All flat surfaces served as storage for random collections of largely nonbedroom items. The bathroom was squalid with dried human body fluids and excrement. This clearly evidenced the true level of mental and physical deterioration Andre had reached.

On seeing the bathroom, my treatment plan for him changed to include a thorough assessment by geriatric mental health specialists.

The second bedroom farther down the hall was used as a combination office and storage area. It was completely filled three-dimensionally, completely blocking his second emergency exit option on that floor.

Strategies

As we completed the blitz, I came to fully understand that Andre had been living for a long time unidentified and untreated with secondary Diogenes syndrome, complicated by what I assessed later met the clinical criteria for Asperger syndrome.

Through the blitz, Andre's profound relationship with paper became increasingly clear. The blitz took two 12-hour days. During that time, Andre would not allow any of the paper to go to recycling. He wanted all the papers put into plastic totes, which he purchased for this purpose. He was resolute. Every piece had to be taken to a storage unit he had arranged. While working on gathering, packing, and getting ready to store all the paper products, Andre and I began to talk about his relationship with paper. He shared with me that he actually had another storage unit already filled with paper that he went to every day to just sit and "be" with his paper, to hold it and feel it. He didn't necessarily read it. The relationship he desired with paper was more tactile and kinesthetic.

In follow-up sessions, it became evident that it was unusually difficult to develop a positive therapeutic relationship with him. I would bring coffee with me as a way to transition to our work tasks. We would often have it on the front steps while debriefing about pressing topics. Then we would go into the house, now just moderately cluttered, and we would select an area to work on. Usually this included the removal of papers, reorganization of items, boxing, getting totes, putting things away. Andre and I worked best with me cueing him about what to do next as we progressed, returning one room at a time to usable space.

We did this every 2 weeks for 4 months to ensure that he maintained the safety established through the blitz. No matter what the item, a fundamental aspect of his relationship with it was kinesthetic and tactile.

Outcomes

Andre could not relate to people, not even his sister. Discussions and conversation were one-sided. The friend he reported having, when he wanted to share some furniture from the upstairs second bedroom, turned out not to be factual, which is why the pieces never left.

In the end, all that he would allow was for us to make him safe for a while. A time soon came when Andre was no longer willing to continue.

Conclusion

I lost track of Andre after that. The prognosis for Andre was poor from the outset. Intensive therapeutic care involving geriatric mental health specialists, as well as treatment by me for hoarding disorder, was what was needed to make any even mildly sustainable progress. Unfortunately, Andre would not accept a referral or allow me to bring him to geriatric-related care. I believe that a diversified treatment care team is the only combination that stands any chance of helping Andre live better.

I remain open to help Andre should he decide to contact me in the future.

Andre's Secondary Diogenes Syndrome Existing Symptoms

- Poor insight or comprehension of public health or safety
- Distrust of society or strangers
- Paranoia or general suspiciousness
- Excessive hoarding or collecting of household items and waste
- Obsessive-compulsive tendencies
- Unsanitary or unsafe living conditions
- Poor nutrition or diet
- Unwillingness to accept outside help or intervention
- Hostility and aggression toward others
- A distorted concept of reality
- Aloofness or detachment
- Extreme social anxiety
- Skin conditions due to uncleanliness
  (Huizen 2016)

Key Messages

1 *To those who hoard to a severe degree*: Understand when you must accept help because regulatory officials are setting requirements. You need to accept the help you need to meet the requirements for the time limits set. Do your best to work with officials, not against them. Otherwise, you delay the inevitable and create an adversarial relationship. It is often *overwhelming* and *frustrating*.

2 The best kind of help and support are people (not necessarily professionals) who:
   ✔ are informed and experienced with the requirements to be met *or* are willing to find out about them;
   ✔ have a *genuine* respect for others;
   ✔ do not believe that they have the answers for other people;
   ✔ are willing to respect, accept, and support your choices as long as those choices do not maintain the excessive accumulation or health or safety concerns; and
   ✔ are willing to be guided by the expert source, such as expiration dates or input from local authorities, when there is a difference of opinion about the fact of something being a health or safety concern.

3 *To those who want to help those who hoard severely*: Keep the lines of communication open and nonjudgmental; but reflecting reality is essential. In my experience, this often requires shifting to adopting a harm-reduction approach. It is at times *overwhelming* and often *frustrating*. Monitor yourself. Set appropriate and healthy boundaries and limits and exercise good self-care.

CHAPTER 11

Professional at Work, Powerless at Home

Secret Lives

Nothing in the world can take the place of perseverance. Talent will not; nothing is more common than unsuccessful men with talent. Genius will not; unrewarded genius is almost a proverb. Education will not; the world is full of educated derelicts. Persistence and determination are omnipotent.

CALVIN COOLIDGE

Nancy

Nancy, a tenured medical school professor and part-time practicing psychiatrist, and I first met during the break at a professional function, where she self-disclosed that she severely hoarded and had spent many tens of thousands of dollars in an effort to get control of her buying and saving compulsions. Many years later, Nancy called me to ask for my help.

Synopsis

Nancy was living a secret life at home while trying desperately to maintain her professional standards at work with her students and patients. The late-night shopping channel purchases calmed her in the short term, gave her something to look forward to, and temporarily filled the void inside her. The consequence of nightly retail therapy was impending bankruptcy, which only escalated her need for more escape through ever-increasing retail therapy.

Problem Overview

Life had taken another downturn. Her twenty-five-year marriage was ending. The house had to be sold because the debt caused by Nancy's hoarding behavior meant that she was not in a financial position to buy out her husband's share.

Background

During our first session while conducting the assessment, Nancy gave me a tour of her 5,000-square-foot home. The living room and dining room were vast rooms filled with clothing, china, boxed jewelry, linens, paintings, children's toys, personal care products, and paper all mixed together in chaotic piles.

The kitchen, hallways, family room, and sunroom were 60 percent filled three-dimensionally with loose personal paper, furniture, food products, empty plastic containers, old magazines, and newspapers, again stored chaotically on all flat surfaces, including the stove and in piles on chairs and the floor.

The basement held her collections, which were professionally organized and stored. They were sorted, packed on shelves, and in stacks six totes high, wall to wall, completely covering all wall surfaces. Nancy was in extreme debt, living paycheck to paycheck because of her compulsions. She couldn't stop buying.

The third floor was approximately 50 percent filled with stacked, packed totes four high. The area most stressful for her to show me was the downstairs spare room and the triple garage, which was three-dimensionally 60 percent filled with unopened DHL, shopping channel, Amazon, FedEx, Purolator, and UPS boxes, to the extent that her Mercedes had to be parked outside in the driveway at all times.

Living paycheck to paycheck, with such a high overhead, was enormously stressful for her. Online packages arrived in multiples daily and added significantly to her stress and anxiety, despite the pleasure and the rush buying had provided just two nights before, during her late-night online shopping activities. Next-day delivery reinforced her compulsive buying by providing almost immediate gratification when the purchases arrived. Avoidance and denial calmed the onset of ambivalence and regret by adding unopened packages to the rising accumulation in the triple garage.

Despite the extraordinary stress she was under, she remained caring and diligent in her professional life as a practitioner. I heard her speak to students and patients on the phone from time to time as she returned messages. She was tireless and patient about providing timely responses to their stresses, concerns, and needs. She spent whatever time was necessary talking to them and helping people manage their moods and medications, no matter how late or what fragile condition she was in personally. She spoke to them gently, warmly, and respectfully. She was skilled and effective at compartmentalizing.

Client's Initial Perspective

Nancy was under extraordinary stress. Options and solutions were running out. In her overwhelmed state, she knew she had created a problem she couldn't solve by herself. She was desperate for help and knew it was not just a question of cleaning up.

Therapeutic Plan

I reluctantly agreed to carry out therapeutic decluttering of the environment before the normal process of intensive counseling. I agreed on the condition that we would continue with counseling once the sale preparation was completed. The first priority then became getting the sorting, donating, packing, and moving offsite to storage completed to make the house ready for painting, staging, and sale as quickly as possible. It was clear that an intensive immediate turnaround of the home's condition was a clear priority for practical financial reasons.

Intervention

The blitz work began.

Strategies

Over 2 weeks, we moved all totes to offsite storage. Then we opened and packed up the shopping channel boxes in the garage. Nancy no longer remembered clearly what they contained and wanted to put all of them in storage so that after moving, we could make decisions later. Based on the contents, there had to be hundreds of thousands of dollars' worth of merchandise in those packages, acquired exclusively through late-night shopping channel or online auction activities.

Dealing with the extreme volume of clothing was a much more difficult matter because Nancy randomly sewed valuables into the hems, pockets, and seams of her clothing. During sorting and packing, we discovered and retrieved valuables that might have gone to donation by mistake. This made the sorting process long and laborious.

She had a severe fear of break-ins now that she was living alone. Her niece came to stay occasionally to comfort her. She was unable to realize that such frequent deliveries by UPS or the shopping channel network couriers might well make her a target for such a threat.

Outcomes

Nancy immediately moved out of the house to keep it pristine following the painting and staging. She lived and slept in her office. Unfortunately, this was not the last setback Nancy would experience.

Conclusion

Counseling to prevent relapse lost its importance to her. I remain very concerned about her current ability to curb her buying habits.

Key Messages

- Hoarding disorder respects no one regardless of financial, educational, or social status.
- Even those who seem to have it all carry their own burdens.

CHAPTER 12

Disabled in Dire Straits

The question is not how to get cured, but how to live.

JOSEPH CONRAD

HOARDING BEHAVIOR CAN HAVE ITS FIRST ONSET when individuals develop a health condition that impairs their cognitive functioning, such as brain injury, stroke, and many other conditions. The condition can also impair their physical functioning and mobility. Alternatively, people may have been living with severe hoarding for some time, but the onset of a disease is the first time they are willing to reach out for help. The disease simply adds to the risk that they have always been living with, bringing it to a moment of truth, because their coping strategies no longer work. In this chapter's story, Cliff's life came to a point where he could no longer avoid or rationalize the Level 5 hoarding severity that he had been living with for more than 20 years. He could no longer turn to his career as the basis for "housekeeping matters" getting ahead of him.

Cliff

Synopsis

Cliff was an accomplished lawyer who developed amyotrophic lateral sclerosis, or ALS (a.k.a. Lou Gehrig's disease). Unfortunately, he had also been living with obsessive-compulsive personality disorder (OCPD) as well as some degree of obsessive-compulsive disorder (OCD) for most of his life. This influenced him to live with absolutes. His absolute focus was on his career, leaving little of him available at day's end. Home life was not a priority; therefore, he absolutely did not attend to it. This resulted in everything else not associated with work being left undone, including dealing with the clutter. Everything in his life that he could influence had to be the way he wanted it to be. The lack of balance in his life had created Risk Level 5 conditions by the time I was called to intervene. As his health and decision-making abilities deteriorated, his level of independent living and ability to enjoy his collections diminished as well.

Problem Overview

Cliff was a 75-year-old lawyer recently diagnosed with ALS when he contacted me. He'd had a long and successful career as a criminal defense litigator. The reason he called me for help was at the insistence of his niece, because he was falling frequently in his home.

Background

When I arrived, I initially found a deferential man with southern charm who was facing an imminent and dramatic progressive deterioration in his health. His deterioration would result in him having to give up his beloved career and an independent life. He resided in a large home but only lived in three rooms on the ground floor, which were hoarded to a Level 4. The rest of the house was a Level 5+. (See "What is Your Level of Risk?" in chapter 2 for a definition of what constitutes each hoarding level.)

Cliff's doctor and his niece, who lived in England, were the only people who knew about his hoarding. He had a wealth of friends and colleagues, none of whom had any idea of the unsafe, unhealthy living conditions Cliff went back to at the end of every otherwise successful, passionately lived day. Both his doctor and his niece shared equal concern for his health and safety, and they were putting increasing pressure on him to get help for his hoarding disorder. They considered it a priority for him to move to a more manageable living arrangement, to sort out the important items, and to clean out the remainder.

Client's Initial Perspective

Cliff shared that, in the past two weeks, he'd had three serious falls in his home. He relied on a walker for safe mobility, but because of the conditions in his three rooms, he wasn't able to maneuver his walker safely. The condition of the home also meant that for the past 23 years, no one had visited him. Sleeping and the occasional meal were the only activities he did at home.

In anticipation of my visit, Cliff opened up to one friend. They had already removed 98 large contractor-sized bags of garbage from the three rooms. Yet, at the time of my visit, the living space was still at an extreme level of hoarding. A pivotal conversation occurred, during our initial session, that defined the central issue of Cliff's hoarding behavior.

I asked Cliff questions to determine which of the three points where a bottleneck normally occurs in hoarding situations applied to him.

To the question "Is acquiring excessively a problem for you?" he answered, "No."

"Is it that once you have something, you have a strong impulse to save it?" I asked. He replied, "No."

"Would you say that making decisions about what to let go of is the issue?" Cliff replied, "No."

"Can you see a contradiction in the fact that you have just removed more than 90 bags of garbage from your house, and it is still cluttered enough that you are falling?" I asked. He broke out into a little grin and said, "That's probably the work we have before us."

Therapeutic Plan

There were no clear and accessible pathways through the rooms. The height of the accumulation was approximately 4 feet in most places. Any partial pathways were so narrow that they were not safe, especially for someone dependent on a walker for safe mobility. Access to various areas of the three rooms required Cliff to step on, or over, things to navigate.

Cliff had a bed that was old and had collapsed in numerous places. He rarely put sheets on it, so it was stained with sweat and caked with dead skin. He had one desk with broken drawers, one salvageable bookcase, some foldable occasional tables, a floor lamp, odds and ends of kitchen utensils, and a few portable radios. Cliff's living spaces also held a significant degree of biodegradables, with accompanying fruit flies, ants, and silverfish.

It is not unusual for depression and heightened anxiety to set in when a person receives a life-changing diagnosis. This was particularly true for Cliff, because the diagnosis meant he would have to give up a much-loved career, lifestyle, and independence.

Cliff's focus on his career was intense and scrupulously precise. This level of focus was in extreme contrast to his apartment. In his living environment if something was dropped, spilled, or broken, it was left where it happened. When he went out, however, he was immaculate and impeccably dressed and groomed.

Intervention

After intensive consultation, Cliff and I developed a plan. He would move into a senior's residence, which would be outfitted precisely to his specifications, with completely new belongings that he would choose with the help of his hoarding-aware friend. Nothing except his memorabilia, books, papers, clothing, and shoes from his current home would go with him due to the condition of everything else.

There was extensive work to do to get the home ready for sale.

Strategies

My team and I went through everything. We cleared the accumulation away from the walls by piling it in the center of the room and set up sorting boxes in the living room along the walls.

Cliff and I planned to go through the boxes during future counseling sessions, once he moved to his new residence. It took four months to get the home ready for sale. Because of the safety issue and his quickly deteriorating health, there was significant pressure to complete the move. For this reason, most of the boxes went to storage.

 Storage units are normally used as a harm-reduction strategy, a short-term stopgap solution while transitioning to a new living situation.

Interestingly, Cliff had almost the same amount of space in the senior's residence he chose as he did in his three rooms. The difference between the residences was that the senior's apartment offered him an excellent quality of life, with enriching resources and services, where he could enjoy the fellowship of his new peers, the pool, and excellent food prepared by a Cordon Bleu chef, while regaling new friends with legal and travel stories.

Every year, Cliff's one indulgence had been to take his niece on an extravagant trip to tour castles and cathedrals around the world, often to new and exotic locations. He felt that each place "required" the purchase of memorabilia. These items were symbols of a life well lived and made up the vast majority of the items he kept. The sheer volume of this collection, however, prevented ongoing access to the memories, which had been the point of buying the items. Together, we brainstormed how to keep these memories accessible and decided to have everything scanned and transferred onto a large capacity external hard drive. I have done this for many clients, and it lessens their sense of loss of happy and meaningful memories.

We helped him decide which pieces of furniture he needed that would fit from a life well lived and worked out a floor plan to assist him and his friend to make workable choices.

Even with these lifestyle improvements, Cliff was losing capacity quickly and experiencing personally embarrassing incidents that would not be acceptable to the residence. We put together a plan to protect his privacy and address these issues on a priority basis, so he wouldn't be shamed and could remain in the residence as long as possible.

Because his illness affected his sleep patterns, he was often hungry when meals were not available. As a result, we agreed to do a little shopping for him. My clutter coaches developed a specialized shopping list because of his increasing difficulty with swallowing.

Letting go of books was especially difficult because he wanted to read and reread them many times, which meant holding on to more books on all topics than his space allowed. Once he finished rereading them, he was willing to pass them on, but only to specific people he felt should have them.

As a perfectionist and procrastinator, Cliff's hoarding was an outward manifestation of the many other unfinished parts of his life—the books he wanted to read but wouldn't devote the time to read; things he wanted to do but didn't prioritize. He wanted love and relationships, but instead, he gave all his energy, time, and passion to proving his self-worth. With all the ways he found to prove himself, he had no time or energy for a well-balanced life, and so he remained a lonely man with no personal life.

Cliff's medical prognosis was dire and progressive. His future was no more than a few years.

Outcomes

The goal for Cliff was to set up a lifestyle that would support him; give him ease, pleasure, and dignity; and make whatever he loved—his books, papers, and tapes—readily available to him in an accessible format. Cliff continued to fall, with increased frequency and severity, resulting in many hospitalizations.

Collaboration with Other Professionals

My crew and I continued to work closely with the residence staff to mitigate Cliff's growing anxiety about no longer being in control while keeping him safe and as engaged in life as possible. We made sure that even as his mobility and decision making declined, his exacting preferences were respected. Despite the profound loss of control in his health and personal functioning, we supported Cliff to feel in control of what happened to his things.

Conclusion

Ultimately, the residence could not accept the liability any longer, and at the end of his last hospitalization for a fall and injury, he had to be relocated to a long-term-care facility. With this move, Cliff began to deteriorate much faster than anticipated. His demeanor and mindset also declined. I continue to keep in touch with him through email.

Key Messages

- Sometimes the best care does not result in a happy ending, and it is necessary to redefine success.
- Working with individuals who live with multiple disabilities that include hoarding disorder requires a multifaceted and holistic approach because of the complexity of these situations. Being able and willing to think outside the box is an asset.

CHAPTER 13

Home Is Where the Heart Is

Disconnecting from Your Environment

I believe your atmosphere and your surroundings
create a mind state for you.

THEOPHILUS LONDON

SOME OF MY CLIENTS, INCLUDING THE YOUNG WOMAN in this chapter's story, tell me that while they were never the best at housekeeping, their cluttering habits got worse and finally met the criteria for hoarding disorder when they became emotionally disconnected from their environment. They no longer saw where they lived as a home. The question is: What would it take for them to reconnect and feel that their home is a safe and happier place, and would that reverse the hoarding?

Raedeen

Synopsis

Raedeen is a young woman who never felt that she quite fit anywhere; not at home, not in school, not at work, and not where she currently lived. The question "Who am I?" became more difficult because there was no safe, calm place where she could figure out this most basic of life's questions, her identity.

Problem Overview

Raedeen had disconnected from her environment. When in quick succession she lost relationships that made her feel connected—her father, her mother, and her pets—she lost her compass and her way. She felt like she was just drifting.

Background

Raedeen was a young woman in her early forties who left a message on my answering machine in a tentative voice, telling me she needed my help but didn't believe that she could let me into her apartment. When I called her back, we agreed to meet at a neutral location. I told her that we could discuss her situation, and if she felt that she was more comfortable after that, and if time permitted, we could go back to her apartment, she could give me a tour, and we could make a plan from there.

Client's Initial Perspective

We met at a local coffee shop over tea. She was impeccably dressed and well groomed, wearing full makeup. We talked for about 45 minutes while she outlined her background and current situation. She was single and had lived alone in the same apartment for the past eight years. She worked full time as a railroad employee. Despite the fact that Raedeen was somewhat anxious, she calmed significantly during our meeting and, in the end, agreed to show me her apartment so we could make a realistic intervention plan.

Therapeutic Plan

It became clear that our therapeutic plan needed to address the following situations.

Raedeen had a ritual that she followed on entering and leaving her apartment. Part of the ritual was to check and recheck that no one was coming out of another apartment or coming around the corner from the elevator. This ritual prevented others from seeing that she couldn't open her door more than 16 inches.

We squeezed into the apartment. There was only one partially free armchair in the middle of the living room. At one end of the living room, blocking most of the window, was a pile seven feet high. It was made up of a chaotic mix of exercise equipment, retail bags filled with unopened purchases, clothing, boxed sets of cooking equipment, dishware, canned foods, and bagged dry garbage. All flat surfaces were covered with high piles of mixed items. There was no clear floor space and most piles were at least a foot high.

Raedeen was not able to cook in the kitchen. Counters were filled with old, moldy, opened, semiemptied food cans and other containers. The sink was filled with water, now gray, and topped with a layer of scum. Dishes and cookware poked out of the sink in places. All counters were piled with largely combustible items. Raedeen told me that she hadn't prepared food in a long time and had no intention to do so in the foreseeable future until the kitchen returned to normal.

The bathroom was cluttered with personal care products and makeup. Items such as empty toilet paper rolls, items that had fallen during use, hairpins, shower cap, pajamas, dropped toothpaste tubes, dental floss, and bags of personal care products were stored in the tub. Raedeen shared that she used to bathe and shower frequently and that she temporarily moved things around to make it possible.

The bedroom was three-dimensionally 60 percent full. It was impossible to tell the size of the bed because one side was against the wall and the piles at the top and on the other side went straight up from and over the remaining side. The only access point to the bed was from the bottom.

Intervention

During our initial discussion, Raedeen told me that the apartment had only been developing into its current condition for the past four years. Before that, while she was somewhat disorganized, she had always managed to maintain things well enough that no one had commented.

As we moved forward over the following two years of counseling, Raedeen said that while hoarding hadn't previously been an issue, a diagnosis of borderline personality disorder had been suspected and confirmed later in adolescence. For most of her life, she had felt insecure and uncertain about herself. Her social interactions were often awkward, and her relationships were not appropriate. There was always drama and crisis in her life, even in her closest relationships.

She realized that her life was out of control and said that she wanted to do something about it.

Raedeen told me that while she had never excessively acquired in the past, for as long as she could remember, she did hold on to things and took care of her things. After many counseling sessions I came to believe that she had undiagnosed obsessive-compulsive disorder (OCD). She told me that when she was younger, she liked to fold her pajamas perfectly and wrap them in tissue paper in her drawer. Further discussion revealed that she soothed numerous other compulsions with rituals.

Raedeen left school early because of difficulties with depression, bullying by peers, and the onset of substance abuse. Later, she returned as an adult and earned her high school equivalency. She was a remarkable, intelligent woman, but she just could not get along with people. She was hypersensitive and seemed to repeatedly attract (or create) interpersonal problems.

Raedeen's mother and father had died within two years of each other a few years earlier. She had been very close to her father. When he died, she felt everything come apart. She began to isolate herself. Emotionally she felt that she had hit bottom. She stopped maintaining her living environment and dealing with everyday life. She felt herself slipping into a deep depression and felt like she never really came out of it. The accumulation in the apartment had worsened a great deal. By the time I met her, she was totally overwhelmed.

After taking time off work to restabilize, when she returned, she felt disconnected and "not quite there." She forced herself to go to work reliably to avoid more problems and to survive financially. She got into frequent minor conflicts with her colleagues. She felt unable to resolve anything, so she began to pretend that nothing had happened; the latest problem was just her habit of exaggerating the worst. One day while sitting in her chair, she suddenly saw things very differently and found herself asking, "When did this happen?"

When their parents had passed away, Raedeen's brother, Dennis, had taken all the family possessions because she couldn't face dealing with closing down the house and settling her dad's estate. During counseling, we made a plan and a list of the items that she would especially like to have to replace the "student quality" furniture she currently had. With few exceptions, Dennis agreed. Before the furniture could be delivered, Raedeen was determined to clean the apartment up, repaint, and make it a nice habitable living space.

Strategies

Although I was concerned that, living in such a compromised environment, Raedeen not use the heat source, there was no accumulation close to the hot water tank, no furnace, and she was more than willing to quickly reduce the overall accumulation to a Level 2 (see "What Is Your Level of Risk?" in chapter 2). Without these changes to her living conditions, I would have informed her that I needed to ask the local fire inspection branch to conduct an inspection and approve the apartment for occupancy, because of the possible risk to herself and to other building residents.

Raedeen was happy to agree, and so we carried out an intensive cleanup, referred to as a *blitz*. We turned the apartment around within a month. We discarded the ruined furniture. Raedeen painted. Dennis delivered the furniture from their parents' home. She and I continued to work on the kitchen and bedroom. We removed boxed items to storage so that the health and safety concerns were eliminated quickly. We did our sorting from the storage unit and had all remaining rooms sorted out and set up again within the next three months.

Outcomes

I worked with Raedeen for about a year and a half. As part of our continued counseling, it was important to determine why Raedeen had disconnected from the apartment. She discovered that she could not live authentically in that apartment. It was not even minimally soundproofed, leaving her feeling like she was living in a fish bowl— unsafe, exposed, continually anxious, and unsettled.

Collaboration with Other Professionals

As comorbid factors became more complex, I suggested that we form an extended care team by including her previous psychiatrist, who had seen her intermittently throughout her adolescence and early adult life.

Conclusion

Raedeen was not interested in finding a new apartment, so we reorganized the layout. We switched the allocation of space between rooms so that her socializing areas were not against walls adjoining other units. Over time, these changes helped give Raedeen the daily sense of privacy, safety, and reassurance that she desired.

Key Messages for Helpers and Professionals

- If possible, be flexible about where the initial meeting takes place when the person has significant anxiety or feels otherwise unsafe.
- Be clear, respectful, and consistent when health and safety issues are concerned.
- Wear N95 masks, booties, nitrile gloves, and protective eyewear when necessary. Model and promote appropriate self-care. Leave some supplies for the resident to use while doing homework tasks, if possible.
- Where heat sources are compromised by accumulation, openly discuss what alternatives need to be incorporated: for example, microcooking for only a defined period and premade food until uncertain or contaminated food prep surfaces are dealt with.
- Encourage residents to maintain a clear bed. People have been injured and even killed by items toppling onto them while in bed in hoarded environments.
- Develop a care team of other professionals if comorbid factors become varied and complex.
- Be respectful and nonjudgmental of diverse lifestyles that do not affect vulnerable others.

- Listen to people to learn about and respect the actual barriers they are experiencing. Help alleviate their expressed barriers. Unless their health and safety or that of others is directly involved, their experience is the agenda.
- Be ready for and manage your reactions to unusual events, such as a cat in the freezer. Do not exaggerate, discount, or minimize these events. With the person's permission, make sure all other professionals involved are made aware. Promote an open communication policy.
- Be clear and firm about your obligation to report if sufficient risk levels exist for the person or others.

Guiding Principles

1 Address and resolve emergency safety issues first.
2 Address and resolve health issues immediately following safety concerns.
3 Help people who hoard realize their vision of how they want their spaces to be.
4 Model appropriate, healthy mental, physical, emotional, and spiritual behavior.
5 Respect your own boundaries and limits amid what sometimes become confusing and chaotic circumstances.

CHAPTER 14

Collateral Damage

Adult Children of Hoarders, Seniors Living with Hoarders, and Neighbors

> No one man can, for any considerable time,
> wear one face to himself and another to
> the multitude without finally getting bewildered
> as to which one is the true one.
>
> **NATHANIEL HAWTHORNE**

HOARDING AFFECTS NOT ONLY THE INDIVIDUALS who suffer from the disorder, but also the people who surround them. Those living at risk are children in a hoarded home (even as adults who have left home), the elderly living with someone who hoards, and anyone living nearby. Being part of a hoarded environment increases the danger to physical safety, as well as to mental and emotional well-being. This chapter examines the collateral damage to the people who are affected by hoarding disorder.

The Forgotten Children

Synopsis

Adult children of hoarders often say that they felt displaced, that they took second importance to the "stuff." What is it like to grow up with so many piles and pathways? What effects did this have on them growing up? What does it take to get past this experience to have rewarding, positive, caring relationships and self-confidence in their adult lives? Many of these parents had complex burdens and challenges, with one or more parent hoarding, and the repercussions on the children vary.

Problem Overview

It is important to understand that parents who hoard are not bad human beings who should have just cleaned up but are complicated, struggling individuals, as many of us are, who often unintentionally left their children with a legacy of pain and unresolved issues of loss and impaired self-esteem.

Helen's Problem Overview (In Her Own Words)

My parents hoarded differently. My father collected cars, metal, and tools, and these items were often external to the house and all over the yard. Because these items were more visible to people, we were usually teased at school about my father's hoard. My mother's hoard was all inside the house. I felt isolated because we didn't have friends come over or have birthday parties. We knew what was inside the house, but we never spoke about it to people outside the home. You can't have close friendships when this is happening. You have to keep it secret.

Client's Initial Perspective

The three words that capture my growing-up years are insecurity, isolation, and confusion. Because of the situation in my house, which included both parents who suffered from hoarding disorder, I felt extremely isolated.

Background

As a child I felt insecure, and this usually stemmed from the blowups around who was cleaning up, or who wasn't cleaning up. There were always fights around the house about who was not doing their job properly. My mother would complain that my father was spending too much money on the stuff he was bringing home for the yard. And my father would complain that the dishes weren't being done and the floor wasn't swept.

I was also confused because how we lived seemed normal. The only way I knew it was bad was by what was said on the school bus. I remember kids laughing on the bus about my dad, and I never knew what to say, to whom. You can't draw in friends because you are afraid to say anything about your life.

I didn't feel very safe, because I didn't know what the rules were, and this proved to be a big burden for a child. I was an outspoken child who often got in trouble and called out the "elephant in the room." This approach did not really do me any favors. I have two siblings, and each one of us dealt with our situation differently. My sister became very quiet and isolated and didn't really talk much at all. I was open and outspoken, and my brother tried to use humor and took on the role of peacemaker.

Many of my dad's friends had what we called *steel gardens*, which is the accumulation of metal. The houses we visited were very similar to ours. So, for the first few years, I just thought this was normal. As I grew and started to have problems with insecurity and felt the need to speak out against things, I would visit my grandparents and see that other people did things differently.

As I got older, I had a hard time trying to justify my situation to people on the school bus. When I was young, I would just laugh along with them, but as the kids got older and crueler, I would speak up and get into fights as I tried to defend my parents. My sister would hide in the corner of the bus, and my brother would start joking with them.

I was trained to never throw out anything. It was a sin to throw anything out because you might need it later. As an adult, I had no training on how to throw out anything, and I tended to go from "I am going to chuck it all" to nothing. I get frozen and can't deal with it.

My parents divorced when I was in grade 3. After my mother left, there were lots of predatory people around the house because my dad suffered from alcoholism as well as hoarding.

My dad was a very dominant and strict person. He liked to control everything, every aspect of his children's lives and every aspect of anyone around him. He felt that his opinions were right, and no one else was right. He was a hyper person who did not stay still for more than 15 minutes at a time, and he was always moving around. He was never diagnosed with anything, but I often felt that the drinking was part of the self-medicating to try to take care of the tendency to be hyper.

Outcomes

I stayed at home until I was 14. My outspokenness always got me more attention than it should have, so at 14 I went to live with my mom. I soon realized that I couldn't stay in her severely hoarded home, and so I was out on my own by age 15.

When I moved to my mom's, it was under very stressful circumstances. She was very casual in her expectations. She thought that children could basically raise themselves, and then she would just send them out into the world. I was a young person who was left with absolutely no guidance. After leaving my father's house, where there was total control, and moving into an environment where there was no guidance, I think what happened to me was an expectation that I was going to live in this hoarded environment and be able to clean it. Mom was hoarding quite extensively at this point, due to loss and other emotional issues.

I didn't have anyone to talk to. At this point, my sister had moved away from my mother's house, and my brother was still living with Dad.

So as a young, confused teenager, I decided to tackle that countertop in the kitchen that was perpetually covered with stuff and get it tidied up for her once and for all. I also knew that I was going to have to tell her where I put all her things when she got home. If I did get a burst of energy to clean up, she would get very upset that the old teapot, which was cracked and broken, was not where it should be on the counter.

At the time, I couldn't deal psychologically with all the anxieties my mother had. She was an unstable bipolar individual who struggled inside and outside institutions, and she was unstable for many years during my life. Situations could flare up quickly and erratically. I never knew what would trigger the upset and crisis about the stuff. As a child I was stuck on the all-or-nothing principle. Do I chuck everything, or do I sort through the items?

Her bed was always loaded with clothes and books. One of my chores was to make the bed, but how do you do this with all the stuff on the bed? If I moved the stuff from the bed, then there would be a blowup about why the stuff was moved. For me at that point, it was just easier to move out than deal with it.

There were three kids in the family. We lived with my father until we were close to 15. Mom then took each one of us in turn. My sister and I moved out on our own within a year. My brother moved back to my father's. I believe she [my mom] suffered from anxiety and ADD, but she also had a huge heart and was a giver. She would volunteer all her time for various causes, but this would take time away from herself, her house, and her kids. She was also susceptible to bargains and discounts. As a parent on a budget, if she saw a good sale, she would buy 20 of the item, even if she did not need it at the exact time. She would buy it if she might need it in the future, and now she got it at a cheaper price. Often she did not use the items before their expiration date. And unfortunately, this buying approach often used up a great proportion of the spending budget.

My dad, although he had his own "outside the home" hoarding issues, could not deal with my mom's mental health issues. He could not stand that the inside of the house was untidy and that he was not in control of her mental health. At one point she went to a hospital for electroshock therapy, and I think he could not deal with that because he did not have any control over it. My mother, on the other hand, has always been subservient to a dominant personality. She is easily mowed over by a stronger personality. The divorce was devastating for my mother, and her hoarding escalated. As soon as she came out of the hospital, from that point onward, she was constantly hoarding. I think it was because she was so lonely, and she was not guided as she felt she needed to be guided.

Every time she would go into the hospital, she would have no belongings. She would try to build a home with a few clothing items, or she would have to rebuild a home with her mother, or at a boarding house. This was devastating for her.

I did have a champion in my court as I grew up. His name was Bob and he was a next-door neighbor. As well, my uncle took over the father role when I was older.

Conclusion

Helen has had to overcome many serious challenges as an adult. She has had the support of a long-term partner, but she prizes her independence because she has always handled life challenges on her own, so she continues to manage on her own.

Mireia's Problem Overview (In Her Own Words)

When I was little, before I was old enough to be invited to other children's homes, I remember being upset a lot because things were so messy and confusing, and my toys always seemed to be lost. As I look back, even when I went to school, I never remember having any friends to play with. My younger sister and I only played together unless we were at the park. I can't tell you why, but I just knew that I shouldn't invite any of the other kids to my house even though we lived nearby. I never felt that I could count on anything being for sure.

Client's Initial Perspective

I actually have four words that describe my growing up years: embarrassment, secrets, uncertainty, and responsibility. I was embarrassed when I realized that we had a shameful secret. I couldn't tell anyone about it, and it made me feel like we were unsafe and different from others, and I felt very alone. I was really confused because I loved my mom and dad and felt that they probably knew best, but how could that be if our house wasn't okay like other people's houses?

Background

When I started school and started to be invited to birthday parties, I remember one day I got hurt at the park. A friend's mom offered to bring me home. I tried to show her that I could walk, but I couldn't and fell down again, scraping my knees. Seeing the blood, she insisted, and I was panicked because all I could see in my mind was the mess behind the front door and the trouble I was going to be in for causing her to see it. I tried to get in first, without her seeing inside our house. I remember feeling ashamed and soiled, wanting to die because of the look on her face as she tried to explain to my mom how I had hurt myself. I decided that from that point on, I couldn't go to any parks and was safest staying alone inside my room. I thought that the story would spread at school, and my shame covered me like a sunburn.

At the age of about 5 I decided that the answer was to start to pick up around the house before Mom and Dad got home from work. I coaxed, bribed, and threatened to tell on my sister and brothers unless they agreed to help me. I told them that if we all did this every day, maybe we could go to birthday parties and maybe even have one ourselves and be like the other kids. They bought my pitch, and we were like a little band of busy bees after school most days. We waited, hopefully, but there never were any birthday parties for us, although for a while we did get invited to a few, until we realized we were expected to invite them to ours. Birthday parties, well, parties period came to an end.

I felt sad, angry, and defeated that when Mom got home, she always made a mess again. I felt overwhelmed and alone with our secret. Dad tried to help a little, but his work was always the most important thing to him. Yet I still loved them.

As I got older, I desperately wanted to please and impress people. I wanted to be the one they thought of first for any little jobs, and so while babysitting, I cleaned their homes and washed and waxed their kitchen floors. They thought I was so grown up, reliable, and told me regularly how much they appreciated me. They told my parents I was wonderful. I felt so good, so calmed, so accepted, and so included in their families and lives, even though there was a cloud over my feeling of being good enough because I also knew I didn't really belong with them or their lovely clean, bright, and shiny homes, where people laughed a lot and ate fresh food, and things smelled so nice. When I got home after being with them, I would run to the bedroom I shared with my sister and begin to clean and organize my side and add the little gifts they would let me have to make my space as much as possible like theirs. If my sister would also join in and help with cleaning up the rest of our room, I would share my "treats" with her to motivate her and share my happiness. If she wouldn't, I would scrape a line down the middle between our beds and declare one side mine and the dirty side hers.

I started to notice how these other families acted and spoke to one another, and I copied how they ate and corrected my grammar. I worked so hard because there was a part of me that feared "our way" was like our skin; it covered us and couldn't be removed. Mom was busy collecting things because they were on sale, someone had offered them to her, or she just knew that someone, if not us, might need them because they were in such good condition. I studied very hard so that I could get a scholarship somewhere and get away as soon as possible.

Things continued to get worse and worse until the fire department and public health made an unannounced visit and said that our home was unlivable. This made me realize that Mom wasn't just lazy or silly or too preoccupied with her stuff; it had to be worse than that—she must be sick. Dad tried to help, but he was still too busy at work to make things change. I began to realize that there were no adults in our family. As I looked around and listened to the officials talk, I also realized there wasn't anyone to help with what we needed either.

Outcomes

I changed my plans, and at 17, I got a full-time job and promised my 15-year-old sister that as soon as I could, we would get a place together. It took me two years of working two jobs, one full time during the week and another part time evenings and weekends, to save enough money to share an apartment with two other girls and to bring my sister, who was finishing high school, to live with me. I still feel guilty leaving my brothers behind. CPS stepped in because of their young ages, and they were put into foster care.

Dad left us. Mom was hospitalized and later evicted, so she had no home to return to. She ended up renting a room in someone's house. When I could, I gave her groceries because I knew she would have spent the little I could spare on stuff, which still remained her first love.

Conclusion

I found someone who counsels people who hoard and adult children of people who hoard and used my insurance benefits from my job to get myself counseling. Now I understand my mom and my reactions well enough to have a life not defined by hoarding, and to shake the indelible shame. It's taken me a while. I still love my mom, but now I also understand that her demons belong to her and that I don't need to please and be perfect to belong and be accepted. I am worthy of love and a good life just as I am.

Timmy's Problem Overview

Timmy, Mike, and Gordie, the children from our story in chapter 6, often feel sad and alone.

Background

Timmy is teased at school because he rarely has the items he is supposed to have. Mom and Dad often rush in with missing schoolwork, lunch, snacks, report cards, or school books. This embarrasses him in front of the other kids and the school administration.

Outcomes

Timmy has awkward social skills and few friends. Because he never had the space to entertain other children, he has had little opportunity to practice the skills of making friends and getting along with others.

Timmy cannot easily manage his feelings. He often acts out in anger.

Conclusion

Timmy, Mike, and Gordie were taken into foster care because the family situation was not meeting their basic needs as children and showed no evidence over the period of family supervision of being able to meet their needs in the future. They have stayed together with one foster family and have visits with their biological parents. Timmy has overcome his aggressive behaviors, developed successful social skills, improved academically, and he has communicated his need for his parents to reduce the chaos he associated with living with them. Mike and Gordie have benefited as well from individualized attention, support, and services to help them meet their developmental milestones. Timmy, Mike, and Gordie's situation is an excellent example of the wisdom of redefining what successful outcomes are. They now live in a stable home environment with the foster family, have mature role models, know they are loved by their biological parents, get to spend positive time with them, and have learned to set healthier personal boundaries and limits.

Therapeutic Plan Specific to Children Growing Up in a Hoarded Environment

Growing up in a hoarded environment negatively affects children's ability to develop healthily in many ways. Below I outline the issues most likely in need of counseling support. The earlier the children can get the help they need, the better the likely outcomes, not just for the children but, by extension, the family.

- How does their parents' inability to demonstrate competence in managing clutter strain and damage the family relationship? Many conflicts arise, and this conflict can often prompt children to leave one parent to live with the other to avoid the situation. These children may fail to learn how to resolve conflict effectively.
- Children can easily fail to learn adequate self-care in the area of managing activities of daily living, especially regarding acquiring, saving, clutter, and making decisions about letting things go. These children may mirror the parents' unhealthy attachment to things (or may do the exact opposite and become adults who are ultraminimalist, with no attachments to those items that can bring joy into their lives).
- When a parent and child share comorbid factors, to the extent that the parent is not able to manage his or her own issues, the child does not have an effective example to use as a model.
- When parents are intensively engaged and active in their communities, possibly as a way to validate themselves as parents of an ideal family, and have a secret

like hoarding at home, they are overcommitting their focus to outside matters while having nothing left for the basics at home. They project the perfect family life to others and create a lack of congruency for their children. Children then must protect the false front and suffer for it in life-damaging ways.

- Children have to lie about the conditions they live in to their community and school. They present one version to the world and secretly live another. They often protect the parents and siblings from discovery. They live hypervigilant lives—always watching to see if someone is approaching the house. Often they live at serious risk of fire and infestation by vermin such as bedbugs, cockroaches, rats, squirrels, and so on. They watch their parents put on a good face in public, and they live in secrecy, knowing the real truth. Often they feel helpless and hopeless, living with anxiety, depression, and other mental health problems. Sometimes they experience an extreme need for order and structure. They react with a fierce protectiveness of their personal space, such as their bedrooms and possessions. They meticulously maintain their personal space while being forced to live with extreme chaos and disorder in the rest of the family space. This experience may provide the foundation for chronic mental health disorders.
- I have seen situations where young children were so desperate that they prompted an accident, necessitating an emergency response and discovery, all the while experiencing fear of discovery and feelings of being disloyal to their parents, other siblings, and the family unit as a whole.
- When children are taken into care, everyone in the family is traumatized. Children removed from their parents experience trauma but sometimes also relief if they experience consistency and predictability in their new environment. They may feel ambivalent when they enjoy part of the experience of being in care but feel torn witnessing their parents' distress.
- In general, many children of hoarders feel that the things the parents keep are more important to the parents than they are, resulting in damaged self-esteem and ongoing separation anxiety. There may be profound, resistant sadness and a feeling of abandonment.

Key Messages

- Hoarding stresses families often beyond tolerable limits.
- It often leaves children's self-esteem damaged.
- It produces resentment and conflicting issues in children of hoarders because the stuff is often seen by them as being more important than the child to the hoarding parent, and they feel they have been abandoned, in some cases, for the stuff.
- Financial resources often go to acquiring things rather than to the needs of the children, or to maintaining a stable, safe, healthy living environment.

- Hoarding affects children's development because there is insufficient space for the family to interact as a unit and as individuals through regular daily functioning, sleeping, preparing food, eating at a table, enjoying a social life together, and so forth.
- When invitations cannot be reciprocated because of hoarding, the family begins to refuse them, causing increased isolation. This isolation has a detrimental effect on the mental health and social functioning of those affected and can often be very damaging.
- Parents who hoard are often in denial. They interpret facts to make their choices livable.
- Children who grow up in hoarded environments may also mimic the beliefs, values, feelings, and habits of their parents and not learn healthy boundaries and limits.

Hoarding and the Elderly

When an elderly person lives with a family member who hoards, he or she can be put at risk due to health and safety hazards which often develop in hoarded environments. Inadequate living conditions and an inability to care for the senior are part of such overwhelming circumstances.

When seniors remain in living conditions compromised by hoarding, multiple risks can be associated with this choice:

- Seniors living in hoarded environments may be at risk of fire, contamination, unhygienic living conditions, and exposure to toxicity (vermin, mouse scat, pet excrement, and unsafe, expired food).
- If they co-reside with adult children who have challenges, elders may feel responsible for the adult child's welfare and maintenance. Their desire to provide care may be beyond their realistic ability to do so.
- Seniors may experience financial abuse if their funds are used to support the other's hoarding behavior instead of maintaining adequate living conditions and care.
- They may be unable to access basic requirements for personal hygiene, such as a usable washroom made inaccessible by narrow, blocked paths or bathtubs being repurposed as storage spaces.
- Seniors may not be able to access home services when needed because service providers are prohibited from entering hoarded environments, or because of

reluctance to call for assistance for fear of being involuntarily removed from the residence once their living conditions are discovered.

- Paramedics and emergency response teams may not be able to get to the senior when needed because of narrowed pathways.
- Medications may be managed poorly because they get lost in the clutter.

Neighbors of Hoarders

Neighbors of people who hoard fall into two basic categories:

1 If the person who hoards has lived in the community for a long time, sometimes neighbors try to help. But normally they have limited ability to monitor and assist even when they try their best. There may be sincere concern for an at-risk neighbor who hoards, and they feel guilt and remorse at having to report that person. This response allows the person to remain unidentified, leaving the problem and risks continuing to worsen on the inside.

2 Other adjoining neighbors are unaware of the risk of flood, poor property management, cross-contamination, infestation, and so forth, that they are living beside. They are therefore not aware of the need to prepare for a crisis and to be ready to respond effectively for their own sake.

CHAPTER 15

The Last Word

SUZANNE AND I FEEL THAT THE LAST WORD should rightfully go to people who can speak firsthand about hoarding and its effect on their lives.

We asked them to consider four questions:

1 What was (is) it like to hoard and live in a hoarded environment?
2 What was the catalyst to reaching out for help?
3 What has helped and what hasn't?
4 If you were speaking with someone as stuck as you were, what would you want to say?

Here is what some journeyers said.

A Few Last Words

BY LUCY, JUNE 13, 2017

When I found myself being totally overwhelmed by the things in my house, I finally reached out for help. I had become stuck, and the mounds just kept getting bigger and bigger. I took a leap of faith and sought professional help, gradually working in partnership so that solutions became clearer to me. I was not a bad person. I needed insight as to what was really going on. Then, with help, I could gradually (not perfectly) move to a less cluttered life.

There is a wealth of experience presented in this book. Take in what you can and try baby steps. When ready, go back and reread another section and make a few more small steps. After all, you didn't get where you are in just a week or two. It was a lifetime that brought you to where you are now.

There is hope. Be gentle with yourself and give yourself a pat on the back for reaching a supportive army of new thoughts to defeat old habits. Change is possible . . . and the keys lie between these covers.

My Environment: A Mirror of My Inner Me

M. M., JULY 2, 2017

1. What was (is) it like to hoard and live in a hoarded environment?

Hoarding is living in a garbage dump.

If I experience chest pain, I worry not about a heart attack but about first responders' unfavorable judgment of me and my living conditions. I have no friends, in part, because friends invite each other to their homes. I also avoid having technicians or work people.

I frequently lose important items, including receipts and medical paperwork. Not too long ago, I started a fire in my kitchen by attempting to use a burner without completely clearing off the stove top.

Hoarding and despair are close cousins. My disgusting environment is, in my own view, a projection of the mess inside my head and what amounts to a deep-seated belief that I myself am garbage and that a garbage-filled environment is therefore an appropriate place for me to be. Given this insight, I would have to conclude that my affliction is one of a spiritual nature—in that it is my downtrodden spirit that has allowed me to live this way.

2. What was the catalyst to reaching out for help?

The mess was becoming more and more of a safety hazard. I realized that I was powerless over clutter, and that my life had become unmanageable.

3. What has helped and what hasn't?

Here are two of Elaine's suggestions that have helped:

First, don't use any burner on the stove unless the entire stove top is cleared off. Sometimes the most basic advice is the best. Never assume common sense.

Second, get a big, outdoor-sized garbage can and contractor-type garbage bags and just starting throwing things away—not fussing over recycling (for now)—because although I like to recycle, I acknowledge that I need to be in survival mode right now, and getting caught up in sorting is not going to be helpful at this stage of my development.

One thing that hasn't worked has been procrastinating on doing the work. (To be clear, procrastination was of course *not* one of Elaine's suggestions, but rather one of my long-standing practices.) I can waste a lot of time on my tablet and watching television—activities that don't require me to take a single step and are usually not uplifting. I (somehow) need to embrace a healthier lifestyle.

4. If you were speaking with someone as stuck as you were, what would you want to say?

First, I would let them know that they're not alone. Second, I would share my belief that based on my own experience, it's too much to handle without help. Third, I would encourage them to seek expert help and let them know about my experience with Elaine. Fourth, if they didn't have the financial resources to seek professional help, I would ask them if they might be interested in joining me in starting a local group of Clutterers Anonymous.* (I have the starter kit.)

"No, thank you": My Journey through the Hoarding Experience

ANONYMOUS, APRIL 27, 2017

"Why don't you have your friends come over afterward?" I asked my then 17-year-old daughter when she informed me of her pending outing with friends.

"Nah" was the typical teenage reply.

"I'd be happy to order a pizza for you and your friends," I cheerily countered.

"No" was the monosyllabic response.

Surely there was another way by which to sweeten the offer to sway her decision. I was genuinely looking forward to the buoyant energy of giggling youth in my home.

"You know, if you guys want to crank the music, then I really won't mind—"

"No, thank you" came the terse, emphatic, I'm-closing-the-door-on-this-conversation reply.

It was at that moment that I knew: She was embarrassed to bring friends into our home. There obviously was a major problem, and it was not of her making.

Born into an upper-middle-class family, well educated, and certainly not without the influence of a neat and organized childhood home, I would never have imagined

---

* See the Clutterers Anonymous website at https://clutterersanonymous.org/.

myself digressing into a home environment of such disarray. Yet here I was, and now my daughter was also being forced to deal with the resulting consequences.

How did I get here? Where was my usual drive to keep things tidy and organized? How could I look past the chaos in my home and not find the will to act? Was I just lazy and unorganized, or was I on my way to becoming one of those sensationalized extreme hoarders depicted on TV? Who had I become, and was I destined to remain that way? Whom could I trust to ask for help?

After the devastating implosion of an unhealthy marriage, wherein heinous abuses had been forced on us, my child and I were forced to embark on a multiyear journey of trauma fallout. This included numerous high-risk behaviors that my daughter had engaged in as desperate attempts to numb her pain while mental health treatments were not available. My own focus was on trying to keep her alive while frantically striving to maintain a roof over our heads, put food on the table, and navigate the incredible and frustrating delays of medical assessments, treatments, social services, and an archaic legal system. Frankly, having the energy or focus to maintain an orderly house wasn't available. Tears, fatigue, and fear have the power to limit one's sight.

Nevertheless, I still had enough pride left to minimize the disarray in areas of the home that would be most readily visible to visitors. Others would graciously assume that I just wasn't the best housekeeper and that I merely hadn't gotten around to "putting things away." However, the hidden alcoves of the house, such as bedrooms, dens, powder room bathrooms, closets, and garage, became the "temporary" storage areas for things that I had promised myself to address later.

In the aftermath of several years of constant stress and incredible financial challenges, I seemed to have lost the ability to focus and make what once had been easy decisions. Items of monetary or sentimental value suddenly seemed to describe almost everything in my home. Strangely, this hindrance only applied to my personal life and not in any way to my corporate environment. My daughter's reaction on that fateful day was the breakthrough moment for me: It was undeniably clear that I needed help.

With great unease and trepidation, I swallowed my pride and commenced the Google search to find help. Under no circumstances was I going to ask family or friends whether they could personally recommend an agency or individual who had insight into my problem. This was my secret, a secret that evoked tremendous personal shame and fear of being labeled something that I just couldn't bear others to think of me to be.

There were several initial unsuccessful contacts that I had made within local community outreach programs. In one case, a young woman with Precious Housecleaning was assigned to me. She was polite, kind, hardworking, and immediately focused on indiscriminately bagging up all that was before her for garbage pickup. She had no concept of understanding that I needed the respect of involvement in this process. After three embarrassing and frustrating sessions of her in my home, I never called to rebook again. I couldn't explain why but knew that this wasn't a healthy or a sustainable approach for me.

So, back to the Google search engine. It was there that I found Birchall Consulting and Associates and linked to the website of Birchall Consulting. What greeted me on the landing page was the following:

Is hoarding or cluttering leaving you feeling . . .

- *Overwhelmed?*
- *Is your clutter getting difficult to ignore?*
- *Are your "things" starting to take over your life?*
- *Is hoarding or clutter becoming a cause for conflict with others?*

These words not only zeroed in on how I felt but also identified the family conflict. Social worker Elaine Birchall was identified as a hoarding disorder and intervention specialist, counselor, and a clutter coach with numerous accreditations and years of experience. Instinctually I knew that it could only be this level of accredited and experienced professional to whom I could extend my trust.

My life changed on the day that I made that call, for it was the catalyst that started my personal journey back to wellness. The supportive, nonjudgmental, personalized initial sessions with Ms. Birchall became the trust and respect-based foundation for the counseling relationship. Our sessions did not merely consist of addressing the clutter, but most importantly, much time was directed at focusing why my behavior had even started. I was provided practical tools by which to make decisions that were once overwhelming. These techniques became integral when working both with her assistance and then eventually when on my own.

Over time, and with incredible insight, wisdom, and empathy, Ms. Birchall firmly guided me back to a state where I could self-manage proper assessment of my environment and take appropriate actions. I was taught to focus on measurable results via standards that are customized to my own immediate needs and priorities. I have gained understanding of what it was that had previously rendered me incapable of maintaining a healthy home environment. I have learned what my vulnerabilities are for relapse, and which actions are available to me for positive and self-empowering prevention.

Although it continues to be my responsibility to maintain diligence during times of emotional vulnerability, Elaine Birchall has assisted me in regaining insight, knowledge, confidence, and my dignity. Without these, I am doubtful that I could have achieved my goals, nor would I be capable of maintaining emotional and environmental health within my home.

Hoarding and all its preceding stages create debilitating levels of unhappiness, shame, compromised safety within the home, and an often unrecognized isolating loneliness. I had an immediate need for effective professional counseling services. These services should be made available from professionals who have proper education and credentials in this highly specific area of mental health. I needed help with the stigma of the disorder, and I needed that help via accurate, accessible information from sound information sources. What wasn't available was adequate access to medical and social outreach programs staffed by people who had an adequate understanding of my hoarding disorder.

Hoarding: A Legacy of Values

K. G., JUNE 23, 2017

My mom's parents lived through the war and Depression. My dad grew up poor and constantly moving before the bill collectors arrived at the doorstep. It makes sense that both my parents had it ingrained in them to not waste anything, to ensure they cherished, honored, and respected what they had. They were not hoarders, at least not in the TV show way. Our home was filled with many items too valued to remove because, let's face it, someday you may need to use it.

My husband has a similar story. His parents didn't just live through the war—they lived it. They are from Eastern Europe. My mother-in-law was a refugee in her homeland. At 6 she and her family left their home with only the items that they could carry. When they immigrated to Canada they could only afford to bring with them the items most precious to them.

My husband and I met when we were both in our early thirties. Each of us had a full complement of furnishings for our apartment. When I met the love of my life, my world turned upside down. Sure he had lots of stuff, but then so did I. Sure his stuff was overflowing his cabinets, closets, basement, but come on, he's a guy.

I moved into his place. All of the things that depicted who I am were divided into his place and a storage locker. They remained there until we were able to downsize. I would not see most of "me" until many years later, when Elaine came to support us.

In all fairness, we did hold a garage sale. That was a struggle. We had lots of "discussions" regarding the doubles—put them in a storage unit or save them for the cottage. The more emotionally connected things made it to the cottage. Since we were two adults, who am I to decide for him what is important or not? That set the tone for our relationship, our "dance."

Our first year together was very difficult because I felt like a guest in his house. I didn't have much input about canned foods long past their expiration dates, large vats of olive oil that, according to him, would be eventually needed or eaten. It was frustrating, exasperating, and hurtful to me that my my opinion didn't matter. I felt that I was not an equal. We were not making decisions together. Looking back with the insight I have gained working with Elaine, I understand a bit more.

When our first child was born, we bought a bigger house and all of the stuff from the storage unit went into the crawl space. My husband created a map of the crawl space, marking it off in a grid on the floor with each square having a number. He then wrote on the map the contents of each grid. That was all great until there was no more space in the crawl space. Items then started to ooze out into the basement, and then it got to a point that there was very little room in the basement, really only a series of paths. We had all this space, but there was never room for anything.

Social functions were a stressful time involving a huge cleanup in the main living areas. God forbid someone mistake the computer room for the bathroom and open the door, as all the residue from the cleanup that we had no idea where to put was in that room. Items went into boxes, laundry baskets, or shopping bags and up to our rooms on our beds. That was the tipping point for both my husband and myself.

With support, he was able to identify that he was dealing with chaotic environments both at work and at home. Since he could not control or change his work environment, he needed to focus on his home environment.

We were sitting in a parking lot taking some time to debrief after a not-so-great session with a marriage counselor. He told me he had something to run by me. He broached the subject of getting a hoarding specialist to come in and help us clean up. I agreed. I was surprised to discover that he felt that I was the cause of our chaotic home.

Enter Elaine. We've been working with Elaine for just over a year now. Is it easy? Hell no! Is it worth it? Hell yes! We have done individual and family work with her. Prior to her coming, I was always second-guessing myself regarding the judgment I had about my husband's items. Again, the mindset of, Who am I to judge what is important to someone else? I wouldn't want anyone deciding for me what is important.

Elaine has been an objective third party. She has been the calm, non-nagging wife voice. She has given him things to think through when deciding how important something is to him. Elaine has also helped me. I'm at a point in my life that all the stuff that was important to me that I boxed up 15 years ago does not have the same meaning and importance it once did. I am able to easily let that go. There are some things that are not so easy. Previously I would have just put them back in a box and kept them until I could make a clear decision, whenever that may have been. Elaine has given me a framework to be able to get clear about why I wish to keep an item, and if I don't wish to keep it, the ability to let it go without guilt or remorse.

This work has been slow. Slower than I had anticipated, but then what do I have to compare it to? Only what I see on TV and that is nicely edited into an hour show with commercial breaks. Also, it doesn't help that we work hard when Elaine comes to our home biweekly, but not much else happens in between that time.

I would love to finish this up by saying that we will get through this together and ride off into the sunset happily ever after. We will get through this, and our lives will look different after. We will not be together.

I have tried, and I am tired. I love him, but I need to love myself more so that I am healthy and able to be the mom I need to be to our children. Currently our goal is to sort through our things and pack what will be moved into our separate homes.

The Domino Effect of Dysfunction

PHOENIX, JUNE 9, 2017

I have named this "Last Word" contributor "Phoenix" because with all the serious generation-to-generation dysfunction and abuse she was born into and thought was normal, once she realized what health was she made all the changes and choices she needed to make to choose a wonderful, loving, supportive stable man for her life partner; has a happy, healthy marriage; and has raised two terrific children— kind, sensible, dependable, and happy.

She has changed the generational pattern she inherited for future generations. Hoarding is her "one more hill to climb."

Hats off and credit to "Phoenix!"

1. What was (is) it like to hoard and live in a hoarded environment?

My house was very full of stuff. It was overwhelming to deal with, leaving me not knowing where to start. I would try to start, but I would not have any success by the end of the day. It affected my life, my family, friends—I would not invite them over unless I spent often weeks preparing. I wouldn't want anyone to knock on my door, or to let them in. I would spend days cleaning up just so that we could have repair people in. The house would still look like I hadn't cleaned because of the sheer amount of stuff in all the rooms. My immediate family understood, but there were points when it got to be too much. They tried, but they weren't too helpful.

The worst moment for me and my family was when our water heater leaked and we tried to get someone to come in to replace it. We couldn't let anyone in for months to check it because the path to the water heater was there but too narrow and embarrassing. We did without hot water for months. We boiled water and had baths that way. We also went swimming weekly and made sure that we had a really good shower after swimming. We boiled water in kettles to do the bare minimum—dishes, preparing food, cleaning up. We washed our clothes in cold water, so that was okay. At least everyone had clean clothes.

2. What was the catalyst to reaching out for help?

I resisted by believing "It could be worse, it could be worse." Actually someone else decided the moment we needed help was now. Someone called Children's Services. They heard our water heater was broken and that we were boiling water. That was a concern. When that happened, it was especially scary and nerve-racking. I was afraid. When they came in and saw the condition of the house, they decided it wasn't safe because there weren't pathways to the doors. It was considered a fire safety concern for us and the kids. They said it had to be cleaned up, and the kids needed to be somewhere else. We went with family. It wasn't abuse, so the kids weren't taken.

It was very hard to make that call to Elaine. I'm used to doing everything myself. I always had to, even growing up; I was managing things for two alcoholic parents. I never really had anyone I could depend on. My parents really weren't there because of their alcoholism, and both of them hoarded in their own way. I grew up in that type of environment, and I kind of thought it was normal. I also blamed myself for being lazy and incompetent. I deeply felt that I should be able to do it all on my own. Another reason I didn't know what normal looked like was that my grandparents, even though I really loved them, were alcoholics and hoarders too. They were organized hoarders, though, committed to keeping things "just in case." We only found out about their hoarding after they died, when we had to close up the house. Glass jars, plastic containers, elastics and twine, and frozen food decades old all kept "just in case."

3. What has helped and what hasn't?

Talking with someone who knows what I have gone through and accepts me for me as I am today, not who I used to be or will be in future, just what I have to give today. Not making judgments, or looking down on me, understanding what has caused this situation.

The support and practical help of friends has also helped. Being accepted after they saw up close how imperfect I am and still remaining my friend after really was humbling. I felt very vulnerable.

Also the donations from my counselors and other clients of things that were helpful to solve a problem I was having, and me being able to help someone else with my donations made everything feel useful, and letting go bordered on being a positive thing. I still have a hard time letting things go if I'm not sure where they will go and that they won't go to good use. I'm getting better at trusting that when my counselor says my donations will be used for a good purpose, that will happen, and I don't get anxious after.

A big cleanup was helpful in one way because we could return home, but not having the time to figure out how exactly I wanted things organized meant that often the organization of things was more someone else's way, even though the helpers knew me and were my friends. I have a family with special needs, and we needed to adapt some things after because my family needed things laid out a different way. After the big cleanup, I had the feeling that I didn't know where things were, even though before everything had been in piles. Piles or not, I felt that I had a better idea of the general vicinity of where things were. I wasn't used to things having a permanent place. Things just got put down, and I counted on my visual memory to remember where to find them after.

4. If you were speaking with someone as stuck as you were, what would you want to say?

When we called for help and Elaine came, it was nerve-racking and scary. I was afraid of being judged. I am always afraid of being judged. I don't ever think I am doing well enough. With help and counseling, I have come to understand that when my life becomes chaotic, with family and personal demands like health needs or activities because of my family's special needs, if I don't keep even a bare minimum of a daily routine, things build up quickly. I don't notice it in time. It's like I have blinders on, and I only notice it when there is a buildup. I fall behind on what I was doing. If I keep a semiregular routine—for example, on this day and in this time frame, I do such and such—it seems to go much better. When my hubby and kids help, that helps me a lot, but it doesn't happen often enough.

I would tell someone just thinking they might need help to just make the call for help but get it from someone who really understands what you are going through. Also just getting it cleaned up might be helpful, but only if you don't have anything else going wrong in your life, especially if you can let things go easily. If you can't let go, it is harder to just organize everything—something has to go. Better storage of all your things is almost never the answer.

The best help is regular help. Longer sorting and decluttering sessions can be exhausting. Start with a big cleanup, but only to the point of returning your home to safety, and then regular counseling and decluttering with someone who really knows about hoarding and can respect and work with your priorities and at your speed.

PART III

Getting There

Resources, Tips, and Tools

CHAPTER 16

Resources

TABLE 16.1

Index to Resources in This Book and Online

RESOURCE	LOCATION	DESCRIPTION
Activities of Daily Living Assessment	Table 2.2, p. 46	This tool helps you assess your ability to carry out necessary activities of daily living. It helps you assess how severely you may be adapting to unsafe and unhealthy conditions due to hoarding.
Animal Hoarding: Devotion or Disorder?	Resource A (available online at jhupbooks. press.jhu.edu/title/ conquer-clutter)	This resource lists five psychiatric models for animal hoarding. (The sixth model describes the commercial abuse of animals for profit.) These psychiatric models may be used to describe the well-established clinical intervention strategies applicable to each type of behavior. This resource discusses overpopulation in shelters and describes the conundrum that municipalities find themselves in with animal hoarding. It also speaks to the criteria for wellness of animals and offers some thoughts on the initial steps people can take if they feel that caring for the animals they have is getting out of their control.
Breathing to Destress	Resource 16.1, pp. 233–34	This user-friendly relaxation breathing technique can bring anyone stressed or anxious back to centered and calm while on the go in any location.

RESOURCE	LOCATION	DESCRIPTION
Building Your Conceptual Model of Hoarding	Resource B (available online at jhupbooks. press.jhu.edu/title/ conquer-clutter)	This comprehensive tool covers an extensive cross-section of life experiences and situations that can influence how you approach your life and your things. The tool can also be used as an interview template by professionals. It is an expanded version of a similar tool developed by Randy O. Frost, PhD, adapted based on experiences that have been expressed to me by my clients.
Calculating Environmental Risk	Resource C (available online at jhupbooks. press.jhu.edu/title/ conquer-clutter)	This tool is designed to help you calculate your risk quantitatively, according to accepted risk factors found in hoarding situations that have a high probability for fire and other safety crises. The more boxes ticked in this checklist, the higher the risk factor is for that environment.
Checking in with Yourself on Danger Signs	Chapter 2, p. 65	This resource offers questions most frequently associated with beliefs, values, fears, and choices that support the existence of hoarding behaviors. The choices you make when organizing your environment can lead to increased risk.
Clutter Checklist	Table 2.1, pp. 44–45	This is a portable user-friendly tool when doing inspections to assess the level and placement of clutter in living environments.
Conscious Acquiring Process	Resource 16.2, pp. 234–36	Using this tool will help you slow down and counteract your inclination to acquire under impulsive influences, substituting conscious choices.
Full Definition of Hoarding Disorder: *Diagnostic and Statistical Manual of Mental Disorders,* 5th Edition (*DSM-5*)	Resource 16.3, pp. 236–37	It is important to have the official definition of hoarding in case full details are important to your situation. I include it for the benefit it provides you in your search for the help you need to take back your life when your things are taking over.

RESOURCE	LOCATION	DESCRIPTION
Dos and Don'ts for Coaches in Hoarding Situations	Resource 16.6, pp. 240–41	This list offers helpful hints to establish positive, supportive working relationships with individuals who are living with the stressors common in hoarding situations as well as to avoid common pitfalls.
Figuring It Out	Chapter 2, p. 66	Questions to ask yourself to self-assess your hoarding behaviors.
Hoarding Disorder and Associated Resources	Resource 16.4, pp. 237–38	A list of print and online resources to help you learn about and manage hoarding disorder.
Hoarding Demographic Measurement Tools	Resource D (available online at www.press.jhu.edu)	This tool I had developed for my hoarding demographic purposes (see the appendix) is so excellent that I wanted to offer it to readers.
Hoarding Fact Sheet	Resource E (available online at jhupbooks.press.jhu.edu/title/conquer-clutter)	This fact sheet is a snapshot of current facts about hoarding. It is a great starting point for individuals who hoard or those who are trying to understand hoarding better so that they can help someone they care about who hoards.
Online Impulsive Shopping (Problematic and Pathological)	Chapter 8, pp. 152–56	This section breaks down three key factors that make people vulnerable to developing an online shopping addiction and offers 10 signs of compulsive online shopping.
Onsite Clutter Coaching Toolkit	Resource F (available online at jhupbooks.press.jhu.edu/title/conquer-clutter)	There are two parts to dealing with clutter. You need help to understand and deal with the underlying reasons you hoard, but then you need to clean up the environment. This tool helps you, and those supporting you, do both.
Problem Solving Using Cognitive Behavioral Therapy	Chapter 4, p. 74	This CBT-based set of questions simplifies problem solving. It was developed originally for emotional and relationship problems but is widely applicable.

RESOURCE	LOCATION	DESCRIPTION
Knowing Yourself worksheets 1–3	Chapter 5, pp. 104–16	Enormous thanks to Jane Burka and Lenora Yuen for their generosity in letting us develop these procrastination worksheets using their work as the basis. These tools will help you identify the barriers that seem so mysterious and ask yourself the right questions to get answers to your procastination behavior. After that, you can get Burka and Yuen's book *Procrastination* to continue working to overcome procrastination.
Are You a Hoarder in the Making?	Table 1.1, p. 16	If accepting hoarding as part of your reality is difficult, try taking this quiz and, if you wish, keep the results to yourself and let the truth sink in. If hoarding is something you need to deal with, reach out for the help you need according to the risk identified in the quiz results.
Environmental Risk Assessment Checklist	Chapter 2, p. 48, pp. 63–64	Safety is always the highest priority. This tool will help identify the risk in your environment.
Bring Home or Let Go?	Resource G (available online at jhupbooks. press.jhu.edu/title/ conquer-clutter)	When the decision about acquiring something needs to be made, these questions will help you stay on track to reach the goals you have set. Making decisions to let things go can be tough. These questions will help you decide the "must have" and the "can go" items. Deciding is still hard, but you can do it.
Sorting Using Elaine's Scaling Process	Resource 16.5, pp. 239–40	The secret to sorting is in the relationship you have with your possessions. This scaling process will help you identify the items that mean the most to you when everything feels special.
My Goals Worksheet	Chapter 3, p. 70	This goal-setting worksheet reminds you that setting goals to broadly balance your life, with joy, fun, play, and work, is vital to sustaining the goals you set for decluttering.

Resource 16.1. Breathing to Destress

There are many online demonstrations of relaxation breathing. Andrew Weil provides an excellent website (www.drweil.com) that describes three different types of breathing—one for relaxation, one for energizing, and one for stress and anxiety. Dr. Weil also demonstrates these techniques in helpful videos on the website. And they *do work*.

1 Relax and breathe deeply through the nose (*not* the mouth) right down to expand your belly (diaphragm).

2 There should not be any noise, pauses, or breaks in the flow of your breath.

3 When you have managed this, start making your inhale breath and exhale breath equal in duration.

4 You may notice a gradual sense of relaxation spreading through yourself.

Autonomic nervous system	• *Supports the functioning of the heart, lungs, circulatory system, and glandular system* • *Has two parts—the sympathetic nervous system and the parasympathetic nervous system—dealing with our bodies' responses to activity (sympathetic) and relaxation (parasympathetic)*
Sympathetic nervous system	Relates to our body's activity response by increasing our heart rate, blood pressure, muscle tone (tension) in the large skeletal muscles, sweat secretion, pupil dilation, and other functions, as well as supplying what we need for physical exertion
Parasympathetic nervous system	Relates to our relaxation response by decreasing our heart rate, blood pressure, and skeletal muscle tone, giving us what we need to disengage and rest, sleep, or digest

- Our mental activities can prompt our sympathetic and parasympathetic nervous systems just as our physical activities can.
- By controlling the rate at which we inhale and exhale, we can balance our sympathetic and parasympathetic nervous systems.

Using 2:1 Breathing to Center Yourself

A yoga technique of 2-to-1 breathing allows us to prompt whichever system we need at the time: sympathetic for action and stimulation or parasympathetic for relaxation and calming.

1 Find a quiet place. If you are shopping, and your cart has items in it chosen in the spur of the moment and not on your list, try a cubicle in the restroom.

2   Focus on a spot in front of you at eye level.

3   Roll your shoulders in circles backward and forward a few times to release tension.

4   Take a few deep belly breaths.

5   Now inhale for three counts opening up the shoulders and letting your chest rise fully.

6   Now exhale for six counts by engaging and compressing the abdominal muscles smoothly as you exhale.

7   You can increase the inhale to four counts and exhale for eight counts to deepen the calming effect.

8   Do this until the adrenaline from the "impulse rush" dissipates and you feel calm and centered.

9   Try this breathing technique when you need energy for activity, such as for sorting and decluttering.

Resource 16.2. Conscious Acquiring Process

This step-by-step checklist to turn back impulse buying is a harm-reduction strategy I developed and have used with many clients who struggle with impulse buying.

This process is meant to:

✔ slow you down;
✔ break the rush of excitement and urgency that fuels impulsive acquisition;
✔ support you to develop other options;
✔ give you time to rationally consider other alternatives without the influence of the roller-coaster rush of adrenaline, serotonin, or dopamine coursing through your body, influencing a rash, impulsive decision you may regret;
✔ support you to make decisions you won't regret later; and
✔ help you avoid digging the rut of hoarding even deeper.

1   As much as possible, take a break from shopping while you learn, practice, and integrate self-regulating strategies. Self-regulating is about making a plan and following the plan most of the time.

2   Plan not to go to stores other than for groceries, unless groceries are an issue for you. Do this by delegating other purchases to family and close friends who are supportive of your hoarding challenges and dehoarding goals. Only delegate to those who are 100 percent behind you, so that you do not have to feel defective, apologetic, or indebted for asking.

3   Even when grocery shopping, start practicing shopping only from a list. Do your best to stick to the list by telling yourself the other interesting items you see will still be there the next time and can be added to the next list.

4 If for an *unavoidable* reason you must do non-grocery shopping, commit to making a list and buying only what is on that list.

5 Before you go through the checkout line, pull over to a quiet spot, look at your list, look at your shopping cart, and if there is anything in the cart that is not on your list, try to make yourself put it back in an effort to practice sticking to the list.

6 Carry the "Bring Home or Let Go?" checklist (laminated, if possible) with you and refer to it to decide your best choice today. Even if an item looks like a good purchase, you can always make that same purchase tomorrow with a new list.

7 If for some reason you absolutely cannot return the next day—that is, if the item is some basic *need* not *want* item (bread, milk, medication, etc.)—leave the basket or cart outside the restrooms or near the checkout, if the cashier will hold it for you for a few minutes while you go outside to get something or use the restroom.

8 Do one of the following:

✔ Leave the building (giving yourself an opportunity to change your state of mind).

or

✔ Go to a quiet place like the restroom. Look in the mirror. Ask yourself if excess buying is what you need to do. Sit and do the relaxation breathing exercises in resource 16.1, "Breathing to Destress." Center yourself. Review the questions once again and review if the additional items are truly *needs* or *wants*. As inconvenient as this sounds, it is an important step to interrupt the "in the moment" impulse decision-making process.

9 *If and only if* you decide that the items are *needs*, add them to your list. Go back into the store and make your purchases.

10 If *any* of the items are *wants*, make note of them for consideration as possible *needs* for future shopping visits, but remind yourself that they are *not needs today*, and so your best choice is not to buy them today.

- Remind yourself that they or something very similar will be available when you do need them.
- If they are on sale, they are not a "good deal" if you are buying them on credit or if you are using cash that could give you a safety cushion against future unexpected financial surprises or needs.

11 This method is not designed, nor advisable, for expensive items, or items you know already are *definite* impulse buys. If you have a particularly strong attraction to something that is expensive or a definite impulse buy:

✔ Remove the item from your cart.

✔ If you can't make yourself remove the item from your cart, be sure to go someplace quiet like the restroom, look in the mirror, and ask yourself what you are doing.

✔ Ask yourself, "Does this choice move me forward or set me back on the goals I am working on?"

- ✔ Do your best to go home.
- ✔ Call a trusted third party and review the "Should I Bring This Home?" question list for acquiring and your reasons for wanting to buy the item(s).
- ✔ Complete a list of the pros and cons of buying and not buying.

12 Try to make yourself sleep on it and wait for the next day.

13 Make a new list and buy from that "considered" list if you still believe the items are your best choice.

14 Slow yourself down. Make your choice consciously.

15 Either return and make your purchases or, if you recognize that the item is an impulse buy and you *resisted* buying it, go look at yourself in the mirror and say:
- "I did it!"
- "I just took a huge step forward to the life I want and deserve."
- Most of all *be very, very proud of yourself.*

Resource 16.3. Full Definition of Hoarding Disorder: *Diagnostic and Statistical Manual of Mental Disorders,* 5th Edition (*DSM-5*)

According to the *DSM-5, hoarding disorder* is defined by the following criteria:

1 Persistent difficulty discarding or parting with possessions, regardless of the actual value.

2 This difficulty is due to a perceived need to save the items and to distress associated with discarding them.

3 The difficulty discarding possessions results in the accumulation of possessions that congests and clutters active living areas and substantially compromises their intended use. If living areas are uncluttered, it is only because of the interventions of third parties (e.g., family members, cleaners, authorities).

4 The hoarding causes clinically significant distress or impairment in social, occupational, or other important areas of functioning (including maintaining a safe environment for self and others).

5 The hoarding is not attributable to another medical condition (e.g., brain injury, cerebrovascular disease, Prader-Willi syndrome).

6 The hoarding is not better explained by the symptoms of another mental disorder (e.g., obsessions in obsessive-compulsive disorder, decreased energy in major depressive disorder, delusions in schizophrenia or another psychotic disorder, cognitive deficits in major neurocognitive disorder, restricted interests in autism spectrum disorder).

Specify if:

With excessive acquisition: *If difficulty discarding possessions is accompanied by excessive acquisition of items that are not needed or for which there is no available space.*

Specify if:

With good or fair insight: *The individual recognizes that hoarding-related beliefs and behaviors (pertaining to difficulty discarding items, clutter, or excessive acquisition) are problematic.*

With poor insight: *The individual is mostly convinced that hoarding-related beliefs and behaviors (pertaining to difficulty discarding items, clutter, or excessive acquisition) are not problematic despite evidence to the contrary.*

Specifiers

With excessive acquisition. *Approximately 80%–90% of individuals with hoarding disorder display excessive acquisition. The most frequent form of acquisition is excessive buying, followed by acquisition of free items (e.g., leaflets, items discarded by others). Stealing is less common. Some individuals may deny excessive acquisition when first assessed, yet it may appear later, during the course of treatment. Individuals with hoarding disorder typically experience distress if they are unable to or are prevented from acquiring items.*

Resource 16.4. Hoarding Disorder and Associated Resources

Books and Reports

- *The Anti-Anxiety Workbook: Proven Strategies to Overcome Worry, Phobias, Panic and Obsessions*, by Martin M. Antony and Peter J. Norton, Guilford Press, 2009.
- *The Anxiety and Phobia Workbook*, 5th ed., by Edmund J. Bourne, New Harbinger, 2010.
- *Attachment in Adulthood: Structure, Dynamics, and Change*, by Mario Mikulincer and Phillip R. Shaver, Guilford Press, 2007.
- *Cognitive Behavioural Therapy: Solve Everyday Problems with CBT*, by Christine Wilding and Aileen Milne, McGraw Hill, 2010.
- *Compulsive Hoarding and Acquiring: Workbook*, by Randy Frost and Gail Steketee, Oxford University Press, 2007.
- *Feeling Good: The New Mood Therapy*, revised and updated, by David D. Burns, HarperCollins, 1999.

- *The Feeling Good Handbook*, by David D. Burns, Penguin, 1999.
- *Feeling Good Together: The Secret to Making Troubled Relationships Work*, by David D. Burns, Broadway Books, 2008.
- *Get It Done When You're Depressed*, revised and updated, by Julie A. Fast and John D. Preston, Penguin, 2008.
- *Get Out of Your Mind and Into Your Life: The New Acceptance and Commitment Therapy*, by Steven C. Hayes, with Spencer Smith, New Harbinger, 2005.
- *The Habit Change Workbook: How to Break Bad Habits and Form Good Ones*, by James Claiborn and Cherry Pedrick, New Harbinger, 2001.
- *Live Your Dreams, Let Reality Catch Up*, by Roger Ellerton, Trafford, 2006.
- *Loving Someone with OCD: Help for You and Your Family*, by Karen J. Landsman, New Harbinger, 2005.
- *Mastering Your Adult ADHD: A Cognitive Behavioral Treatment Program*, by Steven A. Safren, Carol A. Perlman, Susan Sprich, and Michael W. Otto, Oxford University Press, 2005.
- *Mind over Mood: Change How You Feel by Changing the Way You Think*, by Dennis Greenberger. and Christine A. Padesky, Guilford Press, 1995.
- *Mindfulness in Plain English*, updated and expanded edition, by Bhante Henepola Gunaratana, Wisdom Publications, 2002.
- *No Room to Spare: Ottawa's Community Response to Hoarding Plan*, by L. Bonnie Dinning, report prepared for the Ottawa Community Response to Hoarding Coalition, May 2006, www.hoarding.ca/wp-content/uploads/2014/08/no-room-to-spare-report.pdf.
- *Overcoming Obsessive-Compulsive Disorder: A Behavioral and Cognitive Protocol for the Treatment of OCD*, by Gail Steketee, New Harbinger, 1999.
- *Overcoming Compulsive Hoarding: Why You Save and How You Can Stop*, by Fugen Neziroglu, Jerome Bubrick, and Jose A. Yaryura-Tobias, New Harbinger, 2004.
- *The Perfectionist's Handbook: Take Risks, Invite Criticism, and Make the Most of Your Mistakes*, by Jeff Szymanski, Harvard Health, 2011.
- *Procrastination: Why You Do It, What to Do about It Now*, 25th anniversary ed., fully revised and updated, by Jane B. Burka. and Lenora M. Yuen, Da Capo, 2008.
- *The Self-Esteem Workbook*, by Glenn R. Schiraldi, New Harbinger, 2001.
- *Ten Days to Self-Esteem*, by David D. Burns, HarperCollins, 1993.

Online Support

- International OCD Foundation, www.hoarding.iocdf.org, has expert information provided by two internationally recognized top clinical researchers (Randy Frost and Gail Steketee).
- Hoarding behavior and intervention specialist Elaine Birchall, one of the authors of this book, offers advice at www.hoarding.ca.

Resource 16.5. Sorting Using Elaine's Scaling Process

Category 1, 2, 3 = Highest valued category: *I can't imagine life without it; that's how important this item is to me.*

List the *criteria* that make this a 1, 2, 3 category item:

- _____

- _____

- _____

- _____

Category 4, 5, 6 = *This item is important, and if I don't have to sacrifice a category 1, 2, 3 item, I would want to keep as many as I have room for.*

List the *criteria* that make this a 4, 5, 6 category item:

- _____

- _____

- _____

- _____

Category 7, 8, 9, 10 = *This item is nice but not a priority compared to category 1–6 items, and if I have to, I can let them go, hopefully to locations where or people with whom they will not be wasted.*

List the *criteria* that makes this a 7, 8, 9, 10 category item:

- _____

- _____

- _____

- _____

1 Choose an item that is the absolute highest priority of your category 1 items.

2 What gives *this* item such high importance?

3 Feel the feelings connected to this absolute highest priority item. Remember the images connected to its importance.

4 Stay with those feelings, really feel them, and remember what you feel for that item.

5 Now consider which category another item belongs to compared to the absolute highest priority item.

6 What *criteria* account for this decision?

7 If the item is a category 4, 5, 6, based on the feeling it generates, is it closer to a 4 or to a 6?

8 Place it with the other items of the same priority, that is, 4s with 4s, 5s with 5s, and 6s with 6s. Remember: you get to keep as many of these items as you have space for (acceptable space is only where the item would normally be used).

9 If the item is a category 7, 8, 9, 10, then consider where you can let it go to.

Letting go means donating, regifting (if space allows), recycling, discarding, or selling, but the last only if the verifiable value of the item means selling makes sense *and* there is an available market for the item. Otherwise donate to a charity that will give you a receipt for income tax purposes.

Resource 16.6. Dos and Don'ts for Coaches in Hoarding Situations

Here are some guidelines to start off on the right foot and stay there when helping someone in a hoarding situation.

1 Remember, the most important thing people hoarding need to do is change their relationship to their things. Using the strategies in chapter 4, the process of decluttering usually happens more easily. Acknowledge the accumulation, but don't make it the focus in the beginning.

2 Make the people your focus. Ask them how they are feeling about having someone in their home, about you specifically being there, life in general, and only then, how things got to this point.

3 Use whatever term they use for what they do. They may never use the term *hoarder*. That's perfectly fine. There is nothing gained by applying labels.

4 Don't confront denial until you have a solid positive relationship.

5 Language is powerful. Be aware of your personal standards and feelings about clutter and deteriorated environments. Check yourself for possible blaming inferences. No one is at fault.

6 Working in hoarding situations with someone who is anxious and reluctant is frequently tiring and frustrating. Scan yourself for fatigue and burnout. Pace

yourself accordingly. Remember, do one 15-minute work period followed by only one more work period, and only if you can commit to the complete second 15 minutes. Otherwise, stop and take a break.

7 We are entitled to our own thoughts, values, and opinions. We are not entitled to apply them to others who come to us for help. People have the right to live the way they choose, according to their own standards and values. Occasionally, there are consequences for this choice. We cannot *make* others do things differently to save them from the right to learn through consequences. We are wisest and most helpful when we are aware of our prejudices and judgmental internal dialogue. I encourage everyone to consciously repeat to themselves, as I sometime must, "*My personal preferences stop at the door.*" If we fail to do so, we put ourselves at risk of unexpected slips of the tongue, which are demonstrated in our facial expression, tone of voice, and other body language. We will make the other an adversary, not an ally, as we work together.

8 Don't barrage people with questions. Ask what you need to know most, one question at a time, slowly and gently. Give people time to reflect and reply in their own way. Treat every person who hoards as you would want someone you love to be treated. This principle works for the full range of work necessary in hoarding situations, from simple to serious. Sometimes we feel the pressure to make fast and extensive headway decluttering. These are *our* feelings and priorities. It is best not to pass them on to other people. They have their own pressures and priorities.

9 Don't be the expert. Don't let anyone cast you in the role of expert. You are the guide, advocate, and coach.

10 Don't promise things you can't do. Focus on what you can do. Ask what they most need help with. Even if you can help with only a small segment of one of their needs, that is honest progress. Trust will develop from there.

11 Don't bluff. Say what you mean and mean what you say. If you aren't sure, say so. Check your facts when you aren't sure and get back to them.

12 Don't try to buy a relationship with the person hoarding by privately taking sides against enforcement officials or anyone else, even if your personal opinion about the requirements of the authority figures is not positive. Work to build understanding between all parties. With your support, people who hoard need to follow the same rules and laws as everyone else. They are part of society, and special rules do not apply to them. Be aware, however, that with hoarding disorder now in the *DSM-5*, hoarding can qualify as a disability, and they may have legitimate rights to reasonable accommodations.

Appendix

Case Review from Birchall Consulting and Associates, Inc.

THE INITIAL INTENT FOR THIS CASE REVIEW, completed in 2017, was to see how consistent a random sample of my client cases over the past 10 years are in comparison to existing hoarding research. At the same time, Suzanne and I examined any links we could find between Birchall Consulting hoarding cases and their demographics. We do not offer this information as a scientific study. It is simply a snapshot of demographics for 214 cases.* We looked at the following demographic information:

- gender
- hoarding severity level
- age by gender
- dwelling type
- education level
- primary income source
- estimated annual income
- degree of isolation
- other services that had provided intervention
- diagnosed comorbid factors

---

* Participant information used in this informal random snapshot was safeguarded by assigning a data number separate and apart from the physical file at the time the data was collected from the file and entered on the Tool worksheet. The assigned number is not registered on the file itself, so there is no capability for anyone to match the number with the file. For example, there is no way to cross reference Participant 001 with a particular case file. We also chose random samples so that no clients felt exposed— no information relates directly to their file. They may not be a subject of the study, and therefore anyone who is aware of a present or former client of Birchall Consulting cannot conclude that the demographic information collected applies to themselves or the person they know. A copy of the "Hoarding Demographic Measurement Tools" we used for the review is available online (jhupbooks.press.jhu.edu/title/conquer-clutter).

Gender

Table A.1 indicates that women are 2.41 times more likely to request or accept service than men. This ratio does not indicate the prevalence of women who hoard compared to men. It does represent the likelihood of women versus men to seek help. This finding is consistent with the Johns Hopkins Medicine OCD Collaborative Genetics Study (Samuels et al. 2007) and another epidemiological study, which found a significantly greater prevalence of compulsive hoarding problems in men (4.1 percent) than in women (2.1 percent), but these findings are in sharp contrast with clinically ascertained hoarding samples, which are almost invariably predominantly female. Researchers have concluded that perhaps women are more likely than men to seek help about their hoarding problems, which aligns with our data.

TABLE A.1
Seeking Help by Gender

GENDER	PEOPLE SEEKING HELP	PERCENTAGE (%)	RATIO
Male	61	28.5	0.41
Female	147	68.7	2.41
Unknown	6	2.8	0.03

Randy O. Frost, Gail Steketee, and David F. Tolin, in "Comorbidity in Hoarding Disorder," in the *Depression and Anxiety* journal, state that the prevalence of those who self-identify as hoarding was 78 percent female. By inference, 22 percent are male.

Our findings included those who self-identify as hoarding as well as those who contacted me because someone is concerned about their acquiring behavior. Of this cohort, 68.7 percent were female, and 28.5 percent were male. Those who preferred not to identify their gender equaled 2.8 percent.

Hoarding Level

Table A.2 shows that it is 25 percent more likely that a hoarding situation will be at a Level 3 when someone seeks help. If one does not intervene at Level 3, the next most likely point of contact is at a Level 5 (22 percent), and at this point the situation will be a crisis.

Hoarding Level of People Seeking Help

HOARDING LEVEL	PEOPLE SEEKING HELP	PERCENTAGE (%)*
Level 0	6	3
Level 1	1	<1
Level 2	23	11
Level 3	54	25
Level 4	41	19
Level 5	47	22
Unknown†	42	20

* Percentages may not add up to 100 because of rounding.

† Note that 20 percent of requests were by remote methods of contact (phone, email). Even though in all cases, the existing accumulation level was estimated through questions about actual conditions evident to the caller, I was not able to visually confirm the callers' observations.

Age

Table A.3 shows that most women and men reach out, request, and accept service in their forties, fifties, or sixties. It is interesting that people who do not reach out for help and get it in their early forties (40–44) apparently go as long as 10 years before the situation's urgency makes assistance a priority (55–59). The urgency then appears to accelerate for those in the 59–65 age category. Only 6 years later, the next increase in requests for services occurs (65–69). Anecdotally, when requests for assistance are made in the 65–69 age range, they are usually severe situations of Risk Level 4 or 5.

These results are consistent with the findings expressed by Mark Odom in his "Hoarding Interventions" workshop (2011). His slide "Onset of Hoarding Disorder" details that compulsive acquiring onset is in later adolescence. The onset of clinically significant hoarding is in the thirties age range. The average age range when seeking treatment is in the fifties.

Age by Gender and Gender by Decade

AGE	PEOPLE SEEKING HELP (includes unknown gender cases)	PERCENTAGE (%)*	WOMEN	BY DECADE*	MEN	BY DECADE*
Under 20	1	0.5	0	—	1	1 (0.5%)
20–24	3	1.4	3	6 (2.8%)	0	1 (0.5%)
25–29	4	1.9	3		1	
30–34	6	2.8	4	12 (5.6%)	1	4 (1.9%)
35–39	14	6.5	8		3	
40–44	36	16.8	27	34 (15.9%)	8	16 (7.5%)
45–49	16	7.5	7		8	
50–54	22	10.3	17	36 (16.8%)	5	12 (5.6%)
55–59	26	12.2	19		7	
60–64	20	9.4	14	38 (17.8%)	6	15 (7.0%)
65–69	33	15.4	24		9	
70–74	19	8.9	14	17 (7.9%)	5	7 (3.3%)
75–79	5	2.3	3		2	
80–84	5	2.3	3	4 (1.9%)	2	4 (1.9%)
85–89	3	1.4	1		2	
90–94	1	0.5	0	—	1	1 (0.5%)
95–99	0	—	0	—	0	
100+	0	—	0	—	0	—

*Percentages may not add up to 100 because of rounding.

Dwelling Type

At the time clients reached out for help, 30 percent of them lived in three-bedroom detached homes (table A.4). This far exceeds the percentages for the other dwelling types. This does not necessarily mean that larger families requiring a three-bedroom house were most likely to seek help. These results may be a function of the geographic area, as part of my practice is in a lower density urban area with moderate housing costs.

TABLE A.4
Dwelling Types

DWELLING	PEOPLE SEEKING HELP	PERCENTAGE (%)*
Single room or rooms	5	2.3
One-bedroom apt/condo/townhome	28	13.1
Two-bedroom apt/condo/townhome	30	14.0
Three-bedroom apt/condo/townhome	16	7.5
Four-bedroom apt/condo/townhome	2	0.9
One-bedroom detached house	2	0.9
Two-bedroom detached house	14	6.5
Three-bedroom detached house	64	30.0
Four-bedroom (or more) detached house	34	15.9
Other (trailer, house burned, multiple houses)	6	2.8
Unknown	13	6.1

* Percentages may not add up to 100 because of rounding.

Education

Table A.5 supports the point that hoarding does not respect income or education level. It is interesting to note that 35.5 percent of women had a high school education, while 34.2 percent had an undergraduate degree. Among men seeking help with hoarding, 36.5 percent had graduated from high school, and 26.9 percent had completed an undergraduate degree.

Education by Gender

EDUCATION LEVEL	PEOPLE SEEKING HELP (includes unknown gender)*	PERCENTAGE (%)†	WOMEN	MEN
Grade school	11	5.1	8	3
High school	78	36.5	53 (36.1%)	23 (37.7%)
Apprenticeship	0	0	0	0
College	19	8.9	13	6
Professional designation	17	7.9	11	6
Undergraduate degree	69	32.2	51 (34.2%)	17 (26.9%)
Master's degree	17	7.9	10	7
Doctorate	3	1.4	2	1
Other or unknown	2	0.9	1	0

*Some individuals are listed in more than one category, for example, undergraduate and professional.
†Percentages may not add up to 100 because of rounding.

Main Income Sources

In table A.6, the results for pension income are broadly applicable and consistent with the age range of the highest requests for services in my practice.† The labor force in my geographical area is primarily public sector; therefore, it is not surprising to find that 24.8 percent were public sector employees.

---

† Some individuals have more than one main source of income, for example, pension and investments.

TABLE A.6
Main Income Sources

INCOME SOURCE	PEOPLE SEEKING HELP	PERCENTAGE (%)*
Public sector	65	24.8
Private sector	30	11.5
Self-Employed	20	7.6
Paid disability leave from employer	28	10.7
Investments	18	6.9
Provincial or municipal support	14	5.3
Pension	54	20.6
Other (e.g., dependent on spouse or parents)	29	11.0
Blank or unknown	4	1.5

* Percentages may not add up to 100 because of rounding.

Estimated Annual Income

While there is a slight increase in requests for service from individuals in the CDN$30,000 to $50,000 income bracket, there are no remarkable differences up to the $100,000 level (table A.7). This supports the observation that hoarding does not respect income.

TABLE A.7
Annual Income

ANNUAL INCOME (CDN$)	PEOPLE SEEKING HELP	PERCENTAGE (%)*
Under $10,000	8	3.7
$10,000–$19,999	19	8.9
$20,000–$29,999	23	10.8
$30,000–$39,999	33	15.4
$40,000–$49,999	33	15.4
$50,000–$59,999	14	6.5
$60,000–$69,999	14	6.5
$70,000–$79,999	22	10.3
$80,000–$89,999	8	3.7
$90,000–$99,999	10	4.7
$100,000–$109,999	10	4.7
$110,000–$119,999	3	1.4
$120,000–$129,999	2	0.9
$130,000–$139,999	1	0.5
$140,000–$149,999	0	0
$150,000–$159,999	1	0.5
$160,000–$169,999	0	0
$170,000–$179,999	0	0
$180,000–$189,999	0	0
$190,000–$199,999	0	0
$200,000+	7	3.3
Unknown	6	2.8

* Percentages may not add up to 100 because of rounding.

Estimated Total Assets

Table A.8 indicates that regardless of the income levels in the previous table, these same people had minimal assets, indicating equally minimal disposable income. The question remaining is, Did the funds that normally would have represented their disposable income and savings go toward their acquisition behaviors, resulting in their hoarded environment?

TABLE A.8
Total Assets

ASSETS (CDN$)	PEOPLE SEEKING HELP	PERCENTAGE (%)*
$0-$9,999	53	24.8
Unknown	28	13.1
$10,000-$99,999	7	3.3
$100,000-$199,999	24	11.2
$200,000-$299,999	25	11.7
$300,000-$399,999	19	8.9
$400,000-$499,999	11	5.1
$500,000-$599,999	12	5.6
$600,000-$699,999	4	1.9
$700,000-$799,999	3	1.4
$800,000-$899,999	8	3.7
$900,000-$999,999	0	0
$1,000,000+	20	9.4

* Percentages may not add up to 100 because of rounding.

Type of Debt

Table A.9 illustrates that the debt held by most of this sample group was *bad debt*, meaning debt that does not increase net worth or have future value, or debt that the person doesn't have the cash to pay off (per this table, everything other than mortgage debt).

TABLE A.9
Type of Debt among People Seeking Help

TYPE OF DEBT	PEOPLE SEEKING HELP	PERCENTAGE (%)*
Mortgage	94	44
Credit cards	143	67
Personal line of credit	48	22
Income tax arrears	78	36
Other (e.g., property tax arrears, car rental charges, traffic tickets, legal fees, car loans, fines, online charges, monthly expenses not covered by income)	17	8

* Percentages add up to more than 100% because clients may have more than one type of debt.

Number of Daily or Weekly Contacts

Table A.10 indicates that at least 37 percent of those seeking help with hoarding live with someone (in a relationship). Some may be unmarried but have a child or have family or friends who visit at least weekly. We cannot determine if these are vibrant relationships, but at least 37 percent of clients have regular contact with others (such as family, friends, clubs and organizations, volunteering, other forms of social life).

TABLE A.10
Daily or Weekly Contacts with Other People

DAILY OR WEEKLY CONTACTS	PEOPLE SEEKING HELP	PERCENTAGE (%)
0	15	7
Unknown	13	6
1–2	79	37
3–5	62	29
6+	45	21

Despite the above indicators of intact relationships, many concerned calls to Birchall Consulting come from family members, who report being estranged but remaining concerned.

Interventions

In table A.11, the highest percentage of interveners are family members, self-referrals, and professionals. *Note:* A client can have more than one intervention. If more than one intervener is involved, multiple interveners were likely required, probably indicating that the situation was more severe.

TABLE A.11
Interventions

INTERVENTION TYPE	PEOPLE SEEKING HELP
Police	26
Fire	28
Child protection	19
Adult protection	0

INTERVENTION TYPE	PEOPLE SEEKING HELP
Animal protection	5
Housing/landlord	26
Family	81
Friend	17
Self-referral	51
Professionals: social workers, psychologists, senior support, arthritis group, veterans organization	59
Unspecified	11

Diagnosed Disorders

Table A.12 captures comorbid factors significant enough to disrupt treatment or intervention. The most common comorbid factors of this cohort group were, in descending order, generalized anxiety disorder, depression, biological factors, personality disorder, OCD, social isolation, disinhibited social engagement disorder, aging with mobility issues, substance use disorder, acute stress disorder, PTSD, dementia, OCPD, eating disorder–other, adjustment stress disorder, reactive attachment disorder, avoidant-restrictive eating disorder, ADD, borderline personality disorder, compulsive personality and other compulsive disorders, bulimia, ADHD, autism, agoraphobia, anorexia nervosa, Asperger syndrome, acquired brain injury, bipolar 1 and bipolar 2 disorders.

In Mark Odom's workshop slide "Hoarding and Related Conditions" (2011), he cites research indicating that 57 percent of those who hoard meet the criteria for major depressive disorder, and 29 percent experienced social phobia.

Depression presented in 52.33 percent of our sample. Social isolation presented in 16.35 percent. The sample measured social isolation rather than social phobia.

From the same research, Odom cites that 28 percent of those who hoard meet the criteria for generalized anxiety disorder.

In our random sample, 58.87 percent meet the criteria for generalized anxiety disorder. We made the decision to include all nonspecific demonstrated anxiety under the umbrella of generalized anxiety disorder. This might explain the difference between Odom's findings and ours.

Diagnosed Disorders among People Seeking Help with Hoarding

DISORDER (as categorized in the *DSM-5*)	PEOPLE SEEKING HELP	PERCENTAGE OF STUDY COHORT (%)
Depressive disorders	**112**	**52.33**
• *Depression*	112	52.33
Anxiety disorders	168	78.50
• *Hoarding*	-	100.00*
• *OCD*	41	19.15
• *Agoraphobia*	1	0.46
• *Generalized Anxiety Disorder*	126	58.87
Personality disorders	**65**	**30.37**
• *Personality disorder*	58	27.10
• *Borderline personality disorder*	2	0.93
• *OCPD*	5	2.33
Substance-related and addictive disorders	**19**	**8.87**
• *Substance use disorder*	17	7.94
• *Compulsive personality and compulsive disorders*	2	0.93
Eating disorders	**12**	**5.60**
• *Anorexia nervosa*	1	0.46
• *Bulimia*	2	0.93
• *Avoidant-restrictive intake*	4	1.86
• *Other*	5	2.33
Autism spectrum disorders	**3**	**1.40**
• *Autism*	2	0.93
• *Asperger syndrome*	1	0.46
Attention deficit/hyperactivity disorder	**6**	**2.80**
• *Attention deficit disorder (ADD)*	4	1.86
• *Attention deficit/ hyperactivity disorder (ADHD)*	2	0.93
Neurocognitive disorders	**6**	**2.80**
• *Dementia*	5	2.33
• *Acquired brain injury*	1	0.46

DISORDER (as categorized in the *DSM-5*)	PEOPLE SEEKING HELP	PERCENTAGE OF STUDY COHORT (%)
Bipolar disorder	**2**	**0.93**
• *Bipolar 1 disorder*	1	0.46
• *Bipolar 2 disorder*	1	0.46
Trauma and stressor-related disorders	**53**	**24.76**
• *Reactive attachment disorder*	4	1.86
• *Disinhibited social engagement disorder*	30	14.01
• *PTSD*	5	2.33
• *Acute stress disorder*	10	4.67
• *Adjustment stress disorder*	4	1.86
Other notable characteristics		
• *Social isolation*	35	16.35
• *Aging with mobility issues*	26	12.14
• *Biological factors***	78	36.44

Note: Clients in this random sample may have multiple comorbid factors.

* Every member of the study cohort exhibited hoarding behavior and asked for service for hoarding behavior.

** History of generational hoarding behavior.

References

CHAPTER 1. OVERVIEW OF HOARDING

American Psychiatric Association (APA). 2013. *Diagnostic and Statistical Manual of Mental Disorders,* 5th Edition. Washington, DC: APA.

Emergence Health Network, El Paso Center for Mental Health / Intellectual Disabilities. 2018. "Biological Explanations of Obsessive-Compulsive and Related Disorders (OCRDs)." Emergence Health Network. Accessed October 5, 2018.

Feusner, Jamie, and Sanjaya Saxena. 2005. "Compulsive Hoarding: Unclutter Lives and Homes by Breaking Anxiety's Grip." *Current Psychiatry* 4 (3): 12–26.

Hartl, T. L., S. R. Duffany, G. J. Allen, G. Steketee, and R. O. Frost. 2005. "Relationships among Compulsive Hoarding, Trauma, and Attention-Deficit/ Hyperactivity Disorder." *Behaviour Research and Therapy* 43:269–76.

Hwang, Jen-Ping, Shih-Jen Tsai, Chen-Hong Yang, King-Ming Liu, and Jiing-Feng Lirng. 1998. "Hoarding Behavior in Dementia: A Preliminary Report." *American Journal of Geriatric Psychiatry* 6 (4): 285–89.

Iervolino, Alessandra C., Nader Perroud, Miguel Angel Fullana, Michel Guipponi, Lynn Cherkas, David A. Collier, and David Mataix-Cols. 2009. "Prevalence and Heritability of Compulsive Hoarding: A Twin Study." *American Journal of Psychiatry* 166: 1156–61.

Nestadt, Gerald. 2018. "Obsessive-Compulsive Disorders Research: Family and Genetic Studies of OCD." Psychiatry and Behavioral Sciences, Johns Hopkins Medicine. Accessed December 5, 2018. https://www.hopkinsmedicine.org/ psychiatry/specialty_areas/obsessive_compulsive_disorder/research/index.html.

Samuels, J., Y. Y. Shugart, M. A. Grados, V. L. Willour, O. J. Bienvenu, B. D. Greenberg, J. A. Knowles, J. T. McCracken, S. L. Rauch, D. L. Murphy, Y. Wang, A. Pinto, A. J. Fyer, J. Piacentini, D. L. Pauls, B. Cullen, S. A. Rasmussen, R. Hoehn-Saric, D. Valle, K. Y. Liang, M. A. Riddle, and G. Nestadt. 2007. "Significant Linkage to Compulsive Hoarding on Chromosome 14 in Families with Obsessive-Compulsive Disorder: Results from the OCD Collaborative Genetics Study." *American Journal of Psychiatry* 164 (3): 493–99. https://www.ncbi.nlm.nih.gov/pubmed/17329475.

Shaw Mind Foundation. 2016. *Hoarding Disorder*. Newark, UK: Shaw Mind Foundation. http://shawmindfoundation.org/wp-content/uploads/2016/12/Shaw-Mind-Guide-to-Hoarding.pdf.

Steketee, Gail, and Randy O. Frost. 2007. *Compulsive Hoarding and Acquiring: Therapist Guide*. New York: Oxford University Press.

———. *Compulsive Hoarding and Acquiring: Workbook*. New York: Oxford University Press.

Timpano, K. R., C. Exner, H. Glaesmer, W. Rief, A. Keshaviah, E. Brähler, and S. Wilhelm. 2011. "The Epidemiology of the Proposed *DSM-5* Hoarding Disorder: Exploration of the Acquisition Specifier, Associated Features, and Distress." *Journal of Clinical Psychiatry* 72 (6), 780–86. http://dx.doi.org/10.4088/JCP.10m06380.

Winsberg, M. E., K. S. Cassic, and I. M. Koran. 1999. "Hoarding in Obsessive-Compulsive Disorder: A Report of 20 Cases." *Journal of Clinical Psychiatry* 60 (9): 591–97.

Zhang, Heping, James F. Leckman, David L. Pauls, Chin-Pei Tsai, Kenneth K. Kidd, and M. Rosario Campos. 2002. "Genomewide Scan of Hoarding in Sib Pairs in Which Both Sibs Have Gilles de Tourette Syndrome." *AJHG* 70 (4): 896–904. https://www.sciencedirect.com/science/article/pii/S0002929707602973.

CHAPTER 2. ENVIRONMENTAL AND SELF-ASSESSMENT

Burns, David D. 1999. *Ten Days to Self-Esteem*. New York: Quill.

Steketee, Gail, and Randy O. Frost. 2007. *Compulsive Hoarding and Acquiring: Workbook*. New York: Oxford University Press.

CHAPTER 3. GOALS

Doran, George. 1981. "There's a S.M.A.R.T. Way to Write Management's Goals and Objectives." *Management Review* 70 (11): 35–36.

Robbins, Tony. 2018. "Why We Do What We Do." *Tony Robbins Podcast*, 33:21 mins., July 2, 2018. https://www.youtube.com/watch?v=IAavZgI56vE.

CHAPTER 5. PROCRASTINATION

Birchall, Elaine. 2016. "Procrastination: Why You Do It and How To Stop."
Interview with Jane Burka. *Take Back Your Life When Your Things Are Taking
Over*, 54:58 mins., November 2, 2016. https://www.voiceamerica.com/show/
episode/95475.

Burka, Jane, and Lenora Yuen. 2008. *Procrastination: Why You Do It, What to Do
about It Now*. Cambridge, MA: Da Capo Press.

Dweck, Carol S. 2007. *Mindset: The New Psychology of Success*. New York:
Random House.

CHAPTER 6. THE IMPACT OF HOARDING ON FAMILIES

Anonymous. "The Weaver." https://www.poemhunter.com/poem/weaver-the/.

CHAPTER 8. IMPULSE SHOPPING

Andreassen, Cecilie S., Mark D. Griffiths, Ståle Pallesen, Robert M. Bilder,
Torbjørn Torsheim, and Elias Aboujaoude. 2015. "The Bergen Shopping
Addiction Scale: Reliability and Validity of a Brief Screening Test." *Frontiers
in Psychology* 6:1374.

Brand, M., C. Laier, M. Pawlikowski, U. Schächtle, T. Schöler, and C. Altstötter-
Gleich. 2011. "Watching Pornographic Pictures on the Internet: Role of Sexual
Arousal Ratings and Psychological-Psychiatric Symptoms for Using Internet
Sex Sites Excessively." *Cyberpsychology, Behavior, and Social Networking* 14
(6): 371–77. doi:10.1089/cyber.2010.0222.

Drummond, D. C. 2000. "What Does Cue-Reactivity Have to Offer Clinical
Research?" *Addiction* 95:129–44.

———. 2001. "Theories of Drug Craving, Ancient and Modern." *Addiction* 96:33–
46.

Franken, I. H. 2003. "Drug Craving and Addiction: Integrating Psychological
and Neuropsychopharmacological Approaches." *Progress in
Neuropsychopharmacology and Biological Psychiatry* 27:563–79.

Laier, C., M. Pawlikowski, J. Pekal, F. P. Schulte, and M. Brand. 2013. "Cybersex
Addiction: Experienced Sexual Arousal When Watching Pornography and
Not Real-Life Sexual Contacts Makes the Difference." *Journal of Behavioral
Addictions* 2:100–107.

LaRose, Robert, and Matthew S. Eastin. 2002. "Is Online Buying Out of Control?
Electronic Commerce and Consumer Self-Regulation." *Journal of Broadcasting
and Electronic Media* 46 (4): 549–64.

Rose, Susan, and Arun Dhandayudham. 2014. "Towards an Understanding of Internet-
Based Problem Shopping Behaviour: The Concept of Online Shopping Addiction
and Its Proposed Predictors." *Journal of Behavioral Addictions* 3 (2): 83–89.

Schöler, T., and C. Altstötter-Gleich. 2011. "Watching Pornographic Pictures on the Internet: Role of Sexual Arousal Ratings and Psychological–Psychiatric Symptoms for Using Internet Sex Sites Excessively." *Cyberpsychology, Behavior, and Social Networking* 14:371–77.

Sodano, R., and E. Wulfert. 2010. "Cue Reactivity in Active Pathological, Abstinent Pathological, and Regular Gamblers." *Journal of Gambling Studies* 26:53–65.

Thalemann, R., K. Wölfling, and S. M. Grüsser. 2007. "Specific Cue Reactivity on Computer Game–Related Cues in Excessive Gamers." *Behavioral Neuroscience* 121:614–18.

Trotzke, Patrick, Katrin Starcke, Astrid Muller, and Matthias Brand. 2015. "Pathological Buying Online as a Specific Form of Internet Addiction: A Model-Based Experimental Investigation." *PLoS One* 10 (10): e0140296. https://www.ncbi.nlm.nih.gov/pmc/articles/PMC4605699/.

Trotzke, Patrick, Katrin Starcke, Anya Pedersen, and Matthias Brand. 2014. "Cue-Induced Craving in Pathological Buying: Empirical Evidence and Clinical Implications." *Psychosomatic Medicine* 76 (9): 694–700.

Valence, Gilles, Alain D'Astous, and Louis Fortier. 1988. "Compulsive Buying Scale." In *Compulsive Buying: Concept and Measurement*. Sherbrooke: University of Sherbrooke. Accessed at ShopaholicNoMore, February 2011. http://www.shopaholicnomore.com/wp-content/uploads/2011/02/Valence-Scale-with-scoring-11-item2.pdf.

Wei, Marlynn. 2015. "10 Signs You're Addicted to Online Shopping." *Psychology Today* (blog), November 4, 2015. https://www.psychologytoday.com/us/blog/urban-survival/201511/10-signs-you-re-addicted-online-shopping.

CHAPTER 10. A LIFE STORED, NOT LIVED

Burka, Jane, and Lenora Yuen. 2008. *Procrastination: Why You Do It, What To Do about It Now*. Cambridge, MA: Da Capo Press.

Huizen, Jennifer. 2016. "Diogenes Syndrome: Symptoms and Treatment." *Medical News Today*, December 11, 2016. https://www.medicalnewstoday.com/articles/314595.php.

APPENDIX. CASE REVIEW FROM BIRCHALL CONSULTING AND ASSOCIATES, INC.

Frost, Randy O., Gail Steketee, and David F. Tolin. 2011. "Comorbidity in Hoarding Disorder." *Depression and Anxiety* 28 (10). 876–84.

Nestadt, Gerald. 2018. "Obsessive-Compulsive Disorders Research: Family and Genetic Studies of OCD." Psychiatry and Behavioral Sciences, Johns Hopkins Medicine. Accessed December 5, 2018. https://www.hopkinsmedicine.org/psychiatry/specialty_areas/obsessive_compulsive_disorder/research/index.html.

Odom, Mark. 2011. "Hoarding Interventions: 90 Minute Workshop on Hoarding Disorder and Effective Interventions." Boston University, December 2011. https://www.nationalcouncildocs.net/wp-content/uploads/2013/11/Odom-2011-Hoarding.pdf.

Index

self-neglect, 23, 172, 181, 184

self-regulation, 154, 234

selling items, 81–83, 134, 240

senile squalor syndrome. *See* Diogenes syndrome

seniors, living with a hoarder, 203, 212–13. *See also* aging with mobility issues; Diogenes syndrome

sentimental items, 18, 30–31, 162, 167, 194

separation anxiety, 211

serotonin, 146, 234

service programs, 129–30, 133, 182, 212–13, 243, 244

shame: breaking cycle of, 91; and children of hoarders, 149, 207; and compulsive shopping, 141, 153; as obstacle, 2

shifting items, 16, 79–80, 84

shopping: conscious acquiring process, 140, 146–47, 230, 232, 234–36; potential for hoarding self-assessment, 16, 17; sharing purchases, 151–52. *See also* shopping, compulsive

shopping, compulsive: and anxiety, 140, 153; conscious acquiring process, 140, 146–47, 230, 234–36; online, 139, 152–56, 187–89; self-assessment, 154–56; strategies for, 139, 140, 145, 146–47, 148, 150, 151–52, 155–56, 233–36; triggers, 145

shovel-outs. *See* interventions, intense

sleep, 147, 235

SMART goals, 67–68, 69–70

smoke detectors, 63, 64

social anxiety, 153, 181, 184

social isolation, 28, 254, 256

social phobia, 28, 254

sorting. *See* scaling process

stairs, 54–55, 63

Steketee, Gail, 238, 244

storage spaces, 45, 144–45, 194

stoves, 51, 63, 64

strategies. *See* coaching; de-cluttering; harm-reduction strategies

stress disorders, 254, 256

structural integrity risks, 38

substance use disorder, 254, 256

success: defining, 3, 195; fear of, 96–97, 105; keys to, 13; *vs.* pace, 90. *See also* goals

support. *See* coaching; helpers; mental health professionals

suspicion, 172, 181, 184

T

10 Signs of Compulsive Online Shopping, 154, 156

Terri example, 10–11

things: commonly hoarded, 17–18; determining permanent places for, 74–75; saving patterns, 30–3; scaling process, 76–92; shifting, 16, 79–80, 84. *See also* things, relationships with

things, relationships with: aesthetic attachments, 31, 162, 168; attachment formations, 30–31; as barrier to discarding, 83; changing relationships to, 1–2, 3, 240; intrinsic attachments, 31–32, 162, 168; respecting yourself, 75, 91–92; saving patterns, 30–31; scaling process, 76–92; sentimental attachments, 30–31, 162

tics, 28

time: compression of, 176–77; and inherited items, 170; pace of de-cluttering, 75, 76–78, 79, 89–91, 241; processing, 87; and procrastination, 99, 114–15; and removing items, 82, 83; and setting goals, 68, 70

Timmie, Mike, and Gordie example, 121–30, 209–10

Tolin, David F., 244

toppling risks, 54, 62

Tourette syndrome, 28

triggers, 145

tripping hazards, 58–59, 61, 63

trust, fear of, 105

2-to-1 breathing, 233–34

U

unresolved grief, 30–31, 131–32

V

vermin, 13, 57, 63, 137, 212

vision (for home spaces): helping find, 1, 29–30, 166, 202; understanding accumulation, 73

void/longing, avoiding, 78, 90, 169

vulnerability: and loss, 33; and procrastination, 104; as risk factor in hoarding, 26, 28

W

wants *vs.* needs, 151, 235

waste and attachments, 31, 167

water heaters, 49, 50, 63, 64

water softeners, 50

Where Are You on the Path to Hoarding? (table 1.2), 19–20

wishful thinking, 69, 94–95, 114

worksheets: Knowing Yourself, 104–16, 232; My Goals, 69–70, 232; Onsite Clutter Coaching Toolkit, 71, 76, 231; Problem Solving Using CBT, 74; scaling process, 79–80

Y

Yuen, Lenora, 93, 95, 96, 100, 232

About the Authors

ELAINE BIRCHALL is the director of Birchall Consulting, which is dedicated to helping those with hoarding disorders achieve control over their possessions and hoarding tendencies. The founder of the Canadian National Hoarding Coalition and host of the radio show *Take Back Your Life When Things Are Taking Over*, she earned her master's degree in social work from Carleton University. As a hoarding behavior specialist and clutter coach for more than 17 years, she provides training, consultations, and counseling to people and organizations across North America.

SUZANNE CRONKWRIGHT, a technical writer and editor with over 35 years' experience, earned her honors bachelor's degree in psychology from Wilfrid Laurier University. She is recognized for her ability to translate complex technical information into simple, clear procedures.